RAIDING SUPPORT REGIMENT

RAIDING SUPPORT REGIMENT

The Diary of a Special Forces Soldier 1943–1945

Bombardier Walter Jones

First published by University of Plymouth Press. This edition published in the United Kingdom in 2023 by The Devonshire Press, Knowles Hill Road, Newton Abbot, TQ12 2PW, United Kingdom.

ISBN PB 978-1-73944-026-8
ISBN HB 978-1-917152-12-9

© The Devonshire Press™ 2023

The rights of Walter Jones of this work have been asserted by his family in accordance with the Copyright, Designs and Patents Act 1988.

A CIP catalogue record of this book is available from the British Library.

Publisher: Paul Honeywill
Editor: G. H. Bennett

All rights reserved. No part of this publication may be reproduced, stored in a retrieval system or transmitted in any form or by any means whether electronic, mechanical, photocopying, recording, or otherwise, without the prior written permission of the Devonshire Press. Any person who carries out any unauthorised act in relation to this publication may be liable to criminal prosecution and civil claims for damages.

Cover image: 3.7-inch gun on the island of Vis off the coast of Yugoslavia, August 1944.

Typeset in Adobe Garamond Pro 11/14pt. Printed by Print on Demand

The diary reproduced here appear as unedited text, apart from minor changes made to date formats and corrections to typing errors found in the original.

Unless stated all images are in the public domain. UK photographs are taken prior to 1957 and created by the United Kingdom Government and are in the public domain. All recent images have written permission of the Jones family.

Contents

Albert Jones 8

G.H. Bennett 12

Joining The Raiding Support Regiment 18

Daily Life At Nahariya 40

Deployment 44

Europe Again 48

Yugoslavia 52

Vis 54

The Murder Of German Prisoners 76

Death On The Island 80

Two Deserters 86

The Run Up To D-Day 88

The Raid On Brac 92

Return to Vis 116

The Aftermath of Brac 120

Ravnik 122

Wounded in Action	132
The Raid on Korcula	136
Return to Ravnik	146
Return to Italy	152
Albania	158
The Ambush	166
The Attack on Sarande	172
Corfu	188
A Small Italian Town	198
Another Sort of Engagement	202
Signals Over Salermo	206
Hospital	212
Lake Comacchio	218
Operation Impact Royal	230
Operation Roast	238
Return Home	258
Reference	268
Bibliography	272
Index	274

Walter Jones

Foreword
Albert Jones

We were standing at our front door in Liverpool – my mother, brother Walter and I – when a neighbour, Mrs Fields, came up to us in tears. She was carrying a telegram that said that her son Ronnie – a former school friend of Walter – was missing, believed killed in action in France. The timing could not have been worse: we were on the doorstep to say goodbye to Walter, my mother was already trying hard but unsuccessfully not to cry. Walter was returning to his unit after embarkation leave, and we had no idea when – or if – we would see him again.

Ours was just one among the many families divided by the war. We were lucky: we all survived, our mother living just long enough to see Walter return. But many families did not – and no family that came through the war was ever quite the same. When World War II began on 3rd September, 1939, Walter had already volunteered for the army while my brother Harry and I, aged 14 and 11 respectively, had been evacuated to the country. Wal – he was always Wal at home to distinguish him from our father, who was also Walter – had been a hero to me as a child: I tried to write like him, I was a jazz fan and an avid Everton supporter. Although we three brothers attended the same elementary school and spent our pre-war family holidays together in Lytham and in southern Ireland, our age gap (or so it seemed then) meant that contact was brief and infrequent – he was still our 'big brother' – and we did not start to get to know each other as friends until we were approaching middle age. There was a succession of reasons: in the early part of the war our meetings were restricted to his rare spells on leave, then the family moved away from Liverpool in the hope (a vain one as it turned out) of escaping the worst of the Blitz. By the time Walter had been demobilised I was in the RAF, and by the time I was demobilised he had moved to make his life in the south of England. Then I emigrated to New Zealand (where, like Walter, I became an accountant) and by the time I returned 11 years later, he and his family lived in Devon.

It was only then that we started to make up for lost time, and I have many happy memories of those years: of shared humour; of 'Middlesex Sevens' weekends; of indulging our mutual love of jazz; and of visits to Liverpool with Harry to visit ageing relatives and watch our beloved Everton. Other treasured memories of our adventures together include a 'family history' tour that we three made to southern Ireland, involving copious tastings of the local brew and our installation as 'Freemen' of

Drogheda, our mother's home city; and in later years, a trip to New York, Washington, Philadelphia and to our joint musical heritage, New Orleans.

For many years, he had talked to me about those precious (and illicit) diaries that he had carried with him throughout the war. They fitted neatly into the battledress pocket that was supposed to hold his First Aid kit – fortunately he was never injured. But it was not until he was winding down to retirement some 40 years later that he felt compelled to begin the organisation, revision and research necessary for the completion of his memoir.

By the time the work was completed he had written half a million words – five times the length of this book. It was a happy coincidence that much of the research was done at the Public Record Office in Kew – a short walk from where I lived at the time.

It was one of the great disappointments of his military career that when there was an urgent need for bomber crews to begin, finally, to carry the war to the enemy, he was the only one among his group of colleagues to be turned down, which he always assumed was because of his schooling. In many ways it may have turned out to be a blessing, not only because it probably improved his chances of survival – Bomber Command had a less than 50% survival rate – but also, if he had been accepted, we would have been deprived of this fascinating and moving account of Walter's war.

Albert Jones

Gun Crew

Introduction
G.H. Bennett

The Second World War witnessed a steady growth in the number and use of Special Forces units such as the Special Air Service (SAS), Special Boat Service (SBS), the Long Range Desert Group (LRDG) and Popski's Private Army. The harsh climate and special nature of the battlefields in the Middle East were the cradle for emergence of units such as the SAS and LRDG. It took a special kind of soldier – highly self reliant, physically and mentally tough – to operate in the desert with minimum levels of support. Most special units were short-lived expedients to address particular tactical circumstances. Their personnel were renowned for their toughness, skill and ruthlessness. Their leaders, such as David Stirling of the SAS, would establish considerable reputations for their tactical vision, soldierly qualities and powers of leadership. By their very nature, Special Forces were lightly equipped. Whether for reconnaissance purposes or surprise attack, Allied Special Forces relied on speed, surprise, camouflage and evasion.

In 1943, the war shifted dramatically as German forces in North Africa were defeated and Allied landings took place in Sicily and then in Italy.

Italy changed sides in the war, and the failure of the German offensive at Kursk signalled that the tide had turned on the Russian front. An Allied second front in Western Europe was eagerly awaited, especially as the progress of the fighting in Italy proved disappointingly slow and costly. From Western Europe to the Russian front and the Mediterranean, it became clear that the Germans had shifted to a defensive stance and were busy fortifying their positions. Raiding by lightly armed Special Forces remained an option in areas such as the Balkans where the enemy's hold was tenuous, but even here it was recognised that it might be worthwhile to provide raiding forces with at least a few heavy weapons. The British Army was perhaps a little behind others in this respect. The Americans, the Germans and the Italians had recognised the need to have heavy weapons that could be transported across even the most difficult terrain. They developed both weapons and special units that could operate with heavy weapons in the most mountainous regions of Europe.

The decision to form a Raiding Support Regiment in 1943 to supplement the firepower of British raiding and Special Forces was recognition that Allied Forces were about to fight on fresh battlefields set amidst landscapes that held their own particular tactical and material challenges. The regiment would be divided into five troops armed with mortars, heavy machine guns, American-made 75mm howitzers (designed for mountain use) and extremely rugged, Italian-made, anti-tank guns. The regiment was made up of volunteers from Middle Eastern Command, and it would never see action as a whole. Parts of the unit would be sent to support Partisan forces off the coast of Yugoslavia in February 1944 while the rest of the regiment stayed in Italy. Later, elements of the regiment would fight in Yugoslavia, Albania and Greece. In 1944 the regiment would become embroiled in the Greek civil war as it fought house-to-house against the forces of the Greek Communists of ELAS. When the fighting in Europe ended, the Regiment was prepared for deployment in the Far East. The dropping of atomic bombs on Hiroshima and Nagasaki, and the Japanese surrender, came before the regiment had deployed. Instead it found itself heading back to the United Kingdom where it was demobilised. The Raiding Support Regiment was short-lived and all but forgotten in most of the post-war accounts of fighting in the Mediterranean.

One of the members of the regiment who would return to the United Kingdom in 1945 was Bombardier Walter Jones. He maintained a diary throughout the war, even though this was against King's Regulations. Going to considerable trouble to hide the diary, he would use it in the 1980s to write down his memoirs.

Jones, who had been working in the City of Liverpool since he was 14 and was at the Liverpool Cotton Exchange in 1939, had joined an artillery unit of the Territorial Army three months before the outbreak of war. In so doing, the 5 feet 8 inch, 9 stone 9 pound 19 year old went against the wishes of his mother and father. His father had served in the King's Liverpool Regiment in the First World War and was not keen to see one of his sons following in his footsteps with a war looming in Europe. Joining the 66th Anti-Tank Battalion of the Royal Artillery, Jones felt an immediate sense of disappointment:

> "There were no anti-tank guns to train on, nor any other weapons for that matter. No equipment whatsoever! Neither were there any professionally qualified army instructors. Officers and NCOs… were being selected and appointed on the strength of interviews,

which fortuitously threw up a few middle-aged, time-served Reservists who had hastily answered the call to return to the colours… Emerging with rank from the interviews however, were many incompetent misfits possessed with insufficient credentials for leading men into a cinema, never mind a war."[1]

The outbreak of war did not bother Jones. It offered the young Liverpudlian the chance to impress his mates and girls with his uniform and also the promise of some very new experiences. He later confided, "1939 was a lark: a novelty so dramatically removed from the mundane, prospect-less and repetitive routine of the office."[2]

Jones spent the winter of 1939-1940 in training in the north-east of England. The horrors of war were for a time hidden beneath the false quiet of the 'phoney war' and the fun of being away from the routine of office life. Then in June 1940 elements of the regiment were unexpectedly moved to Rugeley in Staffordshire. Jones found himself tending to the needs of Dunkirk evacuees in a tented city on the edge of the town. Jones recalled "listening to these men knocked the bravado out of us: their stories frightened us. Singing 'Rule Britannia' was not going to be enough, after all."[3] As the Battle of France gave way to the Battle of Britain, with the Regiment moving to Bawdsey in Suffolk, the war got steadily closer to Jones. The threat of enemy invasion seemed very real. On one occasion an enemy aircraft attacked the truck that Jones was driving and he was witness to several dogfights between British and German aircraft. After witnessing the devastation of Liverpool and Coventry in late 1940, he volunteered for aircrew duty as a "positive opening towards taking part in the war."[4] His educational background and lack of qualifications (having left school at 14) meant that he was not accepted for aircrew. He remained with the Royal Artillery, spending much of 1941 on the coast of Sussex waiting for an invasion to break the monotony. It was not until news that the Regiment was to embark for the Middle East in early 1942 that Jones felt his desire to see action would finally be realised.

Arriving in May, the Regiment took no part in the Battle of El Alamein. Thereafter the German Afrika Korps was in retreat and on its way towards ignominious defeat, caught between the British and the Americans in Tunisia. Cut off from replacement tanks and fuel supplies, the Panzer Divisions of the Afrika Korps became shadows of their former selves. Jones felt as though the war was in danger of passing him by completely as thousands of men in Middle Eastern command awaited redeployment to other theatres of operations. However, in October 1943 the door of opportunity, the chance to get into battle at long last, opened up for Jones in a rather unexpected way. His military career moved in a very different direction and at a very different pace: for the remainder of the war he joined the Raiding Support Regiment.

Later in life Walter Jones, at 66 years of age, would rediscover his wartime diaries. Urged on by his three daughters, and by a desire to show his younger brothers Harry and Bert the kind of war he had had, Walter Jones began to write. He was also impelled to write because so little attention had been given to the activities of the Raiding Support Regiment. His memoirs were written with the benefit of his diary, on which he would draw heavily, records from the National Archives in London, and on various secondary accounts. At his death on 8 August 2001 the memoirs remained unpublished and in various stages of drafting. The task of editing has involved considerable reworking of the paragraphing to get the memoirs into book form. Beyond this, the words are those of Walter Jones, unless explicitly identified otherwise.

G.H. Bennett, Plymouth

"One of the members of the regiment who would return to the United Kingdom in 1945 was Bombardier Walter Jones. He maintained a diary throughout the war, even though this was against King's Regulations."

Joining The Raiding Support Regiment

The fateful notice had appeared on the order board. Volunteers were required from Middle East army personnel for special service operations 'behind enemy lines', an essential condition being an undertaking to submit to training as parachutists. Recruits were sought from all ranks and from across the whole spectrum of skills and trades, although a preference was stated for those experienced in handling small boats and horses or mules. Heroics didn't enter into it. Futility, boredom, purposelessness and a simple, understandable desire for change eventually prompted my application, and I was not untypical.

These appeals for volunteers had appeared before but were usually so specific in their requirements as to seriously limit the number of qualifying applicants, whose rare and valuable skills self-snookered their requests behind the ball of a Commanding Officer's regimental possessiveness. The difference this time was that only obvious rejection by a selection board could baulk the application. So other dissuasive measures at retention were tried. I was offered Sergeant status. But the appeal of action at last – and cloak and dagger, adventurous action at that – appeared to offer greater fulfilment than promotion and I have never regretted my decision. Well, perhaps never is untrue.

Three weeks later, on 13 November 1943, I was back again in Beirut's transit camp for the momentous interview which would decide my future Army activities. After years of trying to become involved in the action, selection for the avenue most likely to lead to it was positively anticlimactic. It seemed that only hints at lies were necessary to secure my acceptance. What did I know about small boats? Well I had been born and bred in the port of Liverpool hadn't I? Had I any experience of handling horses or mules? Hadn't Aintree racecourse been on my very doorstep? And didn't my mother actually work for its owner, Mrs Topham?

Lord Haw Haw, that traitorous perpetrator of propaganda for Hitler, is reported to have said on the radio that the newly formed regiment I was about to join, the Raiding Support Regiment (RSR) was made up of alcoholics, criminals and misfits, whom other units in the Middle East were glad to be rid of. As usual there was a modicum of substance in the information Germany had scooped up in espionage's most fertile territory, the Middle East. Certainly, recruitment was hardly discerning. The Beirut interviews were a classic example of going through the motions. I cannot recall anyone being rejected: perhaps it was thought that parachute training itself would be the ultimate eliminating criterion.

In fact the Beirut interviews were not the casual affairs they had appeared to be… At the time I was quite unaware that recruitment was taking place almost simultaneously for the Long Range Desert Group (in its new, airborne special operations role) and for the Special Boat Squadron. I have no information to support my theory but I feel sure that these two units had the pick of the specialists in their particular talents and aptitudes, leaving the RSR, like the German propaganda broadcasts stated, with what was left of the pickings – the misfits. Adding weight to this presumption was the earlier call for interview of two of my friends: they had both previously been on a signaller's course and had duly returned qualified as wireless operators. As it turned out, five other members of my regiment were also selected for RSR. So it was that the trundling train, transporting the successful volunteers from Aleppo in Syria to a transit camp at Haifa in Palestine on 25 November 1943, carried more hope and expectancy than remorse or resignation.

A vehicle arrived the next day and took us a few miles north along the coast to an obviously freshly created tented-camp near the German-Jewish seaside village of Nahariya, the first headquarters of the brand new Raiding Support Regiment. It was the first time we had heard the name of the newly formed unit, the novelty of which was – almost literally – sickeningly imposed on six tentative young men in search of unifying stability, by the dismaying chaos and indifference of our reception. We could hardly be expected to make allowances for the uniqueness of the situation. But we should have. What other regiment had been formed without even the nucleus of an existing administration? The 'suspicious stranger' syndrome was instantly evident among us in a way that one might expect… only in a transit camp full of alien (to each other) servicemen. Each of us later confessed to a deepening unease during that first day in the RSR. Similarly though, we each found little difficulty in rejecting any notion of backing out, although we knew that we were permitted 'second thoughts' at any time up to the successful completion of seven training parachute descents from a plane. Two shillings, a day's extra pay for a trained parachutist, was the ostensible incentive given for wishing to 'sweat it out'.

Day two at the camp was even more demoralising than the first. Having learnt that the new Regiment's establishment comprised five "Batteries" – an Artillery term – I imagined wrongly that as a gunner my niche would be found in either the Anti-Tank Battery or the Mountain Battery of 75mm gun-howitzers.[5] Neither Battery wanted me. I found myself allocated to the Anti-Aircraft Battery, whose mightiest weapon was the 0.5 inch Browning machine gun – an infantry weapon which could be utilised for air defence by the provision of a mounting pedestal.[6] That 'could be' is significant: the pedestals were still being pleaded for (to British Military Headquarters in Cairo) in mid-January 1944, and did not arrive until a few days before 'C' Battery left Palestine for an unknown destination on 27 January. But then, what good were mountings without Brownings? They had not arrived until Christmas Day! Such was the start of the RSR. Muddle, uncertainty, recrimination and secrecy. No weapons, no equipment, no premises – not even for trench latrines.

Adjacent acreage was occupied by the newly mustering Special Boat Squadron, formed from volunteers and remnants of the Special Air Service, which, having been formed in the Middle East, had mostly been sent home to start training and recruiting for the bigger things to come across the English Channel. The SBS camp confirmed my notion of its elitist status over the RSR: their communal premises were hutted structures. Cookhouse, mess rooms, canteens, latrines and medical room; all were solid brick constructions.

Training had to be concentrated wholly on the physical aspect of preparing for parachute jumping courses, and to that totally absorbing objective our energies were enthusiastically directed. It was one compelling feature of those first two weeks of December 1943 and the only one, it seemed, that the Regiment was adequately equipped for at that time. Rightly or wrongly, we regarded the hardship as an essential, perhaps deliberate, part of that training. The roughest country was found for a progression of forced marches with loaded packs and small arms over 9, 12 and 15 miles on alternate days, always finishing with a swim in the still Mediterranean from the excellent, sandy beach at Nahariya. Non-marching days were crammed with strengthening and agility exercises. Assessing things after a week, preoccupation with physical fitness obscured almost everything else from my mind. Camp discomfort, equipment scarcity, the random dispersal of even the few friends I had arrived with, and the dearth of any mail or of any amenity (other than the evening portwine imbibing sessions or the uncertain possibility of some ancient movies in Nahariyia village itself) assumed insignificance when related to the coveted goal of that eagerly awaited summons to the airfield at Ramat David, for the parachutist qualifying course. The completion of the 25 mile route march in easy style must have convinced me that I was ready, lulling me into a mood of premature self-congratulation and resulting in a shameful over-consumption of port wine that evening. Maudlin self-pity – caused by an accumulation of factors though mainly the certainty of another Christmas away from home, among virtual strangers at that – seemed temporarily to have relaxed the stiff upper lip. It's the only excuse I can think of. I deservedly suffered next day.

Hurling myself into the training over the following few days conspicuously promoted a cheerier mood, with smug pride exuding from diary entries about success at cross-country runs, swimming and football. .. Worse was to come. On 16 December the weather changed dramatically and dominated everything. The rain that gives Palestine its greenness, and had given rise to stories of monsoon-like storms which we had begun to consider mythical, started that day and heavily influenced everything from that day on. Training came to a halt, tempers frayed and discipline all but collapsed, as survival in already chaotic conditions became almost a personal matter. The camp was on a sloping hillside. Consequently, the rain, of torrential proportions, flowed through the camp as if the hilltop was an overflowing reservoir. We resited tents until the utter futility of the exercise became disconcertingly apparent. Flowing water spilled over the hastily deepened trenches around our tents, necessitating the digging of a canal through the tent also. Trying to find a dry area for our ground sheet and blankets became impossible. Perpetually wet, and surrounded by ankle-deep mud, we were virtual prisoners in our tents. After four continuous days of such conditions, the cheering news was broken to me that I was on the next course for Ramat David on the morrow, 20 December 1943. I think I could have uncomplainingly tolerated anything that nature was prepared to throw at me in those 24 hours, but escape was blissful.

Parachute Training

Although the weather had changed but little, my arrival at Ramat David, less than 20 miles away, represented a transformation equal to another world. For a start, we were accommodated in hutted billets where soaking wet clothes had a reasonable chance of drying before being worn again. But above all, there existed an undoubted uplifting of morale at the sight and sound of planes; at the presence of huge hangers (where training could cock-a-snook at the elements) and of Royal Air Force expert personnel. There was the excitement of reunion conversation with men from our unit who were already at variously advanced stages of their courses and who, without exception, effused with stories of the jumps they had already executed and thrilled us with their anticipation of those to come. The weather had held up their jumping too. Although they warned that the week or so of physical training ahead of us made Nahariya's PT seem like maypole dancing, the prospect became hourly more exhilarating. The real truth of its value lay mainly in its difference: it gave added zest to our exertions, particularly when the urgency became more apparent. To condense the normal six weeks parachuting course which prevailed at home to a mere 10-14 days, implicitly to have us operational for the harassment of the enemy in the Balkans as soon as possible, provided the rare incentive of purposefulness to add to unbounded enthusiasm.

A group of 10 men constituted a 'stick' in parachuting parlance, and I found myself in Flight Sergeant Kent's stick – a training group which was to remain together for the whole course. Not unexpectedly, a spirit of competition was fostered, both between and within sticks, which instilled pride at being one of Kent's Angels rather than a Dixon's Demon.

Many of the men had arrived at RSR woefully unfit, and there had not been time for Nahariya's training to remedy much before they met Ramat David's onslaught. They suffered. For me it was the exercises that hurt – the jumping from various heights and moving trolleys and the imperative forward rolling which had to follow. We rolled the day-long.

The ideal descent, we learned, called for a forward-facing landing which required a roll from the left or right side on contact with the earth – to minimise injury from jolt – by the instant wheeling effect of rounding the body through using, in turn, the outside of slightly bent knees, thighs, hips, back and shoulders in as gradual a flow of contact as possible. Hence the accent on collapsed rolling.

The much less physical skills of plane exits and descent control had to be learned too. Flight Sgt. Kent almost apologised for the use of Lockheed Hudsons at Ramat David; hardly the ideal plane to jump from, but seemingly the only aircraft available. The barely five-feet-high door, the width of one man on the side of the fuselage, presented all manner of exit problems, so our training simulated the real thing by repetitive jumping from the door of a grounded Hudson fuselage. Without the realisation of the all-important hazard of the rushing slipstream of air which emanated from the engines, it all seemed so simple.

Descent-control was much easier to rehearse with reasonable realism. Two actions towards landing survival (at worst) or perfection (at best) could be performed by a parachutist once his canopy had opened. He could make a turn and he could correct unreasonable backwards, forwards or sideways 'swing' or, to give it its technical term, 'oscillation'. Turning was effected by reaching above the head with both hands, grasping the binding of the parachute's rigging lines, pulling down, and at the same time crossing one hand over the other, as on a playground swing, to execute a full about-turn. Practice from a parachute harness suspended from the hangar roof made everyone quickly proficient in this particular skill.

All of this implied that there would be plenty of time available between leaving the Hudson and reaching the ground, but when we learned that most jumps were made from a height of 1000 feet and that the average time for such a descent was a mere 23 seconds, most of us guessed that we would need that long to decide whether we were approaching backwards, forwards or even upside down, let alone whether or not we were swinging! We recited, to boredom, the recommended rhyming mnemonic: "elbows in – shoulders round – feet together – watch the ground". We visited the parachute packing shed to see the WAAF (Women's Auxiliary Air Force) girls carrying out that critically important task of correctly folding, stowing, tying and enclosing those vital nylon panels and rigging lines within the canvas pack upon which our lives would depend. The cheerful confidence that radiated from the girls and the stringent packing regulations which, among other surprising things, dictated the immediate halting of packing when the temperature was found to be outside certain specified limits, were very, very reassuring. Those regulations minimised the risk of a build up of static electricity in the nylon. Static was the parachutist's greatest enemy, being the main cause of the dreaded 'Roman Candle' – the instance in which the nylon stuck fast to itself and failed to separate, even in the rush of air, as it streamed behind the doomed wearer like an oversized scarf or the cascading firework it was so aptly named after. There was a Roman Candle fatality whilst we were at Ramat David, and one of our own officers was killed there in that way a few weeks later on 14 January 1944.

Monday 27 December was pencilled in as the date for our stick's first jump but on 23 December, a gale of terrifying proportions put the kybosh on that day's programmed jumping by the previous course, adding to the backlog caused by earlier bad weather. With Christmas intervening, I had my doubts about performing any jumps in 1943. Christmas Eve brought fulfilment expectantly nearer, however. Kent's Angels were suddenly summoned to a warmed-up Wellington bomber on the airfield for our 'air experience' – a first flight for each of us. In the modern world's universal, daily acceptance of jet travel as commonplace, it is difficult to explain the measure of thrill which that first take-off provided for the group of young men in 1943 who, only a month or so earlier, had no chance of ever taking to the air. That dilapidated, pensioned off Wellington, which gave every indication of falling to pieces as it taxied to take-off, was converted into a magic carpet to paradise in the minds of a dozen or so starry eyed innocents, by the confident, almost carefree, approach to the matter by the RAF crew.

We ought to have been frightened. I'm sure we were. There seemed hardly anywhere safely secure upon which to place one's feet: it seemed to have the scantiest of superstructure, a shortcoming made disconcertingly worse by the huge exit hole in the floor! I thanked God that we were to jump from a side door. I doubt if I could ever have gone out of a floor exit, though thousands of earlier-trained parachutists did. With barely anywhere else to look out of the plane, that seemingly magnetic hole attracted everyone's reluctant attention. "See that reservoir down there?" Flight Sgt. Kent bawled his question more as an instruction. We submitted "Yes!" in lying unison: we weren't seeing anything 'down there' if we could help it. "When you come up for your jumps in the Hudson, the red light will come on just after we pass it. A few seconds after that the green light comes on and out you buggers go!"

I suppose our air experience lasted no more than 10 minutes. Thrilling as it was, I have never considered it served any useful purpose whatsoever, whereas using a Hudson might have given us some feeling about the approach to the dropping zone (DZ) and particularly about the slipstream. "Down there is Nazareth," pointed out our instructor more in the tone of a tour guide. The dawning reality of spending Christmas in the land of the Bible had a sudden and emotional impact. There was plenty of beer sunk in Ramat David's canteen that Christmas Eve. Thoughts of returning to that wretched, meagre camp at Nahariya, the next day, for God-knows-what sort of Christmas dinner, suggested that we should celebrate while we could.

25 December 1943 dawned startlingly beautiful, sunny and warm and remained so all day. Our much-maligned regiment really confounded all advance criticism by arranging to combine Christmas dinner arrangements with the SBS in their coveted mess hall, and in providing an excellent meal with all the trimmings – including booze. In truth, booze dominated the whole day so that the Army's magnanimous decision to send BBC crooner Judy Shirley to sing to the troops came rather amiss, since her voice could not be heard over lecherous, ribald, unrestrained suggestions until even her personal safety seemed in some doubt before the officers conveyed her to the haven of their Mess. Much steam was let off in a 50-a-side rugby match, where the ball mattered much less than deliberate wallowing in the squelching mud which a week earlier we had been bickering and complaining about. When spectators joined in, or were hauled in, the melee got rather out of hand, with duckings in a swollen stream, provoking counter-duckings until it became a mass drunken brawl-game. The first signs had appeared of the collection of reprobates which was the RSR. In mitigation, I suppose that there had to be a modicum of reckless abandon in each of us or we would not have opted out of safe units.

Boxing Day was a 'training-free' day spent in anticipation of the parachute jump which was to come sometime soon. I have often been asked if I found sleep difficult on the night before my first parachute jump. I can honestly answer that I had no trouble whatsoever in sleeping soundly. Coolheaded courage? Not a bit of it. I slept well because I didn't know I was jumping the next day. At 0430 on 27 December, the hut's slumbering silence was broken by the premature reveille inflicted by the excited Flight Sergeant, announcing unexpected jump facilities due to a sudden reduction in the wind velocity. No breakfast, no shaving, just "get dressed and into that bloody truck outside."

At the packing shed we drew our parachutes from the stores, fitted them on our backs, shortened a strap here, extended one there, and slotted their metal end-tabs into the quick release box near our bellybuttons. Each pack was then checked meticulously by Flight Sgt. Kent. We joked nervously about who'd got the Roman Candle one and about how silly we looked in our circular, canvas, rubber-filled, protective hats —which resembled a two-inch deep sponge cake wrapped around one's head – with canvas sides meeting under the chin where there was a stud fastening. Daylight had appeared before we reached the aircraft, where there was some anxiety about the latest wind speed figures being marginally above the 15 miles per hour recommended maximum for non-operational jumps, but at last we were in the Hudson and receiving our final briefing from 'Kenty'. We would go in slow-pairs; that is to say there would be five runs over the dropping zone, with No. 1 and No. 2 jumping at the first run. There would be no great emphasis on speedy exits for the first jump, the normal necessity for operational parachutists to land as closely together as possible being, for once only, ignored. When the red light flashed on at the door he would call "action stations, No. 1" and expect No. 1 to take up his trained, half-crouched position at the door with fingers lapped outside the door entrance, with which to eject himself with all his strength from the plane into the body-weight-supporting slipstream, immediately on his green light-prompted command of "Go!"

He would give the same commands for No. 2 whilst the green light was still on, so requiring close backing-up in the plane. He wanted clean exits: half-cock, shambling, testing the water, peeping walk outs would end in disaster, as the slipstream would catch hold of any loosely protruding limb and cause it to spin the body back against the fuselage and possibly, though God forbid, against the plane's tail, where severe injury would be almost certain and entangling the parachute rigging lines an unthinkable possibility. Once floating under our air-filled canopy, we were to listen to the megaphone-amplified voice of the dropping zone officer, who would supplement our own observations about any corrections we might need to make to our landing.

As Kenty clipped the end of our static lines to the rigid metal rod in the plane, I understood better why military parachutists use the static line chute and not the self-operated ripcord (free fall) chutes. With so much to sweat over, it was sensible to be relieved of the critical operation of pulling a rip-cord. The static line, attached at one end to the rod strongpoint in the plane and at the other to the back panel of the parachute, would expose the chute to the atmosphere automatically, as falling body weight broke the graded series of strings which detached the back panel from the parachute pack. The military objective was perhaps even more important: a uniform length of time between exit and the opening of the chutes means closer contact as a unit on the ground.

The Hudson was airborne and soon cruising at the optimum jumping height of 1000 feet. The jokes had stopped, as much from the inability to think of any at such a time as from the dry mouths which would have found them difficult to relate anyway. I had been allotted the No.4 position in the stick – second to go in the second run. Preoccupied with my own personal crisis, I cannot remember much about the first two disappearing except for Kenty's near maniacal "Go!" and his undisguised pleasure at their exits, as the Hudson banked for the circuit which would straighten out for my run. Two things had already surprised me. Firstly, the Hudson's 'door' to which I have already referred, was not a door at all – it was an open doorway. The actual door was probably on a metal scrap heap somewhere, abandoned for the rest of the war as useless or simply in the way. The other remarkable thing was that our respected, fearless dispatcher was not wearing a parachute. He had stood in the doorway from take-off, looking like a bored bus conductor awaiting passengers, until standing aside for the first exits, giving us more palpitations for his safety than for our own. Worse than that, after 1 and 2's departures he sat sideways in the doorway, his back pressing against one side. He then wedged himself with one foot against the other side for leverage as he proceeded with tug-of-war intensity to haul in the discarded static lines and back panels of the first two jumpers, against the possessiveness of the howling slipstream.

I didn't need to look out for the reservoir. When the Hudson straightened up after its tightly banked circuit around the DZ, even Flight Sgt. Kent's nod and smile towards No. 3 and myself were superfluous. I had remembered how the plane had cut back its airspeed just prior to the first pair's exit and I recognised that rather alarming juddering as the pilot strove to achieve minimum airspeed. We sidled towards the door, someone called "good luck" from behind us, whilst Kenty's last advice was "Go out like the first two and you'll be fine." The red light came on. "Action stations No. 3." He was in position. I shuffled to where he had been standing. Green now!

"GO!" He vanished – and I filled the vacant aperture. "No. 4 GO!" I surged out into space, not consciously aware of carrying out any of my training instructions. For a second I was weightless, reclining horizontally on the intangible couch of the slipstream. Then, without any sensation of falling or of tugging or buffeting, I imagined that I might have been in Heaven itself for all the dramatically contrasting peace and serenity in which I found myself. Perhaps I was in Heaven? Had the Roman Candle been mine? The noise and vibration of the plane was a world away: never a glance towards its remote flight direction: never a thought about such an object's part in my being where I was. The ease of it all! The tranquillity! Then, the view! Bird's eye, yes that was it; the magnificent view. How many seconds did he say from a thousand feet – 23? Must be longer! In fact, I don't think I'm coming down at all. Didn't Kenty say he would see us all later at the drop zone to see if we agreed with him that it was the second best sensation in life? Well, I know that a walking fish and chip supper with salt and vinegar on – and eaten with the fingers out of a newspaper – takes some beating, but this is quite superb. Kenty was right – nearly as good.

"No. 4!... No. 4!" God, that's me! Oh, it's the chap down there with the megaphone. "Good exit No. 4. Keep coming as you are." Keep coming? How the hell could I help but keep coming? Oh, I see. No need to make a turn, he means, no oscillation. I'd forgotten about that. In fact, I had forgotten everything about the rules in my unbridled happiness. But I will never forget the dramatic change of realisation from dreaming that I might be suspended in space forever to the fact that I really was coming down – and quickly. Indeed, for the last 50 feet I was sure that the earth was coming up to meet me halfway, as the speed of my descent became relative and I braced myself for what was supposed to be equivalent, on average, to jumping from a six foot wall. The reality was more like stepping off the back door, and I rolled more from condescension than necessity – a gesture which earned me the accolade of "an excellent landing" from the ground-control officer and added a boost to my rampant ego.

Pressing and turning the quick-release box freed the webbing straps, which had hitherto attached the chute to me. Holding on to a strap, I raced around the rapidly filling canopy and collapsed it before it became faster than me, in its wind-assisted mobility. As soon as it was crumpled into a reasonable bundle, I deposited it and myself into the waiting truck as instructed. The truck would take the whole stick back to the airfield packing shed for another issue of parachutes for our second jump immediately. It didn't happen that way because of an unkind windspeed, which was a great pity since the mood I was in would have kept me jumping all day. For all the embellishment, for which I apologise, the fairly terse diary entry for the day takes some beating: "It's the grandest of all feelings. Don't remember coming out of the door but managed to make an excellent landing. Thrilled beyond expectations – can only remember laughing all the time, especially when ground controller complimented me". Which I suppose only goes to show that a bit of praise now and again is good for morale.

Back at the hut, one bed without any kit on it… Oh, God! Not a casualty? He had been RTUd (returned to unit) – the instant fate of a jibber: one who could not bring himself to go out of the door. A collective silence was broken by a relieving snort from his former near neighbour. "Well! I'm glad it was that loud-mouthed bugger!" We endorsed that view. But not without sympathy, and perhaps even admiration at the courage required of such a tormenting decision – after all that arduous training. We marvelled incredulously too, at the extraordinary sensitivity of the Army in ensuring that he was off the premises before we returned: a very deliberate policy which we were to encounter again.

The cynicism which service life bred, however, alternatively suggested that the Army had the jibber's feelings less in mind than the need to avoid contaminating the rest of us. Take your choice. Whatever one's feelings in that minor drama, they could not compare with one's attitude to a mass-jib of 18 volunteers (including three sergeants) who applied for and received their Return to Units from Nahariya before even transferring to the airfield at Ramat David! Something wrong with recruiting, or a persuasive barrack-room lawyer at work?

Free from duty, we went into Haifa for the rest of the day. Strangely enough there is no record of celebration but there are two probable reasons for that. With only one of seven jumps completed, it might have been tempting providence to congratulate ourselves too soon – after all they don't bring out the champagne on the completion of the first lap of a Grand Prix. I think it likely that the risk of a hangover was not considered an ideal approach to our second jump next morning. There was also the more prosaic explanation – we were skint after our Christmas indulgence. Whatever the reason, the film The Man who Came to Dinner received our attention and it was a first rate show.

Tuesday 28 December dawned windier than the day before and with no hope of parachuting. We were, if you'll pardon the expression, left in suspense. Wednesday morning was just as grim as the weather forecast, but with the promise of better things in the afternoon. This kept us in camp on standby with fruitful consequences in the afternoon – our second jump. Fast pairs from 1000 feet. I knew much more about this one. More aware of my exit; more certain that I did do things correctly on my first jump from instinctive execution of thoroughly instilled training practices. Arms tight by my sides, legs pressed together and a really forceful thrust away from the Hudson, that astonishing second of encumbrance in the slipstream, then again the uncanny, contrasting, library silence. Where did the noise go? I looked around and could neither see nor hear any trace of the plane. Very strange, but each of us experienced it. There was much more sensibility about coming down this time too. I was soon aware of a backward approach to the DZ, and had executed a complete reverse turn smiling the while in self-congratulation before my megaphone mentor could issue the instruction. I had another uneventful landing. That evening I finished the diary entry with "I'm really happy about this – enjoyed it immensely."

The rain was belting down the next morning but apparently this, by itself, is no barrier to parachuting, so our early dismay at the likelihood of further postponement rapidly changed to unrestrained glee at the arrival of the trucks. We did two jumps that day – one immediately after the other – slow and fast fives from little under 1000 feet. The first was an appalling effort. Apart from a thunderclap wallop of a landing, on the a backward swing of an oscillation I had failed to correct (having missed the ground by a foot or two on the forward swing), I had already earned black marks for an earlier misdemeanour. Whilst in the plane, after Flight Sgt. Kent's thorough inspection, I had surreptitiously released the press-stud fastening of my protective headgear to ease the tightness and the sweating. In the excitement of the collective venture of going out in a five-stick, I forgot to refasten it, with the consequence that it disappeared in an instant. I rightly incurred the wrath of the ground controller, who noticed it immediately and made no bones about telling me through the megaphone. The reprimand was continued on the ground and he was not amused by my replying that I was relieved to find that I had lost only my hat – at the time I felt sure it was my head which had been wrenched off! My stupidity, I recognised, could have had serious consequences – particularly with regard to my atrocious landing, with an unprotected head. With another set of parachutes we were in the air again for our fourth jump. Suitably chastised and subdued, I ensured that my behaviour was impeccable this time, but as luck would have it number four was the perfect jump anyway and totally incident free. Soaking wet, I experienced the carefree joy of a victorious Boat Race crew's cox emerging from his ritual ducking.

Four done, three to come, the last of them to be a night jump. And tomorrow was New Year's Eve… I didn't sleep very well – not a noteworthy fact in itself – but I learned only later that statistics show that most jibbers make their momentous decision after their third or fourth jump, once the reality of what they have been doing had impressed itself more forcefully up on their minds and the time for a final decision was at hand. Jibbing had never entered my mind, yet I cannot explain that restless night unless it was excitement at the possibility of having the final jump on my birthday. New Year's Day had fired my imagination and was driving my mind in rehearsing the composition of my proud letters home.

The morning's conditions were not very favourable but it was decided to try, with eventual successful consequences. Jumps numbered five and six were completed in quick succession after much puzzling circling of the DZ without explanation from the crew or dispatcher. In the fifth, drifting took me a long, anxious way off target, landing me heavily on unyielding rocks – well outside the huge, more comfortable DZ field. Being in the middle of a 'fast tens' stick, it can be imagined that most of us were thus off course. Maybe, when one considered the odd antics of

31

the oft-circling plane, the pilot had something to do with it. Whatever the explanation for my fifth jump's traumas, number six was uneventful. Speculation about the night jump buzzed around when, on returning to the huts, we were confined to billets. It was a dreadful afternoon of waiting. We asked ourselves, wouldn't it be extraordinary for anyone to make three descents in a single day? Apparently it would. Most extraordinary. Tenterhooks was putting it mildly. We could be in an elitist minority. We could be celebrating the New Year as it should be celebrated.

It really was a spontaneous cheer which erupted when, just before darkness fell, Flight Sgt. Kent burst in with "OK lads, it's on!" We were in the truck almost before he had finished the sentence. It was pitch dark when the Hudson took off, after Kenty had explained that this was to be the jump which would most likely resemble the conditions of a night-time drop in enemy occupied territory. A fast stick of ten, keeping as closely together as possible and dropping from a mere 500 feet, demanded an immediate assessment of our descent progress from observation of the solitary flare on the DZ. We were to assemble together as soon as possible after landing by calling the number of our next mate in the stick, then report together to the ground controller. Whether it was from feelings of satisfaction at the imminent completion of the course (which would put another inch on my chest), or perhaps the total obscurity of danger in leaping into the darkness, I knew not – but I ejected myself from the doorway of the Hudson with extra physical vigour and zealous optimism.

It was a strange, lonely experience to be suspended above the earth, knowing that I could neither see a living soul nor be seen. I pondered that, if this had been my first jump, there would have been more justification for believing I was Heaven-bound. Where was the damned flare? It must be behind me... Yes, at the right rear... a turn's necessary... got to feel for the webbing straps... got one, got two, now... Before I could apply any pressure at all I was down harmlessly. Five hundred feet does not allow for any dithering. Whether I landed forwards, backwards or sideways, I know not. I was safe for the reason that night jumps are invariably safer – because one's tried and tested landing position is sustained throughout the descent. Daytime's reaching for the earth tempts supple, bent legs towards vulnerable rigidity.

I collapsed my chute, calling at the same time at not much more than a whisper for No. 8. He acknowledged almost at the same time as I answered No. 6's call to me. In seconds we were together, chattering exuberant nonsense. We had reported to the ground controller before the absence of 9 and 10 was noticed. The ground controller decided that, as the exercise was over as a secret mission, he could shout, "You there, 9 and 10?" "9 is," came the immediate reply from the total darkness, "but I can't find 10." Our alarm skimmed the icing off the cake. We all called out for 10, begging God for an answer and losing our tempers. The controller took over: "One more call then we search." No response ensued. "Right, chutes in the truck then come back here." Flares were lit from the solitary landing beacon and torches were produced for just such a disaster. We lined up at finger touching distance and moved off in the dense darkness, with the controller only occasionally calling and the rest of us observing agreed silence, straining our hearing for a call – however feeble it might be – and each one of us dreading that the discovery of a crumpled body should be made at his unfortunate feet. We searched systematically, and then we searched randomly without success for perhaps half an hour, when the controller decided that the whole camp would have to be mustered to join the search – after he had checked on the possibility (which had not occurred to us) that No. 10 might have jibbed and still be in the plane.

At this juncture, a voice – a seemingly ghostly voice – froze each one of us to the spot. "You lot looking for me? No. 10, like?" He emerged from the blackness with his bundled-up chute grasped to his body. "I thought you might be worried. Got caught up on the plane, you know. Must have been a couple of miles away before the bloody thing shook free. Then I got this lift. I've been as quick as I could." He related his remarkable story endlessly as he walked toward us. We wanted to be mad at him until we realised that his elated animation was no different from ours, but he had more to be grateful for to the Gods. His providential escape only enhanced our celebratory booze-up in the NAAFI canteen. I did not get drunk. I wanted to savour the rare enjoyment of achievement and to glory in my new status.

Weather Disrupts Training

The euphoria generated by having won our 'wings' incurred a considerable dent immediately on our return to the camp at Nahariya on New Year's Day. Very little had changed. Certainly not the weather, and the weather impinged on everything at unprotected Nahariya. It was natural for us to suppose that nobody cared and, although officers suffered equally badly, they were targets for our bottled up, seething discontent, which blamed them for doing nothing to arrange for our reasonable protection from it. Forty years later the regimental war diaries at the National Archives at Kew showed me that our seniors were actually risking accusations of insubordination at the time, with their forthright representations to Middle East HQ at Cairo on our behalf: "Batteries will not be ready... After three weeks of rain, no drying, bathing, hot water facilities... impeding training." The strongest possible stance was taken on 21 January 1944, however, "It is once more stressed that a camp of this nature and on this site is the worst place imaginable in which to organise and train a new unit for early operational target dates. They cannot give due care and attention to their training when they are wet through, lacking in changes of clothing and boots and have nowhere to go except a cold and draughty canteen hut or a soaking wet tent which may or may not stand up against the daily and nightly storm." The Acting Commanding Officer sent that one. Similarly, it is also easier now to understand Cairo's attitude at the time. Obviously, a new, permanent – or even semi-permanent – camp would not be built in the wilds for a unit as ephemeral as ours. We were required to be in Europe as soon as possible, not swanning around in the Middle East – and we were 'swanning' weren't we? To GHQ Cairo, the weather was just bad luck, and was probably considered an exaggeration anyway. One can imagine the comfortable occupants of Cairo's cosy office premises sneering, "Wish they wouldn't keep on about their wretched showers up there in Palestine. Aren't they supposed to be hairy-chested paratroopers, anyway?"

Back at Nahariya, one could detect an air of urgency. Weapons and equipment had begun to roll in, adding to the frustration of having nowhere to muster a group of men together for training purposes, except for the rare, opportunistic occasions when the storms actually abated. Even then, officers had to act rather gingerly: there are limits to the number of times you can expect men to sit or lie on wet ground, to enhance their skills at operating and maintaining unfamiliar weapons, without arousing their fury. Genuine military operations are a different matter.

Explosives Training

Some batteries – or major parts of them – were sent off to other parts of the Middle East to train. The feeling grew that their readiness was less critical than 'C' Battery's – the one I was in. Yet, amazing as it seems to me in retrospect, we learned some more about our main weapon, the 0.5 inch Browning machine gun in which we soon developed a respectful confidence. We had a short course on explosives and demolition, and we suffered demoralising lectures on what our duties were on being captured. The explosives course is worth a mention, if only because it was the one activity for which the weather was actually beneficial – at least from the safety aspect. I cherish the memory of that course's first practical exercise; the setting of a fused detonator in a handful of plastic explosive, the ignition of the fuse and the withdrawal to a safe distance for the resultant explosion. NCOs from the Royal Engineers were our excellent tutors from whom we learned the first, cardinal rule for all explosive settings – "Never run away from a charge." The theory is that it should never be set on so short a fuse as to need to do so anyway, but the maxim's main concern is the avoidance of panic in others who may be unaware of the fuse's time setting.

Towards practical indoctrination of the discipline of this dictum, 30 or so of us were placed in a straight line, with fingers just touching and thus a double arms' length apart, and facing a parallel marked line 15 paces away, in open ground. We were each given half a pound of plastic explosive (looking and feeling like fresh, mouldable putty), a detonator (resembling, in size and appearance a standard cotton reel or bobbin), a length of fuse (similar to modern coaxial aerial cable) timed for a 10 second duration and finally a box of special fuse-igniting matches. Our instructions were brief and unambiguous. We were to set the detonator firmly into our lump of explosive, gently push the length of fuse cable into the hole provided in the detonator (like in our cotton reel), then advance with our 'bombs' to the marked line, together in line and keeping our distance.

Distance between us was again checked before we each obeyed the instruction to place our bomb on the ground on the line and directly at our feet. "Now take out one of your matches, but do not strike until I give the command for you to do so." Perfectly clear so far. The Sergeant instructor next reiterated, "I do not want to see anybody running – remember that!"

"You have all seen what a lit fuse looks like, so I don't want to see any unlit fuses that you 'thought' were lit when we retire from the charge."

"You will now kneel down with your matches ready."

"When I give the command 'Strike' you will strike your match on your matchbox, ignite the fuse, and when you see it lit and 'fizzing' you will retire to your 'start' position in orderly fashion – no running."

"You have each got 10 seconds, which is about twice the time needed to walk briskly back to your start mark."

"All ready, then?"

A quick glance along the line confirmed that we were each hovering over our bombs with matches poised.

"Strike!"

I brushed the match against the abrasive side of the box. Nothing happened. Nerves perhaps? One second... I tried again. No ignition. Two seconds... Must be a duff match, fiddle in the box for another – Hell's bells, my fingers are shaking... Three seconds, four seconds... Why won't it ignite? God! The bloke's fuse on the left is fizzing only five or six feet away from my head – and he's walked almost halfway back! I struck the match successfully and applied the flame to the end of the fuse wire... Come on for God's sake, ignite, FIZZ! Five seconds, six... the one on my right is fizzing now. No running, remember. NO RUNNING? That's a laugh. The stampede back to safety would have put to shame the Charge of the Light Brigade.

It was a disgraceful exhibition of timidity – he said so. Only nine out of 30 had been lit and had exploded. Whether by accident or not, the Royal Engineers had given us a simple lesson in psychology – in human frailty. There had been nothing wrong with the matches or the fuses, as we proved minutes later after we had witnessed the minimal effects of the explosions on the muddy earth and executed the tiresome misfire drill. We had been guilty of panic and of engendering panic. On the third trial of the exercise one hundred per cent success was achieved. From that moment on, explosives and demolition and the sophistication of such things as time-pencil fuses became a subject of fascinating interest to almost all of us, exemplified later in the year by the almost daring contempt for the rules so clearly enunciated by those astute and much underrated men of the Royal Engineers.

Escape and Evasion Training

The high ranking officer, who had been sent from GHQ Middle East to depress us with the conduct expected of us as prisoners of war, paradoxically cheered us with the implications of imminent involvement in hostilities. It was difficult to decide whether to applaud or rebuke High Command for imposing on us so negative a subject, but I suppose in the spirit of boy-scout preparedness it had to be delivered simultaneously with the surprising issue of what was described as an escape kit. The other point in its favour was the confirmation that we were rather special. No other units that we had heard of had received items which indicated the likelihood of action behind enemy lines, which suggested a fair degree of individual independence and implied almost certain co-operation with Partisan organisations.

In logical terms, it was sheer pessimism to envisage a situation calling for any of those objects – a file, a crude compass and a map of the Balkan countries – but their issue redeemed some of GHQ's otherwise besmirched reputation, in their concerns for our welfare. The four-inch-long file was wholly concealed in a flat, innocent looking strip of rubber, which had been designed to fit snugly in the pleat of the field dressing pocket of our battle-dress trousers in the hope of avoiding detection in the normal frisking. My trouble was that it added further rigidity and bulk to a pocket already bulging with my forbidden diary, to the point where a passing medical officer might one day suspect one of the most frightening examples of unilateral hernia he had ever diagnosed – and without the removal of the patient's trousers at that. So I found another home for it – the file, I mean, not the diary.

The compass was at once simple, yet quite ingenious: a two-part brass trouser button (on the face of it) which obviated the need for sewing. With the two parts separated by the trouser material, the spike on one part clicked into the recess in the other, effectively locking the button in an almost irremovable position. The recessed half of the button had been magnetised and marked with a tiny luminous spot to indicate north. One simply had to place the magnetised part on the spike of the lower part to see it swivel instantly to indicate the direction of magnetic north. Useful to know in a blind trek for freedom.

The map had been printed on one side of an otherwise innocuous looking, folded field handkerchief. The unmistakeable utility of these items hardly warranted even the few words of explanation which they produced. Perhaps the promise of the future issue of gold sovereigns, as universally accepted tender for emergency purchases in countries where wartime internal fiscal and political chaos had rendered their national currency worthless, posed more questions than the speaker answered. But both speaker and recipients seemed to be reduced to embarrassed speechlessness (at least initially) by another item issued. The conjecture, the jokes and the moral sensitivity which the personal issue of a couple of packets of rubber sheath contraceptives later provoked would make an interesting book in itself. Suffice it to say that none of the escape items issued were to be 'exposed' before our arrival on the scene of military operations.

Morphine tablets comprised the final means of 'escape'. We were instructed in the dosage for relieving extreme pain – and how much it would take to kill. I imagine that this was to beat the Germans to it if they appeared to be intent on carrying out Hitler's declaration of 18 October 1942: to treat all Commando-type infiltrators in occupied countries as spies and execute them. Fortunately, his instructions were not always carried out.

The exclusivity of our unit gradually became more outwardly noticeable, with the issue of gear which advertised to all in the Haifa area that ours was a somewhat distinctive military role. Our secret existence had obviously been exposed, so what did it matter if the hitherto exclusive beige berets of the Special Air Service suddenly appeared in greater profusion? Although we had become part of a Special Services brigade, the regiment acquired its own rather eye-catching, coloured cap badge emblem depicting a winged torch, and showing the capitals RSR with the biblical legend from St. Paul's first epistle to the Corinthians, 'Quit you like men'. It is true that the wags and the detractors soon fastened on to the word 'quit' in its American usage, rather than 'acquit'. All this, together with a Commando dagger and our smart, brown, calf-high South African Army boots (instead of the black, standard issue Army clod-hoppers) unfortunately prompted a swaggering braggadocio in some of our more aggressive types. Long before it had a military reputation, the Regiment developed an unenviable one of loutishness through aggression, vandalism, drunkenness and looting, which suggested an undisciplined rabble rather than the crème de la crème esteem which the speciality of our training claimed for us.

Daily Life At Nahariya

After constant pressure and in a rare gesture of conciliation, the War Department decided to erect a galvanised structure around and above our latrine bench seats, so that a visit to sit over one of the roughly hewn holes in the bench became more private and less of a risk of contracting pneumonia. That we should come to curse the protection will, I know, brand us as perpetually whining denigrators of all authority. Never satisfied! It wasn't that at all, really. It was simply that our protection from the elements simultaneously provided shelter for the scorpions, of which there were an abundance at Nahariya at that time. They seemed to like the surroundings too. It has to be regretted that the obviousness of this logic of nature was not perceived as readily as it should have been. We do tend to learn from painful experience. It took several days – or nights, more correctly – for us to learn not to sit out after dark unless in dire straits, and only then after burning off with a match or candle the scorpions invariably lurking beneath the rim of the seats. Those first few nights of learning left enduring memories of terror-stricken shrieks of pain piercing the night air, followed by silhouetted images of fast disappearing victims, scurrying over the skyline, sometimes wearing trousers, sometimes not, heading in steadfast urgency for the Medical Officer's tent for treatment to parts normally recognised as private and vital.

I was lumbered with a fair share of guard duties at Nahariya, which in mid-January were more than somewhat onerous due to the astonishing insecurity of weapon and ammunition storage, the scattered nature of the camp site and – a rare phenomenon – the presence of the mules needed for the training of the mountain artillery battery. The wide dispersal of these sites warranted three simultaneous sentry patrols, so that it was a comparatively large guard of nine other ranks and two NCOs which was needed every 24 hours. Each sentry did two hours on, four hours off.

On one memorable night I was the junior NCO on a guard commanded by Corporal 'Spike' Kelly, a redoubtable character yet possessed of a puckish sense of humour. As luck would have it, or perhaps more in the spirit of comradeship and sympathy which always seemed to be directed at men on guard duty, we received a tip-off from an officer's mess orderly, at just about dusk, that the orderly officer of the day had been drinking heavily and boasting to his fellow officers that he was going to catch the guard 'on the hop' that night. Thus the sentries were especially vigilant and the rest of us remained impeccably, correctly dressed, even whilst resting, as we waited the inevitable shout from the guard-tent sentry, "Guard! Turn Out!."

It was a few minutes after midnight when the call came. I cannot imagine that anyone could ever have seen a slicker, quicker turnout despite the inky blackness of that night. With Kelly on the extreme right, six sentries and then myself on the far end in one straight line, we must have displayed a formidable challenge, even to one determined to find fault, as we presented arms with Grenadier-like precision on Spike's command.

With the help of a tiny, weak-batteried torch he surveyed us and weighed into Spike with nebulous complaints and criticism that had obviously been rehearsed even before he had left the officer's mess tent. With commendable restraint, Spike held his tongue and allowed the tirade to run its term, answering only with his name when demanded for the purpose of it being recorded on a 252 (Army charge sheet) for "this disgraceful guard." The only two complaints we took seriously were claims that the sentry guarding the mule lines could not be found and the one on the weaponry had been caught smoking whilst on sentry – both names he demanded for going into 'the book'. Spike agreed to my checking after the officer had gone: the first sentry challenged me alertly at a point some fifty or so yards from the animals; the second sentry was a non-smoker. Army injustice at work again.

With the commotion over, I persuaded Spike to bed down for the first doze of a couple of hours whilst I took charge – a time-honoured bending of the rules. He agreed, and after divesting himself of most of his bulky kit he settled himself down on a groundsheet and blanket on the tent floor and was soon asleep. Not one of us had reckoned on the Orderly Officer coming back again, as he did half an hour later, though fortunately he was correctly challenged. "Guard! Turn out!" We had been caught literally napping. The turnout was a trickle as those who had been asleep fought off their drowsiness. Spike was well away: I had to shake him before I dashed out. I told him briefly I would take the guard commander position on the right so that he could have a few more seconds in which to don his gear, and slip quietly into my position on the left of the guard in the darkness and hubbub whilst I stalled the orderly officer.

He was not going to be easily stalled. The torch shone in my face. He swayed slightly.

"I suppose you realise, Kelly…"

"Jones, Sir," I interrupted.

"…that you're expected to be alert for 24 hours a day, and if you call that turnout being alert Kelly…" "Jones, Sir," I said again.

"…you're going to learn what a turnout …"

He stopped.

"Why do you keep saying, Jones?"

"It's my name, Sir."

"Oh, so it's Jones now is it?"

"No, Sir"

"NO, SIR?" he echoed. "NO?" again.

"Well, I mean not just now Sir. It's always been my name".

"Then why did you tell me it was Kelly a few minutes ago?"

"I didn't, Sir."

"YOU DIDN'T?" He was echoing again.

"Do you realise what you're saying, Jo-, Kell-…?" His voice trailed away.

"Yes, Sir. You were speaking to Corporal Kelly a few minutes ago. He's Guard Commander: I'm NCO marching-reliefs. Corporal Kelly has had to go to the latrines and I have properly taken charge."

His confusion compounded by drink, he decided that he would inspect the guard one by one again, and as I was about to fall-in behind his slow, staggering footsteps, I felt a tap on my shoulder. Spike, who had heard the goings-on, was wide awake and presentable, having slipped round the rear of the line. He surreptitiously pushed me out of the way, indicated that I should sneak around the rear of the sentries to my rightful place at the far end of the line, which I did, then himself silently followed the officer's slow, pernickety process of criticising of each sentry's faintly torch-lit appearance until he reached me. Seeing the two stripes on my arm he pounced:

"Ah! So you're back at last, Kelly!"
"No, Sir, I'm Jones, Sir, and I haven't been away."
"You're WHAT?… WHO?"
"Jones, Sir."
"No, you're not. You're Kelly."
"No, Sir, I'm Jones, Sir."
"Then where the hell is Kelly?" he snarled victoriously.

"I'm right here, Sir" calmed Spike, sounding like a comforting night nurse answering the cry of a feverish patient, from less than a foot away from the left ear of a very bewildered officer. The effect was startling. I think he thought the DTs had finally got to him. He staggered off into the night, pausing and turning towards us just once to threaten that every one of the guard would find himself on a charge in the morning. We did not. Nothing more was heard of the incident about which, at the time, I felt furious, but which subsequently caused some mirth.

Deployment

The days after our final, gruelling, three day, fend-for-yourself exercise in the hills (and in the inevitable pouring rain), our confinement to barracks heralded the momentous journey to pastures new – Port Said. The transit camp at Port Said did not hold much appeal, either in anticipation or in reality. The nothingness of Port Said is reflected in the absence of any diary entries for the five days of our stay. Furthermore, I remember nothing of it except for its significance in the long road home from Asia to Europe.

On 1 February 1944 we boarded a troopship, the MV *Dilwara* along with hundreds, possibly thousands of other troops, thus suggesting a mass military movement rather than a stealthy landing of Specialist Forces. Guesses were limited therefore to Italy or Tunisia as a possible base for our operations but as always, guesses they had to be. There were even some optimistic souls who imagined we were destined for Blighty, to prepare for the ultimately inevitable landing in northern France if the war was going to be won. It was a theory which collected some credence as we sailed, then hove-to to assemble into a sizeable flotilla which, when it did move-off, proceeded only to Alexandria to merge with an even more substantial waiting convoy. Acclimatised to troopship conditions, and aware that our sailing westwards in the Mediterranean indicated a short trip, the horrors were relatively minimal. It was a fairly relaxing trip, allowing plenty of time for meditative stocktaking – a pleasing contrast in itself after what had been a couple of months of feverish activity. I could reflect on being pleased about many things. I derived considerable satisfaction from coming through the personal challenge of parachuting without anxiety, regret, or more importantly, injury.

Another measure of our good fortune had taken a little longer to positively manifest itself: I had been allotted a first class gun crew. There were four Scotsmen (three from the same heavy anti-aircraft artillery unit, who had already been overseas for three years) and a Cockney. The Scots were a delightful mixture of talent and personality, who were already close friends of deep understanding. Archie Lundy, a Lance Bombardier and therefore my deputy, combined handsomeness and athleticism with high intelligence and wit: he could be a voluble man, particularly where his principles were at stake. William Laird Brown, sometimes Bill, sometimes Tony (a derivation of Twinny – he had a twin brother) but more often Topper, displayed an outward appearance of calm and even (I always suspected, deliberate) slow-wittedness. This totally belied his keen mind, mischievous sense of fun, dedicated ideals, ready perception of duty and, perhaps even more so than Archie, his superb prowess. Both Archie and Topper would have become automatic choices for any football team, which the Battery, or even the Regiment, would field if ever we had come together again as a whole.

Bert Roger, their friend in arms of many years, was a vastly different kettle of fish. A droll, dour sage of a man, Bert was by far the oldest amongst us. Combined with his longer background of civvy-street working life as a stockbroker in Glasgow, his ubiquitous, tranquilising pipe and his economy of words and physical exertion, this made him seem like a displaced aristocrat. He succeeded in making one feel guilty for allocating to him any manual – or menial – task that might soil his hands. In truth, he never dodged his fair share but still managed to convey that he lived in a cruel world. His torpid approach to exercise and his slight, lethargic stature made me wonder admiringly about the suffering he must have endured during his parachute training. In Willie Kirkwood, the fourth Scot, we had a rogue. An undisguised product of the worst slums in "No Mean City", Willie had the guile and cunning which every outfit needs for acquisitive, fair-share survival in an often cruel, competitive world. Charlie Winch, the final member of the crew, was a Londoner. After surveying the other gun crews I had no doubt whatsoever that I had fared best in the lottery. Our whole relationship was totally devoid of the dispute and rancour that seemed to affect the other crews. We trained without the need for any spoken reminders of rank or of our interdependence on each other.

The progress of the war had also begun to justify cautious optimism by February 1944, as our majestic convoy sailed unmolested. The Russians continued to roll back the enemy's eastern front and had already crossed the pre-war Polish frontier. The Americans were beginning to alter the balance of power in the Pacific. Allied progress in Italy had been slow-but-sure up the Adriatic. Whilst the bombing of Germany intensified from Britain in closely co-ordinated operations of the RAF and the US Army Air Force, the air assault on the Balkan countries and Central Europe was under way from newly operational bases in Italy. At about the same time, Churchill and Roosevelt were announcing a measure of success in the Battle of the Atlantic, with the news that merchant shipping losses were 60% less than those of the previous year. The only dampener on all this optimism was the knowledge that my movement would indefinitely disrupt the flow of letters from home. The immediate future held only bleak prospects for personal communication.

"We bonded. We polarised… We learnt new vulgar songs, one of which was to become our notorious signature tune."

Europe Again

After landing at the Italian port of Bari we spent most of the day draped over the rails awaiting landing orders, gazing compulsively at docks, desolation and, for the first time, masses of lolling, mildly inquisitive American army men strewn amongst stacks and assemblies of guns, ammunition and miscellaneous supplies vital for the prosecution of a war. The whole scene was one of assembled power and resources – a further reminder of the volume factor in the American contribution to the Allied war effort – which, with the assortment of shipping itself, paradoxically created gnawing misgivings at the vast, unmissable target it presented to an enemy air attacker.

Presumably, the Luftwaffe were more vitally engaged elsewhere. However, somebody in authority must soon have experienced the same anxieties as myself about the dockside breach of all we had been taught about dispersal, for our disembarkation with only battle-order kit, was followed by a march of a couple of miles or so, without complaint, to some open land which did not deserve its description even as a 'temporary' transit camp.

The diet of hard rations was soon supplemented with unsolicited contributions from friendly, curious and bountiful American soldiers, whose spam made a change from bully-beef and whose frank, open warmth of approach made a surprising change from the usual mutual initial suspicions which operated when British units met.

If we envied them their kit and supplies, we could at least take some comfort from our special-forces equipment being vastly superior to that of ordinary units of the British army. Bedding-down that night was a perfect example. Our lightweight, snug sleeping bags offered a better guarantee of quality sleep under our easily portable two-man bivouacs than did the poor bloody infantry's blankets under the stars. Truth be told, sleep did not come easily on that first night back in Europe after almost two years. Danger had nothing to do with it: the battle for Italy was too remote to be heard. When I think now of the thousands of lives that were lost in the long struggle for the conquest of Italy, which went on until the last day of fighting in Europe, I imagine that each one of those who died spent their first night in Italy in similarly disturbed, optimistic excitement at the prospect of being pointed in the right direction for home. I think I was rare though in also finding space in my thoughts for regrets at leaving the Middle East, and a dreamy, unrealistically optimistic ambition to return there again under different circumstances.

With typically unquestioned military mystery, a fleet of lorries arrived the next morning bearing the rest of our personal kit from the *Dilwara*. After we had boarded the vehicles as bidden, the convoy then set off northwards along the Adriatic coast road for sixty or so miles to a small port called Monopoli, where we were billeted in reasonably comfortable, if overcrowded, conditions in a school building at the town's outskirts. Monopoli, being some thirty miles south of Bari – which we knew had been taken by the Allies within a few weeks of the landings in Italy in September – appeared to show few of the outward signs of the ravages of war but, being typical of the neglected towns of southern Italy, nevertheless had the appearance of a sad, down-at-heel countenance of deprivation. I had not then heard the northern Italians' jibe about the south but if, as the yarn goes, one did draw a line across Italy from Rome to Rimini to find something of Africa below the line, I have to say that my first impressions of Monopoli's people would have enhanced the reputation of Africa in my reckoning. Everyone had heard of the charges of cowardice, duplicity and chameleon loyalties directed at the Italians. Contact and recounted experiences had provided some justification for those criticisms yet, appropriately prejudiced as I was, my first association with Italian people at Monopoli in February 1944 was an enlightening, pleasurable experience oddly inconsistent with my posture of belligerence and disgust towards a bitterly scorned enemy of five months earlier. Alerted to all their wiles, I still discovered a charm in the Italians with whom I came into contact at Monopoli which remains inexplicable. The sceptics would, no doubt, point out that we were at Monopoli for only twelve days. In that short time we discovered hairdressers, tailors, embroiderers (who copied and reproduced our 'wings' and cap-badges with amazingly deft artistry), photographers, restaurateurs, and, of course, vino barmen who created our first and lasting taste for the pleasures of vermouth. And, believe it or not, there was already in Monopoli an established YMCA where 'chars-and-wads' (teas and cakes) could supplement the mainly unsatisfied appetites remaining after our army meals.

We bonded. We polarised. We had fights among our tense selves and we had near-mutinies in frightening bouts of ill-discipline and insubordination. We played football matches and had cross-country runs. We learnt new vulgar songs, one of which was to become our notorious signature tune. It was a remarkable twelve day episode.

"We were heading to the assistance of the Yugoslav Partisans, whose leader was a mysterious character called Tito."

Yugoslavia

I have not recorded, nor can I remember when or how I became possessed of the information that enemy occupied Yugoslavia was to be our destination. On 18 February all the fun and high-jinks were interrupted, and we were rather hurriedly taken by road to Bari to unload a ship laden with our guns and supplies. The writing, if not in manuscript, was on the wall. We worked with an enthusiasm that day which equalled for impact the startling effect of our first glimpse of an Italian city.[7]

Two days later, we set off by sea on board LCI (Landing Craft, Infantry) No. 260. LCI 260 had sailed from Monopoli's slightly ruffled harbour on Sunday morning 20 February 1944 into a turbulent Adriatic, bound (we had actually been told!) for a destination in 'enemy waters', but the Navy crew soon had misgivings about the storm which had developed at sea. The result was that our progress to the north was cut short and the haven of Bari's docks was soon sought, to the intense satisfaction of the many who were suffering from seasickness. The anticlimax might have been distressing had not our superiors, with commendable appreciation of the situation, allowed us ashore in Bari for the day under threats of unimaginably dire penalties for any blabbing of our projected enterprise – a laughable precaution, since none of us knew of our destination nor of our role. So the day, which started with cloak and dagger potentialities, culminated in an enjoyable appreciation of most of what city life could offer.

Topper and I saw two films that day: Ball of Fire and Air Force, neither of which made any lasting impression on my memory. However, by contrast, we did make the pleasing discovery of Spumanti – a poor-man's and then-ignorant-of-any-other-man's champagne – and enjoyed excellent food at one of the several forces' canteens, already well established in a city teeming with British and American troops. The true extent of what a fortuitous bonus that day in Bari had been became clearer the next day when, after we had slept in bunks in cramped conditions on the boat, it sailed into frighteningly stormy waters of at least equal ferocity to that of the previous day. We were under orders that apparently forbade any further delay in meeting the timetabled arrangements for reception at the other end.

Vis

During the course of the day long voyage, the information was revealed that the 'other end' was a Yugoslav island off the coast of Dalmatia called Vis[8], which was occupied by a small garrison of Tito's Partisans.[9] It was the only island – perhaps the only populated part of Yugoslavia – not already held by the Germans.[10] During the latter part of 1943 the enemy had extended its total mainland occupation of Yugoslavia, invading and taking possession of the other islands in the Dalmatian group, strengthening control of the Adriatic supply seaways and denying the Allies the use of the islands as platforms for any optimistic mainland invasion aspirations of their own.

As the briefing unfolded that day, my zest for adventure began to be overtaken with qualms of repeating recent Mediterranean military history. If, as seemed likely, the enemy could have taken Vis as easily as he had occupied Brac, Korcula, Solta, Hvar, Mljet and the other Dalmatian islands, was he not waiting for the Allies to repeat the folly of Crete, Kos and Leros before swamping the island with his superior military might, in order to collect prizes from the garrison of a poorly supplied Yugoslav brigade of resistance fighters, reinforced with British troops and their valuable equipment? The Germans could actually see Vis from their other island bases and had mainland airfields a mere ten minutes flight away: our logistical links were half a days sailing away in Italy, through seaways where the relative strength of naval power was finely balanced.

The remnants of No. 2 Commando, licking their wounds after a mauling at Anzio, were the first integral British Army unit to arrive on the island, among a plethora of advance parties from Commando and anti-aircraft units, with a mission to defend the islands at all costs. 'C' Battery's hurried presence in its anti-aircraft role reinforced my niggling misgivings. Our knowledge of the significance of the operation was scant, but it would be unfair to attach blame or shame to any party for that. It had taken several courageous, diligent, undercover British military missions, parachuted and then secreted deep into mainland occupied Yugoslavia from 1941 to 1944, for the Army to be sufficiently convinced of the situation to enable them to report to the Prime Minister. We were heading to the assistance of the Yugoslav Partisans, whose leader was a mysterious character called Tito. Partisans to us then meant any resistance fighters – guerrillas in fact. But in Yugoslavia the name 'Partisans' served to distinguish Tito's devoutly Communist band of fanatical fighters from those other Slav opponents of German occupation who were imbued with strong Royalist leanings. Their leader, an ex-regular army officer of the pre-war Yugoslav monarchy, General Draze Mihajlovic, had chosen the name 'Chetniks' for his band of followers.

It is probably overly simplistic to state that both factions, whilst seeming to operate from the start with a single common objective, were violently opposed to each other. The British military missions, paradoxically not wholly manned by true military types but liberally sprinkled with men of the Special Operations Executive, had revealed that Partisan/Chetnik differences were not limited to ideology. Both factions were jockeying for position after the war by destroying each other in the second battle (their civil war) before the first battle (for freedom) had been won by the ejection of Nazi occupiers. Pledged to support Yugoslavia, Britain initially infiltrated token material consignments of arms and supplies by nocturnal air and sea-drops to the royalist Chetniks. It was doubts about the effectiveness of their use against the common enemy that had prompted the formation of several British military missions. The missions' reports justified Churchill's anxiety. Mihajlovic represented no effective resistance to the German occupiers with whom he shared a mutual antipathy towards Communism. Indeed, frequent instances of collaboration with the enemy were revealed as the Chetniks craftily conserved their resources for the ultimate internal fight for power.

Another dormant, simmering and opportunistic faction of Yugoslavian politics had seized upon Hitler's invasion as a heaven-sent opportunity towards furtherance of its claims for the separation of Croatia from the state of the South Slavs. As fascist as Hitler or

Mussolini, their leader Ante Pavelic had enjoyed for years the protection and patronage of Mussolini within Italy's frontier, awaiting stroke of good fortune such as Hitler's invasion had presented. Always reluctant members of the collection of South Slav states which constituted Yugoslavia after the First World War, these radical Croats known as the Ustasi lost no time in pledging support to the invaders, and in currying favour by perpetrating atrocities and injustices against Serbians, in particular, to a degree which made Hitler's men seem almost angelic.

We knew nothing of all this when LCI 260 stealthily negotiated the last few miles of the voyage, through black Adriatic waters to moor at the sheltered jetty of Komiza – the western port of Vis island – at 23:00 on 21 February 1944. Neither did we know that within 12 hours, Winston Churchill would announce to Parliament that future assistance by the Allies to Yugoslavia would be directed wholly to Tito's Partisans. It was a purely military decision: to hell with the post-war political implications. If the Partisans were killing Germans, they were the ones worthy of support. To have been otherwise influenced by fears of post-war communism would have made a mockery and a nonsense of Western reliance on, encouragement for and support to the Soviet Union.

My first glimpse of the Partisans, in the minimal amount of artificial light necessarily risked to facilitate unloading the LCI, made me glad they were on our side, and even more glad that they seemed to know that we were on theirs. For a start, they all appeared to be huge, bulkily framed individuals who strangely belied the deprivations of three years of occupation. Their peculiar assortment of uniforms (mostly acquired from captured or killed Italians and Germans), their purposeful demeanour and conspicuous, bristling armoury of pistols, grenades, knives and ammunition, presented a fearsome aspect reminiscent of Hollywood's version of banditry in the Mexican mountains. But there was a major difference: they were not all male. In our low lit surroundings, only voices distinguished male from female. A surprising revelation!

Only the briefest of nodded instructions were possible as British Navy officers nervously indicated that a rapid discharge of our cargo of armaments and supplies would help their chances of sailing clear of enemy patrolled waters, before daylight's dawning exposed them in their dash back to the relative safety of the eastern Italian coastline. There was no doubt about our being welcome, however. The Partisans radiated a ready friendship and respect, which required no knowledge of each other's language for its communication. They set about unloading the ship with a frenzy and energy which was breathtaking, and which soon had the LCI's crew smiling again and the rest of us wondering and worrying about how we would have managed without Partisan help. In a fraction of the time allowed for the off-loading operation, the jetty was littered with our gear and the vessel was quietly chugging its relieved way into the darkness, leaving us with a strange feeling of being abandoned. Our silent, valedictory waves to the crew and their reciprocation seemed to imply a mutual recognition – though I suspect an exaggeration – of each other's danger.

Our officers, having been briefed by advance-party colleagues and a Partisan interpreter, had been able to tell us that we were to spend the rest of the night in a schoolroom in Komiza. Morning, we learned, would signal our move over the nearby mountain range onto the island's central plains which we were to defend. Each man loaded up with as much equipment as he could possibly carry – in addition to his own not inconsiderable personal kit and small arms – and set off in a silent, single-column stagger to follow the Partisan guide, who incidentally carried more than any of us with apparent ease. Our instructions were to maintain silent, visual contact with the man ahead of us so as to avoid losing our way in the veritable maze of haphazard housing. This was a positive discouragement to dallying so that, loaded as we were, not even the cold February night air could neutralise the clinging, sticky sweat of our heavily burdened hike.

The reason for silence escapes me now as much as it did then, because I remember experiencing one of those out-of-place giggling fits born of musical comedy male voice choruses (typical of The Pirates of Penzance or Maid of the Mountains) as fitting the occasion more appropriately. After a few minutes of what seemed like mountaineering, there was no mistaking a bustling, whispering hubbub coming from the rear of the column. I was glad when it caught up with me: even more so at being softly told by one of our officers to halt and rest my load. He passed me and continued up the hill into the night accompanied by a voluble, agitated but unintelligible Partisan who disappeared with him into the alien darkness. After what could only have been a couple of minutes they returned – leading the column down the hill. "Some bloody fool took the wrong turning and was leading us out of town," came the explanation. Actually, the 'bloody fool' was Topper Brown. With his head down he had followed on the heels of a crossing Partisan who was obviously going about his own business and had thus innocently diverted us away from the schoolroom, where puzzled waiting Partisans could only ponder at how a supposedly efficient troop of elite British military forces could find itself childishly lost so soon after its arrival on their tiny outpost of an uncomplicated island. Topper was never quite allowed to live it down.

It was 02:00 before we simmered down, snugly enveloped in our lush sleeping bags on the congested classroom floor, but slumber did not come easily. Poster pictures of Tito and Stalin glared down from every wall, heightening the sense of adventure and stimulating conversation about the unusual nature of our mission. Morning could not come soon enough. Curiosity could only be satisfied with daylight's revelations. We washed, shaved and breakfasted (on 'compo' rations) under the intense gaze of admiring Partisans who jabbered with unintelligible but obvious approval at our arms and equipment and, I suspect, at our mere presence among them. I wondered if they had slept at all. We, in turn, wanted to see their island and, barely able to contain our curiosity, we hastened out individually into the alleyways of Komiza.

There was to be no hanging around for us. I cannot remember how our weaponry and stores were transported to our destination, four or five miles away over the hills and onto the island's central plain, but we marched on the road. The island's roads were then little more than dusty tracks, which for the first mile of steep ascent out of Komiza were mere ledges cut out of the rocky hillsides in a series of blind bends devoid of any edge marking or safety barriers. In most places it proved difficult for jeeps to pass in safety. The heavier vehicles, which were to arrive later on the island, created more fear from the likelihood of a precipice-dive ending than the threats of a German invasion. Tracks, which had been good enough for peaceful islanders for hundreds of years, had immediately become dangerously inadequate – or certainly were to do so within a few weeks of the Allied garrison's consolidation.

It was an exhausting climb, justifying the abandoning of any pretence at orderly marching until the seemingly scooped-out and levelled plateau of cultivated vines had been reached. Even then, our officers had problems in restoring discipline among the moaners, who seemed to imagine that troop-carrying vehicles should have been miraculously produced for our transportation. Aware of our village destination, our leaders were soon able to encourage us to renewed effort by identifying it from their maps. Once it was within sight, the village of Podselje became an easily attainable goal to surprisingly revived, swinging, singing marchers.

With the flash of the magic wand, which in wartime always seemed to arrange these things, billets were found for the near forty of us. Where the displaced occupants of the dwellings had been moved to I never knew. The contours of the hillside arranged our house of three levels to have its entrance on the middle floor, directly from the lane that gave access to the village. The lower floor was a storage place that housed everything necessary for the making and storing of wine. Its double-door garage-type access (which I never saw unlocked) would have opened onto the next lower lane. Ours was the last house of the village on the western side, a fact which contrived to help the Partisans decide that the levelled area just outside the house's entrance door would be our common meeting place for evening vino-drinking, singing and dancing sessions.

But on that first day of such accord we also had to be reminded why we were there. Gun sites were decided upon, resited and changed again, so that most of the day was spent abortively in roughly levelling areas for our Browning machine gun, its pedestal and ammunition in readiness for the imminent action. News of German aircraft, shipping and troops assembling on the mainland had given every indication of an early attack on Vis. Sited at staggered levels on the hillside, our six guns enjoyed uninterrupted coverage of the whole central plain of the island, most of which was within effective range of the weapons. It meant that from that moment on, each gun would never be unmanned. This presented little difficulty, inconvenience or acrimony during daylight hours, but for the twelve-hour night shift two men had to forsake the relative comfort of their billets and occupy the gun-site in wakeful alertness on a two-hours-on, two-hours-off basis.

There began an arduous era of vigilance which guaranteed that insomnia was never likely to be a problem to contend with during our stay on Vis. I put Charlie and Kirky on for the first night and spent the hours after midnight wishing I had put myself on, as I listened to torrential rain tippling down. It took very little imagination to picture their helpless exposure on that cold, unprotected site on the hillside and to appreciate the absurdity of either of them even unrolling his sleeping bag. Sleep was an impossibility.

I knew that their misery would have been completed by the awful change in the weather coming on top of their envy at easily hearing the sounds of revelry emanating from ourselves and our Partisan hosts, who had been determined to introduce us without delay to the warmth and fervour of their patriotic songs and dances and to their mysteriously unlimited supply of the island's vino. It was a memorable night. Certainly, communication was difficult but the early evening had yielded a commissar character called Srdan Serdar whose better than passable English appointed him henceforth as interpreter, counsellor and friend. The nearest our language could approach to the pronunciation of his Christian name was Sirjon, by which he was thereafter known.

Sirjon was something of an enigma. Whilst preaching Communism for all he was worth, he paraded an aloofness of suave superiority over his comrades which stamped 'class' over his every gesture. Snobbery might even be near the truth. Probably in his late twenties, Sirjon's handsome Slav features were enhanced by vanity expressed in a sartorial elegance so un-guerilla like as to suggest the very privilege which Communism's levelling was held to reject. He wore an immaculate Italian officer's uniform and resplendent, glistening boots. Despite the slightly niggling nausea that his presence induced, Sirjon was our willing and helpful source of information and our introduction to local customs and to his Partisan colleagues. Suggestions that he was a plant among us were probably true, but I saw nothing sinister in that: life without him at Podselje would have been much less rewarding.

The mixture of ethnic origin and age range, and the high proportion of females that comprised the Partisans with whom we were linked, combined to produce initial surprise among us at the heterogeneous assortment that our new friends obviously were. It shouldn't have done. Where whole communities had been ejected from their own mainland or island homes, grateful to be alive and united in passionate resolve to destroy the enemy responsible for their dilemma, niceties of recruitment would have been absurd. Capacity to contribute towards the struggle was a matter ultimately influenced in any event by the will to survive.

Women could fire a sten gun or throw a grenade as well as most men could; girls and boys could carry messages; old men could cook or perform a hundred and one other supportive tasks. This army was, in truth, a mobile fighting community which could not afford passengers. It added to the admirable family feeling which attended that first welcoming gathering at Podselje.

Their singing, imbued with passion and executed with an obviously inherent feel for harmony and unselfconscious desire for performance, is a memory I shall retain until I die. Sirjon readily complied with my request for the phonetic translation of the words of our own favourites among their songs. Despite our relative vocal inadequacy, within days we were singing 'Partisani Nasa', 'Dalmatinsca', 'Domovina' and others with such proprietary pride as to make our mock marching – exaggerated left-foot stamp – flatteringly compulsive.

Life on Vis was every bit as unusual as one would have expected it to be. The only life-giving properties that the island possessed were grapes, wine and water. The latter was to run out first. Every other basic item of supply – food, clothing, equipment, ammunition, fuel and transport – had to be supplied by sea at night from Italy, by courtesy and courage of the Royal Navy. Similarly, the luxuries of life like mail and my hopes of a NAAFI ration of chocolate, non-vino booze or cigarettes, relied upon the Navy's availability and capacity, as well as the caring interest and administrative capabilities of our base-wallah's to supply us from Bari. Not unnaturally, though probably unfairly, we usually felt that those at base were neither caring nor capable. Such cynicism was not without some justification. When the decision to supply the Partisans began to be implemented, a few anomalies arose from a strange application of priorities. Whilst we, ostensibly on operations, were fed on 'compo' rations or operational hard tack, the Partisans were to receive fresh food wherever possible. There was one particularly galling example of this absurdity: their supplies of flour yielded appetising bread from the island's bakery at Vis Town. It cost us cigarettes (when available) to barter for loaves with the Partisans.

It was the intermingled presence of females in the Partisan army that posed the most questions. No sexual segregation? It suggested all manner of problems, but Sirjon's explanation of Tito's decreed death penalty for both parties for any breach of his strict rules of chastity whilst the enemy was still on Yugoslav soil had sufficient ring of shotgun deterrent about it to make it appear enforceable. Pregnant soldiers were immobile and incapacitated soldiers for a while: babies meant more mouths to feed from already very limited resources. In such highly emotional circumstances temptation must have been difficult to resist, but I learned of few breaches of the rules and certainly did not hear of any executions for the offence.

The immediate practical priority for us was the construction of some protection for the gun and crew from enemy attack, and from the then hostile winter elements. The only building materials available were limestone rocks, dislodged for the planting of vines and the earth-retaining terrace walls built to contain them. Our early pathetic efforts at using them for the construction of dugouts at first puzzled, then amused our Partisan friends. When the consensus seemed to be that we were trying to build a minature 'koocha' (house), we were pushed aside in their competitive desire to take over the task. In no time at all the guns were enclosed to an adequate level, and adjacent two-man sleeping hovels were constructed and roofed. They were palaces when compared with those first few nights of total exposure. Camouflage nets concealed the whole from the cameras of enemy observation planes, or so we hoped.

If my diary at this stage enthused about my good fortune in the quality and compatibility of my gun crew, it spares little in self reproach for my consumption of alcohol. Free availability of excellent vino would be my main grounds of mitigation, but self-condemnation at my abuse leaves no doubt about my guilty conscience at the time: I must stop this drinking. These Partisans are great folk but they won't take any 'no thank you'. I might add in defence that I drank no more than the rest of us – and certainly much less than did the hardened Partisans – but it was an era of unprecedented imbibing which I appear to have wanted recorded.

When the mail started to catch up with us after a week on Vis, a whole new enthusiasm pervaded the venture despite the frustration of the obvious restrictions which influenced the newsworthiness of our replies. There we were in the most intriguing situation of our war – something to write about at last – but it was wholly forbidden to drop even the remotest hint of our whereabouts! Even the address allocated to us for use by our correspondents (Raiding Forces, advance HQ, Force

133) conveyed nothing. For many months our correspondence merely confirmed our existence, with trite and boring repetition padding out the lines.

The population of Podselje was further swollen at the beginning of March with the arrival of a detachment of 43 Royal Marine Commando, which by its very presence served to dilute the attention which we had received from the Partisans. It did not dilute the vino, but helped to disperse the pressure to consume it. More importantly, it demonstrated the build-up of Allied troops on the island which then totalled two Commando units, a Royal Artillery Light Anti-Aircraft Battery (No. 101), a light Field Ambulance Detachment (No. 151) with a surgical team, a detachment of No. 10 Commando (Serbo-Croat speaking) and a detachment of an American Special Operations Group. Tension began to grow in direct ratio to some reliable reports of German troop concentrations on the mainland, so that practical training had an urgent sense of purpose about it. The more we fired the Browning the more we liked it: the more too that the crew proudly absorbed the praise for its handling. Guard duties became less of a bore or chore when a genuine turnout was anticipated. Only the incessant rain, I felt sure, was keeping the enemy from trying a landing, so that when an island-wide alarm was sounded on the calm night of 14/15 March each of us was pumping his personal reserves of adrenaline ready for action. The Germans didn't come.

However, whispers had been circulating. The talk was of a Commando reconnaissance party having landed on one of the German-held islands with a raid in prospect. The force that landed on the island of Solta at around midnight on 18/19 March from two LCIs, certainly arrived unnoticed by the German occupiers. Indeed, the ease with which most nocturnal landings could be effected on any of the Dalmatian islands was to become a feature of the series of raids that followed. Great credit for this is due to the co-operation of the Yugoslav villagers. It would have taken divisions of troops to have effectively patrolled those hundreds of miles of coastlines, of which back-of-the-hand knowledge was understandably reserved to the Yugoslav population of those isles. That population became the eyes and ears of the Partisan forces. Nevertheless, the Germans on the islands initially displayed a military naïvety, which suggested that when Himmler was boasting to the world of his knowledge of the strength of the Allied force on Vis (on 11 March 1944) he must have forgotten to tell his local troops. Perhaps it was imagined that we were there for defence only. On Solta, the attackers ought to have been expected.

The reconnaissance party of some few days earlier had produced an exemplary dossier of information, but it had run into a German patrol and had had to leave behind one of its officers, as a wounded prisoner in possession of copious notes and diagrams of nought but military significance. Yet after Colonel Jack Churchill led ashore 180 or so of his No. 2 Commando, together with a similar number of men of the US Special Operations Group who were supported by 47mm guns, medium machine guns and mortars manned by men of the 101st Anti-Aircraft Battery and 43rd Marine Commando, Heavy Weapons Group, they were able to disembark, cross the island and settle into agreed positions around the German-garrisoned village of Grohote without detection. The initial attack, just after dawn, proved to be a total surprise to the enemy whose retaliation was slow and seemingly half-hearted. Their reaction to a loudhailer call to them to surrender to British forces was, however, equally half-hearted, despite the noisily proclaimed threat of an imminent raid on the village by the Royal Air Force from bases in Italy. Perhaps it was a sledgehammer to crack a nut, but when 36 fighter-bombers arrived precisely on time and proceeded to devastate Grohote, it is doubtful who were the most surprised but it terminated the operation. Loudhailer calls enjoyed a better response this time.

The Allied raiders took back to Vis around 100 prisoners, having already buried six victims of the onslaught. Allied casualties were two killed and about twenty wounded. Solta, for the time being, was bereft of Germans. It was an excellent start to raiding which had two important effects. Firstly, it necessitated the enemy's strengthening of the defences on each of the islands, thus achieving one of the main objectives of Allied presence in Yugoslavia – the tying down of more and better enemy forces in Dalmatia – but secondly, as a consequence, it made future raids that much more difficult and costly for the Allies. If one paused to cogitate on the element of surprise to which the raid on Solta, owed its success, perhaps the fifth columnists in our midst would not have imagined that the British could have been so stupid as to hold an Anglo-Yugoslav concert in the schoolroom at Podselje on the same evening that many of the defenders of Vis were stealthily stepping ashore on Solta.

I have to admit though that the concert was a tremendous success, apart from the temporary nuisance of a troublesome minority of RSR drunks who were metaphorically, then literally, carried away. It was the emphatic and ultimate icebreaker in tri-partite relations between Partisans, commandos and RSR in Podselje. What mattered was our singing of 'Partisani Nasa' and 'Dalmatinsca' in Serbo-Croat and their renderings of 'Tipperary' and 'You are my Sunshine' in English. The diary is almost emotional: "A fine feeling now exists between ourselves and the Partisans. There's something wonderful about these folk – I would like to go on fighting with them until we have liberated their country."

However, this perfect picture was disturbed by an unwelcome development. Someone must have spotted the inequality in the calibre of the gun crews, for on 19 March Charlie Winch was taken away from me, made up to Lance-Bombardier and, in a minor reshuffle, replaced by an Irish lad named Paddy Haden. Charlie strengthened Fred Butcher's crew – my loss, Fred's gain – but it was a compensation to see Charles get some deserved promotion. Paddy was a likeable lad, tentatively acquiescent to a point near to characterlessness until he felt the reassurance of acceptance, after which he contributed his fair share of constructive opinions to add to a rare quality of enthusiasm for hard physical graft. Whether his rather droll humour was delayed whilst he settled in or if it naturally matured from contamination by the rest of us I never knew, but he soon emerged as a laconic comic who thereafter regularly amused us with apt examples of a perceptive wit. He immediately raised with me a subject which it was my duty to initiate and on which I usually procrastinated. "You'll be wanting my next of kin," he said as he produced a scrap of paper bearing his father's name and an address in Monastriden, County Sligo. What prophetic instinct prompted his uncharacteristic blundering into a topic as taboo as a soldier's will leaves me bewildered. Within a year he had been killed.

With Paddy joining us, the crew had a League of Nations look about it: four Scots, one Irish and me. Friendships were developing too, from living in close proximity with other crews. Among the gun commanders, Jimmy Irvine, a sergeant from the same regiment as Topper, Archie and Bert, was almost inevitably drawn towards my bunch. In a praiseworthy attempt to prevent boredom before it set in, the powers decided that some of the flat plain below our gun positions should be cleared of vines and levelled to provide a football pitch. It was a job which was tackled with more enthusiasm than might have been expected, considering the limited tools at our disposal, but it produced an excellent example of teamwork between the Partisans, commandos and RSR, and we found an enhanced camaraderie in toiling together. The resultant, grassless, full-size pitch provided countless hours of pleasure (and sometimes fury), but I also think it clinched somebody's notion of the potential for building a rough airstrip on Vis.

Royal Air Force advisers had been on the island since January, and early discussions had taken place between Brigadier Fitzroy Maclean and Randolph Churchill about Vis' secondary potential as an 'aircraft carrier'. I am convinced that the impressive sight of the rapidly created, level football pitch provided the final nudge for the experts to order the vines' clearance for a narrow runway of some 1000 yards alongside the island's only noteworthy road. We played our first football match on the new pitch on 19 March against the Commandos (43RM) who thrashed us 5-2: it was to be a week or two before the air-strip had its christening. Christening with landing planes that is.

On the night of 22/23 March Jerry decided to mark it first and so turned out to bomb it. Either the daily visitor high in the sky in a reconnaissance plane had spotted it with his camera or Sirjon's 'five columns' were at work again. It was the first real air raid on the island and whilst one could expect attention to be given to the two towns of Vis and Komiza, the enemy must have known about our presence on the plateau to justify a few bombs there. I think there were casualties in the towns that night but it was by no means a heavy raid, the nearest bomb to our position falling 1000 yards away. There were probably no more than five or six planes involved. The first real air attack came a few nights later on 27/28 March when Podselje was clearly the target for up to twenty bombers, although the towns copped it too.

It was a terrifying onslaught, about which we could do nothing because the effectiveness of our Brownings was limited to 1000 yards – a fact which infuriated the Partisans who felt we should be blazing away randomly and harmlessly into the night sky, as indeed were they with their small arms, mostly sten guns with a range effective at less than 50 yards. It was the first instance of disharmony between us, about which they were totally irrational. It marked an irreconcilable difference of approach between our 'whites of their eyes' training in the economy of ammunition and the unnecessary revelation of our gun positions, as opposed to their principle of blazing away regardless.

Parachute flares had first been dropped to illuminate the target, after which the bombs rained down on the tiny village at will without impediment. I'm told that blanket bombings of cities breeds a fatalism from feelings of dispersal – "I'd have to be really lucky to avoid catching one out of this lot, when there's so many of them [bombs]." When one is part of a relatively small and specific target, and a helpless, unprotected one at that, even the heathen resorts to the last line of defence – prayers – and so I did. As always in a crisis, some praiseworthy human qualities emerged. For me, the most lasting memory of that night was the work of a man I had barely been aware of before. Ray Fishwick, our seconded medical orderly, had hitherto been a mere name to me. My admiration for his dedication, knowledge and skill bordered on hero worship after that night, as he recruited us and bossed us around as assistants in tending the wounded. Out of it came the discovery of a mutual rapport, and consequently a close friendship, not at all diminished by his hometown being the other side of the Mersey – Wallasey.

Daylight – as it always does – eased our worst fears. Barely a house had escaped some damage but only three or four had disappeared after direct hits. Wisely, most of the occupants had deserted the village when the first bombs exploded, so that although most of the casualties were found on the hillside, their dispersal had prevented the toll which would have resulted from direct hits on overcrowded houses. But it was bad enough. Three RSR men had been killed, as had three Commandos and four Partisans. I have no record of the number wounded but I know that Ray was away for days whilst he helped at the hastily improvised operating theatre in a house near Komiza, which had been converted into a hospital. It is an extraordinary truth that, until the air raid, I had not given a thought to the significant absence of an RSR medical officer. Had I done so, I would firstly have dwelt on how or why he should have been with us when some of the Regiment had already been dropped into Greece to help the guerrillas there, some were still in the Middle East and some at Bari in Italy. Secondly, I would have asked whether we were attached to the 43rd Royal Marine Commando for medical services. I never knew. After the raid I cared not: Sergeant Ray Fishwick was good enough for me. Without being aware of any particular leanings of Ray's politics, I found myself infuriated at the social system that excluded such a natural doctor from actually being able to be one because his general educational qualifications were deemed inadequate.

If the raid found for me a good friend, it also produced a bitter enemy – or rather, it confirmed one. A diminutive, mouthy Welshman, whom I shall call Thomas, had crossed my path in near conflict since our days at Ramat David. There was never anything that I remembered which justified violence – just a taunting aggression in which he saw fisticuffs as the only solution to any contrived disagreement. Only the certain knowledge that I was being provoked had postponed the bout, but my inner rage at the lout simmered at the mere sight of him. I often think that I would have done mankind a service by killing him that night, as I could easily have done without question amidst the turmoil of the raid; and I came very close to it.

Ray was treating a Partisan girl who lay on the hillside in some terrible distress, with a piece of shrapnel lodged high in her inner thigh. Two male Partisans were at her head comforting her. In response to Ray's call, I held the leg and the torch whilst he cut the trouser leg away, baring in the process the private parts of the girl's body. I couldn't watch; I would like to say wholly on the grounds of decency but I knew too from Ray's gasp that the wound was not a pleasant sight, and my squeamishness might have rendered me useless. At this point Thomas arrived on the scene and his opportunistic voyeurism produced remarks which would have been disgusting at any time or place. There and then, they were vulgar, inhuman and the antithesis of therapy to the poor girl, whose ignorance of English was no barrier to an embarrassed understanding of the leering tone of the words. I got rid of him, exchanging language that has no place in a narrative intended for my grandchildren, but I knew from the hate in my heart that the showdown was not far away. By then I was looking forward to it.

Two nights later I think I willed it to happen. There had to be a physical resolution: I knew too well that to use my rank to charge him with insolence or insubordination would have solved nothing. He'd had his usual skinful of vino and was being as objectionable as ever in the billet, whilst most of us tried to lapse into the precious sleep which was at such a premium on Vis. Resigned to the conclusion that the time had come, I did not mince words in telling him to 'shut up'. Darkness could not obscure his instant, belligerent sparring stance at the foot of my palliasse on the floor, as with a sneering taunt he enquired about who was going to shut him up. That apt distortion of Shakespeare's Henry VI came to mind as a maxim of self-preservation:

> "Thrice armed is he who hath his quarrel just – But four times he who gets his blow in fust."

At the same time as I announced that I was taking on the job (of shutting his mouth) I leaped from my sleeping bag, grabbed him by the ankles, yanked him off his unstable feet and pounced on him. I realised with some relish that here was my first chance to use the lessons of my 'Tough Tactics' course a year earlier. I had my arm crooked around his neck in an instant and as I forced his face to the floor I could feel the rest of his frame squirm upwards as his legs frantically crabbed around to bring his body to face the same direction as his head – front down – to avoid having his neck broken. In that position I then levered my body against the floor to apply all the strength of my shoulders in tightening the screw of my right arm, by then reinforced with my left, around his neck. In such a position he was helpless, and I knew I could have killed him in just a few seconds. So did he. Everyone else in the room realised it too and had yanked me away from Thomas before more damage could be done. He was suitably cowed and feigned bewildered drunkenness in submitting to his bed whilst I remember feeling strangely cheated, having decided to embark on the showdown – a rare flash of temper for me – and a callousness to be emulated only once.

There has to be one thing said in Thomas' favour: he could have reported me and had me busted to the ranks. I sometimes wonder if that might not have been better than his future attitude towards me. His arm-on-shoulder, gesture of friendship was bad enough but his frequently quoted, nauseous "We understand each other, don't we, Wal?" emphasised the accidental truism of the statement. Fortunately, his belonging to another gun-crew meant that, with irregular guard duties on our respective guns, our only proximity was confined to rarely coinciding nights in the billet. Small mercies.

The air raid proved the inadequacy of our protection in the gun pits. Digging-in was not going to be easy in the rocky hillside so someone suggested requisitioning explosives, which to everyone's surprise miraculously materialised without delay. Plastic too! The stuff we had trained with in Palestine. The opportunity for putting our demolition training into practice added excitement to necessity, although the juvenile amateurism of our early attempts at blasting out the rock causes me to wince even now. We progressed from ignorance to reasonably deft skills, and then to reckless flippancy as each gun crew gradually reduced its fuse time before evacuating the site prior to the explosion. All the recognised safety rules were broken in a childish frolic which we thought at the time constituted fun. Not only was there inter-gun competition for minimal, last minute, 'chicken-style' vacation of one's own site, but the game gradually extended to suppressing warning of a lit fuse to adjacent crews in anticipation of the fun at seeing them 'scarper' in response to one's frantic five or six second shouted alarm – from a safe distance, of course. Ah! The ignorance – or innocence – or stupidity – of youth!

March 1944 ended on a high note – well, several notes really. The Army Post Office boys seemed to have found us at last. The receipt of seven letters from Anne bridging a couple or three weeks' correspondence affirmed that letters must have been accumulating. Seven! Seventh heaven, again! Those letters, and others from my parents, brother (Bert), Big Mac, Wally Robinson and George Green, each conveyed concern at the absence of news from me, which tended to neutralise the joy engendered by the receipt of such gems. Circumstances had reduced my normal output but I was bitter to think of the anxiety created through all of my letters having been held up for so long. I regret not having recorded something of the contents of their letters, beyond "he seems to be doing ok" in reference to Mac's, but I suppose seven passionate letters to a starry-eyed, love-denied young man of 24 did have the unforgivable effect of dumping other news that day into the pit of ordinariness. Nevertheless that day's mail, coinciding as it did with a short period of stability after months of mobility or imminent mobility, was the spur I needed to motivate the pen again. Without the courage to take on the censor even by hint, however, inspiration was tiresomely dulled by being limited to small talk. Archie, it seemed, had had more success in managing to drop sufficient innocuous clues for an uncle of his to collate and cleverly deduce from them where we were.

Life with the Partisans soon returned to pre-air raid amity. Close friendships began to develop. Kirky, the rascally Scot, became a popular favourite with them for reasons which we never found apparent, unless it was his readiness to have a go at the Serbo-Croat language. Sirjon helped him, but how they communicated in English I shall never know, being consistently unable to understand his Glaswegian dialect myself. Probably due to his diminutive stature the girls almost adopted him, so that in the evening song and dance sessions he was usually supported by one on either side of him in circle-style dances where gender played no part in one's position in the ring. To those tough, buxom girls that was no problem. I recall one evening when vino had laid him to bed early, news of which would not deter the girls. Unselfconsciously they entered the house, dragged a half-revived Kirky out of bed, clad in only his shirt, and danced around him as usual. The dances that night seemed to have acquired a necessity for more supported leaps in the air than normal, guaranteeing that Kirky's body landed much sooner than his lighter, and otherwise concealing, shirt. Whoops of enjoyment ensured that no one in the area missed the spectacle.

My particular friend among the Partisans in Podselje turned out to be their storekeeper, Roko. A man about my own age, Roko was the rare instance in the Brigade of being a native of Vis. Indeed, he had lived in Podselje with his aged mother and stunningly beautiful teenaged sister, Milka, until requisitioning of their home had necessitated both mother and sister finding residence in Vis town. Slight of stature, though undoubtedly physically fit, Roko never managed to exude the gladiatorial aggression of most of his colleagues. A possible explanation might be the fact that the enemy had not occupied Vis. Passion for conflict is fed on vengeance. Would not Roko – would not we – have been more hostile protagonists had we lived in enemy-occupied territory, where bestial atrocities committed against our families and friends were the order of the day? Perhaps it was this kindred spirit, this shared understanding which attracted Roko to us, although the reason why my gun-crew was found the most compatible I cannot explain. He tried valiantly to pick up and use as much English as possible, while he probed deeply into our personal circumstances, our way of life at home and ambitions for the future. He seemed to be the only one interested in such matters: that there was any other place in the world beside Yugoslavia and the Soviet Union seemed not to have dawned on the others. I am not sure whether he was particularly good at his job.

On our first visit into Vis town, a couple of miles walk along the twisting downhill road (the alternative was a mile of clambering down the rocky hillside), our prime commitment was to meet Roko's mother and sister. Language difficulties delayed our discovery of the tiny house, accessed by an alleyway. Conditions were not conducive to prolonged social conversation either, but the sad looking, black-clad old lady greeted Tony and me as a mother would. Caring, concerned and almost alarmist, she managed to convey that the war was still far from won and that we must take care of ourselves for the sake of our loved ones at home, for whom she prayed.

When Milka appeared from behind a line of gleaming, clinically clean washing which, in its billowing volume, recalled the Pathe Gazette newsreels of Cowes Regatta, her radiance left us gasping for breath. The main explanation for shock takes nothing away from the sheer, sparkling beauty of the girl: strong Slav features, a flawless complexion, blue eyes and tightly waved blonde hair scintillated all the more with the welcoming smile so typical of Roko himself. It was the remarkable contrast with the Partisan girls' necessarily drab, man-fitting uniforms which created the almost unreal image. Why Milka was not a Partisan I never knew, but her clothesline seemed to indicate that she was performing a usefully accepted service for many, many Partisans, thus justifying her keep. Sun bronzed shoulders, arms and legs, and a shimmering white blouse topping a fresh looking, multi coloured skirt, suggested that we might be looking at an Eastmancolour Doris Day, or whoever the clean-cut Doris Day beauty was at the time. A lifetime of clambering up and down the hillside for shopping expeditions into Vis had given her an alluring athleticism which, although it applied the finishing touch to her physical attraction, she also probably found very useful in escaping male advances. Roko wanted her to take on our laundry, but confronted with the magnitude of the washing-line on that first visit we could not bring ourselves to increase that burden, so we carried on with our own dhobying and darning. One thing which did surprise us was the apparent lack of jealousy of the Partisan girls at

Milka's relative feminine freedom. Whenever she visited the village she seemed to be on the most amicable terms of friendship with all of them. Is it too naïve to suggest that there was a mutual recognition of the necessity of each other's role in the great pattern of things?

The town of Vis spread itself thinly around the whole of the naturally enclosed harbour. Slightly larger than Komiza, the growth of Vis was similarly limited by the steep rise of mountains surrounding the bay. The resultant density of its unremarkable buildings – again like Komiza – nevertheless presented an attractive, maze like assortment of dwellings and ship chandlery premises, with so few cafes or bars as to confirm that this was no holiday island. The considerable length of the quay-side, afforded by the wide encircling of the bay's shelter, provided almost a linear mile of tying-up facilities, which at that time in 1944 appeared to be utilised to the full. The vessels moored along the quay were the power-assisted, sail-rigged schooners which were the lifeline of the Partisan cause in their transportation of personnel (both combatant and wounded) and supplies between the mainland and the other islands. This involved nightly hazardous, cat and mouse voyages of stealth through waters patrolled by German E-boats. The channels between the islands were also packed with the enemy's own flotilla of sailing supply ships, who plied the whole of the Dalmatian coastline. The presence of British Navy motor torpedo boats (MTBs) and motor launches (MLs) had supplemented the bustling activity and atmosphere of the quaysides of both Vis and Komiza.[11] The seafaring Partisans' attire was even less uniform than that of their landlubber colleagues. Most of them seemed to prefer bare feet to heavy boots. Only coloured kerchiefs on their heads and knives in the mouths were missing from fulfilment of fantasy. They certainly looked fearsome enough. I felt sure that our acceptability would have been instant and total had Sirjon prepared for us a Serbo-Croat equivalent of "Ahrr! Jim laaad!

There were two further surprises on our first day in Vis town. Until that day we had not been aware of the American troops on the island. Meeting them was rather like the pictures one sees of opposite tunnelling engineers meeting in the middle. Their greetings were effusive to say the least but unmistakeably genuine for all that. Our beige berets were still a rarity and, although the Americans had met our lads from the Brownings sited on the dominating height of Fort George above the harbour's entrance, they were not going to permit our remaining as strangers. Almost hero-worshipping in their warmth, one could not fail to be affected by their friendliness. These specialist Rangers had been recruited from Serbo-Croat or Greek-speaking American troops, and had already been on the raid on Solta Island.

The second surprise was more of a delayed realisation of something we already knew. It takes some imagining to conceive of life functioning in any community without a currency! Small wonder we hadn't anticipated it. Barter reigned. Cigarettes had become the unit of currency but, in truth, there was a very limited market in goods and services. With food and drink supplied, the absence of consumer goods to buy, except for the luxury of loaves of baked bread, some specialist island booze such as prahva, and perhaps the services of a very ordinary barber to pay for, who needed currency? And who, therefore, needed pay when cigarettes did nicely? Our drawings of Army pay were confined to any allowances we made to dependants at home, contributions to a savings-by-deduction scheme and the unreliably spasmodic NAAFI 'ration' which, if it did arrive, comprised a bottle or two of beer (usually the Canadian brands), cigarettes (in addition to the free issue of 50 per week) and toiletries like soap, razor blades and tooth-paste. In moments of rapturous daydreaming we would speculate on how we would spend our undrawn pay when we were back in Italy.

"The crew of the Liberator had confirmed the disturbing rumours of peremptory Partisan trials of captured Germans, with their inevitable outcome of cold-blooded mass executions."

The Murder Of German Prisoners

On 2 April we had a reminder that the war had wider ramifications than our own insular and relatively cosy island existence. The Allies' capture of airfields in Southern Italy had brought into bombing range many enemy strategic targets in mid- and south-east Europe, such as the Romanian oil installations at Ploesti, heavy industry factories in Vienna's suburbs and rail installations at Sofia. Huge numbers of American Liberator and Flying Fortress bombers, outward bound for these targets, began to fill the daytime sky in formations directly above our island on every day that the weather permitted. It was an awe-inspiring sight (and sound), unfailingly bringing buoyancy to our hearts with its tangible proof of how, after years of defending, we were at last taking the war to the enemy. On that 2 April – a clear, cloudless day – we lost count after three hundred bombers had passed over. We could not have guessed that we would be affected in an extraordinary way with that day's colossal bombing raid that incidentally (it later transpired) was on Steyr in Austria.

The disciplined formations of the outward flights were never quite repeated for the return when, it seemed, it was an every-man-for-himself slog home to base in Italy, some limping and flak-damaged. Some were seemingly lost and some were running short of fuel. Each, one hoped, was bereft of its bombs. Why a Liberator came to be circling low over the island that afternoon was of small consequence at the time. What did matter was that the plane was in serious trouble, with the pilot obviously searching for the safest looking place on the rocky island on which to attempt a belly landing. Our inter-section football match stopped abruptly as we prayed for the pilot to spot and use the adjacent runway. We scattered for our own safety. In his final approach, which initially had looked promising, he appeared to find the descent from the surrounding hills too steep, levelled out, overshot the cleared landing strip and deposited the plane out of sight behind a small copse of trees a mile or so away.

We cringed, awaiting the explosion. It didn't come! Ray Fishwick disappeared at pace into the billet, emerged equipped in a trice, and disappeared again – this time in the general direction of the crashed plane – with two stretchers, his 'bag of tricks', and three volunteer helpers. Still no explosion; no sign of fire either, thank God. Anxiously, we waited for Ray's return – expecting the worst, hoping for the best. Happily, we had worried unnecessarily. The American crew of the crash-landed Liberator had walked out of the plane unharmed and very, very grateful to the skilful pilot who had saved their lives. The comic aspect of the incident is that the crew, as their feet touched terra firma, raised their arms aloft in surrender to the gathering Partisans. The Americans believed themselves to be in enemy territory and had resigned themselves to spending the rest of the war in a prisoner of war camp. Yugoslavia to them was an enemy-occupied country. Their double relief can be imagined.

The next day a route march was unexpectedly arranged for all of 'C' Troop, except for gun-manning sentries, ostensibly as part of fitness training. However, we marched off in the direction of the crashed Liberator in order to satisfy our curiosity. I wondered if the Partisan guards might not have already beaten us to it. In view of the whole crew's fortunate escape we were puzzled at the adjacent, newly dug and crudely covered graves. Booted feet actually protruded, yet Ray had said nothing about ground casualties. Strange... On with the forced march... Down into Vis town, a nod to the Americans playing baseball on the square, then up the hill to Fort George for a brief, pleasing reunion with Bud Minkley and the rest of the RSR gun crews sensibly sited there.

The buzz doing the rounds was sensational. Had we heard of the escaped German prisoners? We had not. Then obviously we would not know how many had been shot by the Partisans as they tried to avoid recapture.

"Oh! Yes, it was towards Rukavac where they caught them," (Rukavac was a village of a few houses in the south-east corner of the island, at a sheltered inlet later to be developed as the landing-craft loading start point for many of the raids from Vis). "By the crashed Liberator?" we enquired. Our question was almost in unison. We knew the answer too. The graves had been explained, as had the identity of their occupants. But officialdom duly confirmed the more serious explanation that eventually found its way through the island commander (Brigadier Tom Churchill) to Fitzroy Maclean and up to Prime Minister Churchill, eventually to

Tito. There had been no attempted escape by the prisoners.

The chance aspect of the revelation is remarkable. The pilot of the crippled Liberator bomber, in saving the lives of his crew, had inadvertently disturbed an execution party congregating in a remote corner of this tiny, rocky island – the existence of which he had probably not known and of whose military or political loyalties he was certainly unaware. One can readily imagine the astonishment of the secret, impromptu Partisan 'court', the firing squad and the bloodthirsty spectators at the sudden, uninvited appearance of an audience from the sky. They were caught red-handed, I suppose you could say.

The crew of the Liberator had confirmed the disturbing rumours of peremptory Partisan trials of captured Germans, with their inevitable outcome of cold-blooded mass executions. Subsequent investigations brought admissions from the Partisans and the disclosure that the nearby, smaller island of Bisevo, ironically famed for its beautiful blue grotto, as the most frequent venue for executions. Allied alarm centred on implied complicity with this serious disregard for the Geneva Convention, for the humane treatment of prisoners of war. Public dissociation was vital, in the interests of Allied prisoners already in German hands and for the future psychological persuasion of enemy troops to surrender with the assurance of correct treatment, as an alternative to the fanatical, costly resistance to be expected from any who knew their capture meant certain death. Tito eventually issued orders for the executions to cease.

Nearly all the activity in early April 1944 was in the air, or perhaps it would be more correct to say out of the air. From our hillside gun positions above the crude landing strip on the plateau, we enjoyed an elevated grandstand view of the comings and goings of planes, whilst smugly revelling in pride at our influential bit-part in the conception of the enterprise and our considerable share of the hard graft unstintingly applied in clearing the vines and roughly flattening – if not technically levelling – the ground. Once its merit had been proved, others jumped on the band-wagon of recognition. Five weeks or so after we had witnessed its first practical use, someone in authority on the island decided to ask GHQ Central Mediterranean Forces for permission for the construction of a landing strip on Vis. Work began on Sunday 23 April. By then we had actually witnessed several life-saving landings (including a Spitfire bereft of undercarriage) and even two take-offs: one successful and one a tragic failure.

"The powerful 3.7 inch anti-aircraft guns had immediately emphasised the practical redundancy of our .50 inch Browning machine guns..."

Death On The Island

One of the US Air Force Lockheed Lightning escort fighters had made itself conspicuous long after the daily, disciplined formations of bombers and fighters had passed over from Italy on their bombing missions – but well before the time we had learned to expect to see their less orderly, straggling return. Showing every sign of wanting, or needing, to land, the pilot made several assessment runs which, even to our inexpert judgement, seemed to be courting disaster if a landing on the plane's three-wheel undercarriage was being contemplated. Our highest ambitions in clearing away the vines had been to assist crash-landers! The stretcher and medical bag were already on Ray Fishwick's shoulders as he hopped about restlessly on our hillside vantage point, trying to assess where his next patient might be likely to come to rest.

In near disbelief we witnessed what was to be the final determined dip from over the eastern hillside into the valley. Every inch of stopping distance needed to be utilised: we cursed the low, stone walls at each end of the strip which had frustrated our further bare-hands clearance. A foot or so cleared the first wall. Great! The plane's wheels touched down perfectly. So far, so good. We crossed our fingers. An obscuring cloud of dust whipped up by the wheels' brakes followed, and then enveloped the screaming plane on its remorseless progression towards the now dangerous far end wall. Not until it ended were we conscious of the terrible noise to which we had been subjected, and the contrasting silence was uncanny. No sound of collision. No explosion! No conversation either – just the tense waiting for the dust to settle. And then the involuntary cheers! Oh! The relief!

The sleek, twin-boomed aircraft gradually emerged from the dust cloud majestically motionless, with its twin noses either side of the central fuselage seeming to snort defiance at the wall a mere yard away. Vigilance on the gun sites was forgotten. Every single one of us raced down the hillside to greet the hero of the hour, the skilful, fortunate pilot whose appearance contributed even more surprise to the occasion. The squat, smiling, Oriental who emerged hardly seemed consistent with the scenario, but there he was – no less English speaking than any other Yank. A Chinese American had dropped in from the heavens. Surrounded by the inanely questioning mob, his answers permeated by ripples of repetition (and doubtless distortion) to the circumference of his well-wishers. Men had appeared from gun sites we had been unaware of.

"He was almost out of gas…"

"He'd lost himself…"

"He wants to know if we've got any gas on the island…"

"He says landing was no problem…"

"He thinks taking off will be a bit dicey…" Taking off! TAKING OFF? That thing would never take-off from here! Of course, he was kidding wasn't he?

When the Royal Air Force co-ordinating officers arrived from Komiza post-haste in their jeep, such experts found the notion even more absurd: "Impossible! Count your lucky stars and leave it at that." The only plane ever to have taken-off from Vis had done so eleven days earlier. We had witnessed that too. A tiny American Stinson Sentinel, with a rather overdone guardian swarm of escorting RAF Spitfires, had made the trip across the Adriatic from Italy specifically – as the smallest operational plane in that theatre of war – to test the rough runway for take-off potential. The Stinson, a wing-strutted monoplane employed militarily only for liaison and observation work, was not much more than twenty feet long, weighed less than a ton and had an average speed of little more than 100 miles per hour. It managed to land and take off comfortably. There was talk of a Spitfire trying it next. But a Lightning! A 400 mile-an-hour lightning! It didn't take an expert to understand the risk. Yet our optimistic Oriental convinced everyone with his unbounded enthusiasm. He joked of his need to get back to Italy that night: "If I don't, the other guys will share out my kit. It's the accepted code."

Refuelled through the misguided efforts of some logistic loon who had anticipated emergencies, and revving, smiling and waving confidently from his enclosed cockpit, his moment of truth had come. Even with the tail planes almost touching the wall, the strip looked pathetically short for a take-off. Positively screeching with power, the plane's rapid acceleration was alarming in its sheer, noisy intensity, yet encouraging in its implied force. Prayers for success were uttered – and answered: miraculously, the wall had been cleared! A triumphant rising stall to the left – spontaneous cheers partially frustrated by the nearness of tears of relief – the impossible had been achieved.

Then disaster. Unaccountably, the plane stopped rising, then dipped out of our vision a mile or so away. Engine noise faded into a silence of suspense. Perhaps it had cleared a fold in the hillside and was now skimming over the sea? Then came the explosion, followed by the flames. We learned later that Partisans had extricated the pilot from the plane before it became an inferno. He died on the way to the island's improvised hospital, a needlessly wasted young life with not an enemy in sight. I know there has to be a modicum of stupidity in all courage, but I still think of that brave fool with admiration.

A few unwarlike matters qualified for mention in my diary in mid-April. The weather began to improve in the direction of our earlier expectations. Our Middle East-acquired tans enrolled on a refresher course and we began sleeping out at night in the newly moved gun sites on the hillsides – as an invigorating alternative to the stuffy, crowded billet. Then there was the first expedition by lorry down to Komiza for shower-baths which, despite the menace of the clouds of road dust on the return journey, warranted the diary entry "I revel in it. It's good to be clean again."

We played the Commandos at football on 7 April and lost 5-2. I played in the team that day. On 8 April we won 4-2. I didn't play. Topper scored all four: a message is there somewhere.

Quite apart from the local daily tonic provided by the sight of hundreds of Allied bombers passing high overhead on daylight raids, the global war news was encouraging. The Russians had advanced on a broad front – in the south they were a mere 25 miles from Odessa. The Allied Armies in Italy were pressing on north-east of Cassino, whilst in the Far East the Americans were making slow but steady progress in gobbling up the Pacific Islands. Britain's 14th Army had started to turn the tide against the Japanese in Burma. We ought to have been pleased but it made our near-passive role of defence harder to bear. If the situation displeased us, imagine the frustration and impatience of the Partisans –

whose desire to eject the enemy (and that meant Cetniks and Ustasi, perhaps more emphatically than Germans) from their beloved country represented more of a vested interest than did our transient presence.

Our news came from a surprising source. Some bright spark (and I really mean that as a compliment) at Commando Headquarters had hit upon the idea of turning out a daily news-sheet from radio information of world news he received from the BBC. This single-page 'newspaper' was distributed to troops throughout the islands. It served to cushion the feeling of island isolation that understandably affected morale. Eagerly awaited each day as 'The Daily Vis-à-vis', it even had a Sunday edition called 'Vis of the World' which, unlike its notorious counterpart, suffered from the lack of opportunity for, and therefore absence of, scandal on the island.

Enemy air raids on the island increased to an almost nightly event, with the two towns of Vis and Komiza the main targets. With heavy anti-aircraft guns on Vis at the time the raids became more spectacular, though militarily less effective. One had the feeling that the enemy wanted to show us that he still had some aircraft available, which, in a perverse sort of way, suited us. Aircraft over the less vital Dalmatia meant fewer aircraft over crucial Italian fronts and the hundreds-of-miles-long Russian front.

The powerful 3.7 inch anti-aircraft guns had immediately emphasised the practical redundancy of our .50 inch Browning machine guns in an anti-aircraft role, and promoted near rebellious representations to our pathetically unenterprising officers to find some infantry roles for this magnificent weapon in raids on other islands. It was ironical therefore that, within a few days, my Browning was in action against enemy planes. At least I thought they were enemy planes.

Even in the half light of dawn, I flatter myself that I recognised the two fighters which cruised from left to right across our gun positions at a few hundred feet as Italian Macchis, but I cursed myself for even that rapid identification taking too long for me to issue fire instructions before they had disappeared out to sea behind Mount Hum, the island's highest point. When, to our disbelief, they came back for an opposite run, the opportunity was too good to miss, so with identification confirmed we let fly. None of us had any doubts that our tracers had hit one of the planes, and watching the immediate evasive action of the two

Macchis we knew we had surprised them. Surprise them we certainly had! Basking in the praise of our rudely awakened officers, and those of our colleagues who would not have been able to distinguish a Macchi from a Tiger Moth, we awaited news of the Macchi's fate.

The field telephone link to Vis town soon produced the answer. Yes, a Macchi had been shot down. It had come down just off the coast and the pilot rescued safe and sound by a Navy Motor launch. He was a Canadian! He'd been flying one of the many Italian planes handed over to the Allies on Italy's surrender.

I wondered why my 'own goal' had not provoked irate condemnation and immediate arrest. What was the penalty for shooting down one of our own planes? I doubted if the rulebooks had a precedent for that. Apparently, there were three reasons for my absolution. Firstly, the planes bore no Allied markings, and since the German Luftwaffe were also using captured Macchis anyway, who could tell whose they were? Secondly, they had made their run across the length of the island a few minutes before the night time curfew for Allied planes had expired. A curfew had been imposed only a few days earlier to allow us to treat as hostile all night-time planes and, in particular, a couple of cheeky Messerchmitts which had made a similar dawn run on a couple of occasions the week before. I was ignorant of the curfew: we simply hadn't been told. The third reason pleased me most. Congratulations were to be passed on to the man who had identified the relatively rare Macchi! My useful hobby had saved my skin in a way I could never have imagined.

April had one other aircraft story to yield. Potential patients for Ray appeared conspicuously in the sky one sunny afternoon. A US Liberator on the home run after completion of its bombing mission made a few low, lethargic inspections of our runway, did not fancy what it saw and headed out towards the sea again at less than a thousand feet. It took us a few seconds or so to realise that it did so on its own: above our heads were eight billowing parachutes bearing the Liberator's crew. Again, we were to witness the double relief of men whose crippled plane had rendered doubtful their safe reunion with terra firma and who had reconciled themselves to certain captivity, until they saw us and heard English speaking voices. No wonder they were elated.

Diary entries for 19 April show another example of my idiosyncratic reluctance to record bad news. Topper must have been taken away from my crew some weeks or so earlier for promotion: it was never necessary to record what a bitterly upsetting disappointment it was to me. An event of such moment as would warrant block-capital entry – but it is not registered anywhere. That entry on 19 April 1944 reveals merely that Spike Skates (one of my colleagues from 102 Battery) who had replaced Topper, probably weeks earlier, was "settling down." Jimmy Irvine was the fortunate recipient of Topper's services – a reunion for those two also.

Two Deserters

The bitter frustration of our waiting on Vis for positive military involvement in the war in the Balkans can be no better exemplified than by one incident involving a soldier named Douglas Rice. Duggie was a popular, likeable, Cockney scoundrel whose reputation for vehement out pourings about our military inactivity was equalled only by those of his close friend, Charlie Parker. Their sudden overnight disappearance in May 1944 was at first treated as some notoriety-attracting prank which, although constituting 'desertion' – a most heavily punishable offence in war-time – was not at that point treated too seriously by our officers. There might be a few men who would desert for reasons of cowardice, but not Duggie or Charlie. It seemed more likely that they had acquired a booze hoard somewhere and had slunk off to a secret hovel to work off their boredom. After the passing of a couple of weeks without news, every one of us began to experience a puzzled concern for the safety of this rascally duo, despite our awareness of their individual and collective enterprise and ingenuity. Small as Vis was, it still possessed a thousand hiding places where anyone could lie low; but this was hardly their style.

Their absence had gone on for too long to represent a mere protest, and they would be too clever not to realise that their discovery or voluntary return to the fold for such a meagre principle would be wholly self-defeating. Their arrest would render military action even more distant: they would be tried for desertion and caged in a military glasshouse in Italy. The passage of a month or so began to remove from our minds the wonder of their disappearance and we were awaiting their requested replacement from Italy, when the siesta of a Podselje afternoon was disturbed by the noisy appearance of a Commando jeep – bearing the flamboyant, unshaven and generally unkempt Duggie and Charlie with as much pregnant mystery as a magician's re-production of his ostensibly sawn-in-half assistant.

Their story was at once bizarre yet, for them, typical; frightening yet enviable; condemnable yet admirable. In their collusive resolve for action, they had stowed away under cover of darkness on a Partisan schooner bound for a who-knew-where clandestine, mainland landfall. When discovered, they had convinced the Partisan crew that they were part of a British Military Mission sent to help to protect Tito during the Germans' most serious campaign of the war to capture the Partisan leader. Duggie's and Charlie's hair-raising experiences on the mainland went some way towards satiating their thirst for action and, I've often thought, would have been worthy of a written amount in their own inimitable, racy language. On balance, they were extremely lucky to have escaped from their running brushes with the enemy and luckier still to have their absences 'overlooked' in view of their 'enterprising' contribution to the war effort. So much fuss was made of them that I wondered why Tito had not struck a special medal for them. They were shining heroes among the local Partisans thereafter.

The Run Up To D-Day

The month of May had started well. The heavy anti-aircraft boys had brought down a plane on the first night of the month, but unlike my effort they had actually destroyed an enemy plane. On the night of 11 May they shot down six more raiders. In daylight, the air traffic was all one-way: literally hundreds of Allied bombers from Italy speckled the clear blue sky as they noisily droned towards targets in mid-to-eastern Europe.

But best of all, May brought believably strong rumours of another pending raid on one of the enemy-occupied islands. The stories permeated down the line (carefully omitting the island's name), fanning speculation about when, where and – more pointedly – involving whom? Whilst it was nothing more than rumour, it pleased us all and kept us on our toes for half the month. Then each gun commander was told to nominate one of his gun crew to fulfil the Troop's single-gun assigned role for the imminent raid. All four of No. 11 Troop's ('E' Battery RSR) artillery pieces were being used. That a mixed machine gun crew should be hurriedly, unfamiliarly intermingled for our initial test of strength before the enemy (instead of using an established crew), merely served to confirm the inadequacy of our officers. We drew lots. Bert Roger, who drew the coveted short straw in my crew, began to examine his food more closely thereafter for signs of poisoning by his envious colleagues.

On 20 May he was called forward and took his leave of us with the buoyant optimism of a child bound for a Christmas grotto, with the good wishes of us all ringing in his ears. He returned the next day – the raid had been postponed – and was then summoned the following day for the real thing. An omen if there ever was one.

The raid on Mljet could hardly have been considered a success, except in the sense of its nuisance value or, as one might have been later forgiven for guessing, as a feint for the more ambitious campaign which would soon follow. I think that the military commanders on Vis must have been affected by some of the impatience which had motivated Duggie and Charlie. With a measure of justification they had relied upon a standard of support and intelligence from Mljet-based Partisans and sympathisers, comparable with the excellence of that which had been encountered on Solta. It was the only occasion when the territory for any raid in the area had not previously been 'reccied' by our own people. On that lapse alone the raid was destined to be a failure. That other factors should compound the unusual shortcomings of the Mljet Partisans was a stark illustration of the theory that when your luck is out, the problems don't come singly.

The plan was to eliminate the German island garrison of about 300 men on a nippy 18 hour surprise 'visit', commencing with an undetected landing at about midnight on 22/23 May 1944. Undetected it was, providentially. Most of the LCIs' landing ramps failed to function properly, seriously delaying disembarkation on the (mercifully secluded) landing beach. This increased the grim feelings of foreboding which were later justified by events.

The codename which had been chosen for the raid was 'Operation Foothound'. Cynics would say that this came comically close to breaking all military secrecy (let alone, common sense) rules by almost labelling the project. Had it been 'Footpound', the nature of the notoriously rocky terrain to be encountered, coinciding with the unfortunate decision to use the occasion for the initial operational experiment in the use of the recently-issued felt-soled 'creepers', might have made it descriptive – and given the game away.

Mljet is a cigar-shaped island, some 25 miles in length (roughly west to east) and about a mile at its widest. Despite being heavily wooded, it is a rocky island with four main peaks, two of roughly 1500 feet and two of little more than 1000 feet, on each of which the Germans had predictably established their main fortified garrisons.

We had reasoned that if the attacking forces could be in their respective positions before dawn, simultaneous onslaughts against the German strongholds by synchronised attacks from Italy-based Spitfires carrying bombs, together with artillery poundings from RSR's 75mm gun-howitzers, would ensure that the element of surprise would neutralise any commanding advantage enjoyed by an enemy with all-round vision from his consolidated, dug-in defensive positions on the peaks. Therein lay the rub.

The two main attacking forces of Commandos were not in position until some five or six hours after dawn due to the inefficiency of the Partisan guides. In short, they got lost and completely missed the paths and tracks. Urgent direct line marches on compass bearings or even on rough guesses became the only panic-driven hope of achieving the start point at anything near to the scheduled time – and with some of it in all-revealing daylight. The effect was to subject the men to one of the most arduous physical undertakings of the Adriatic campaign.

Loaded unreasonably, if unavoidably, with a quota of the mortar ammunition in addition to his own kit and weapons, each man could relate harrowing tales of stumbling climbs and descents over sharp-pointed rocks. Rock and scrub had combined to make a formidable and endless obstacle course which produced vehement cursing against anyone who had contributed any part to the raid's suggestion or planning. The terrain played havoc with the light footwear; the scrub tore trousers to shreds; sweat, cuts, abrasions and fatigue reduced fit men to spent, demoralised automatons, kept going only on pride, discipline and superb fitness.

Apart from the on-time Spitfire attack, only one other aspect of the raid worked according to plan – well, better than planned actually. The precautionary radio communication embargo was extended long after the agreed upon time for the end of the silence: hardly any of the sets worked! Consequently, the afternoon decision to abandon the operation (after only desultory skirmishes resulting from accidental patrol confrontations and speculative artillery salvoes) had to be brought by runner.

Thankfully our casualties were few. Two men had been killed and six taken prisoners of war. The casualties on the German side were unknown, but the pessimism which attended subsequent discussion of the raid suggested that the human balance sheet was no cause for celebration. A few of the Commandos initially reported 'missing' were astoundingly recovered on the landing beach the following night by the redoubtable and resolute Captain Bob Loundon, who had persuaded the Navy to take him out on a motor-launch on the speculative venture of rescuing his thereafter everlastingly grateful men.

When Bert got back to us, his state of exhaustion was alarming – adding pangs of conscience to the folly of my tolerating a lottery to decide that the least fit of us would go. His recovery was, however, rapidly accelerated by his overdone exhibition of one-upmanship.

Ted Stokoe summed up the Mljet operation in his book Lower the Ramps: "For almost 22 hours we had trekked through some of the roughest terrain in the world. Little had been achieved." A friend wrote recently from South Africa: "Yes indeed I was on the Mljet raid and what a shambles it was. We seemed to chase Germans up a series of hills only to see them running down the other side. At least that is my lasting impression." Although he did add: "The only amusing part was when a Sergeant of No. 2 Commando got taken short and modestly squatted behind a wall only to see two Germans approaching. He picked up his Tommy gun, shot them both and continued his business." The last word on Mljet belongs to one of the raid commanders, Major Neil Munro, in his report lodged for posterity in the National Archives at Kew: "It was probably the most concentrated fatigue ever experienced by the Commando."

The Raid On Brac

There was a mischievous suggestion doing the rounds that it was the embarrassment caused to High Command by the Mljet escapade which had prompted, within a few days of its conclusion, the hurried conception of another raid. The urgency that attended its announcement certainly fuelled that theory. Exactly a week after Mljet, all of the Troop's six Brownings were placed on stand-by for 'the biggest job yet': we were to be ready within twenty-four hours!

Fulfilling as this welcome news was, the first worrying misgivings of another scantily-prepared raid took some assuaging. Only when the size of the operation became apparent did the pulses of genuine excitement swamp those early fears. In retrospect, I know those fears could easily have been avoided had we been told the important, if not vital, reason for the urgency and magnitude of the job. A desperately surrounded Tito had signalled in frenetic terms for any diversion from the Vis garrison which might relieve the concentrated pressure on him on the mainland near Drvar. High Command had decided upon Brac with sufficient ostentation to suggest, even to us, that it might appear to be a preliminary to a full scale invasion of mainland Yugoslavia. If we could be expected to believe that, surely the Germans would?

At the time, speculation on the reason hardly penetrated our heads during the excitement of preparation, which seemed to involve everyone on the island – British and Partisans alike. Podselje throbbed. Our Yugoslav friends beamed with happiness, as if the war was actually won. There was very little time allowed for such theorising anyway. On 31 May we were told. The next day, equipped with our Brownings (and wretched pedestals), two Bren-guns, our own personal small-arms, cases upon cases of ammunition, 'compo' rations and water, we were transported to the sea inlet village of Rukavac, which was already agog with bustling activity around as many beached landing craft as its meagre landing points could accommodate.

Oddly enough (odd, that is, in the wake of the Mljet fiasco and the hurried nature of the pending operation), I could not help sensing an atmosphere of cool efficiency and smooth, confident organisation pervading the preparations that day at Rukavac. Perhaps volume had something to do with it: this was not to be a mere dabble. Partisans were there in their hundreds; buoyant, voluble and inevitably singing as lustily as ever. The 25-pounders of a Battery of the Royal Artillery's 111th Field Regiment were being loaded together with hundreds of rounds of ammunition onto LCAs (Landing Craft, Assault) or LCTs (Landing Craft, Tank), creating a reassuring potential firepower with which to bolster the operation. We knew similar activities, probably on a much larger scale, were proceeding on the quaysides of Komiza and Vis town. The Partisan schooner fleet had been marshalled in its entirety to supplement the sizeable Royal Navy contribution.

Again, there had been some personnel reshuffling and supplementing of gun crews. My diary shows that my crew for the operation comprised Archie, Bert, Paddy, Spike, Charlie (Winch), Tony, 'Gabby' and a character known as 'Dixie' (who could only have been a 'Dean') but about whom, shamefully, I can remember nothing before, during or after the raid. The other two 'borrowed' characters, Tony and Gabby, would have been my own personal last choices. Acknowledged to be indolent, truculent, undisciplined and unamusable, their allocation to me must have been the work of a sadist. I wondered, for what good reason would any sane person place these men in my crew and deny me the services of, for instance, our own Kirky? But then I realised my good fortune in having Charlie and could only rationalise on it being the manifestation of a deliberate policy of equalisation of quality throughout the Troop, at least for operations. Paradoxically, the man I should have known best (apart from Tony and Gabby, of course) was the one I had the most misgivings about. Spike's volatile moods were legendary in our previous regiment together. On a favourable day he could be inspirational, on another downright subversive. I knew I had to keep him usefully busy and regularly – and flatteringly – amused, so that I could maximise the value of his infectious joviality.

The effect of his main obsession, which outweighed all his other interests, I felt assured I could dismiss any qualms about. Females would not feature at all in a hostile military raid into enemy territory – not even with Spike's acknowledged female-divining skills. Involvement, commitment and tenseness would provide their own bucket of cold water, even in the remote possibility of the appearance of any accessible members of the opposite sex.

Operations on Brac – June 1944

Nevertheless, it was a cheerful, optimistic gun crew which boarded a tightly packed LCI 289 in the early evening at Rukavac, whence we sailed in a veritable flotilla of landing craft and schooners at 19:00 in reassuring, enshrouding twilight, having been told at last that we were bound for Brac on a major multi-point-landing raid of considerable magnitude. The stirring Partisan singing had to be silenced lest it heralded our alien approach over a tranquil, sound-bouncing Adriatic. By contrast, the unavoidably audible engines of the vessels of the fleet just went on chugging away. The moon conspicuously silhouetted the landing craft as it bottomed with a gentle crunch onto one of Dalmatia's rare sandy beaches at precisely 01:30 on 2 June. Unopposed, thank God – so far!

Our lips were dry from excitement. We whispered over and over again our various instructions as we shuffled forward in line along the starboard side of the craft towards the landing ramps. Well disciplined, experienced Commandos queued in orderly calm ahead of us: restive, impatient, voluble Partisans tried to hustle us forward from the rear in their hostile, bludgeoning desire to get at the enemy's throat.

The tranquillity of the situation was strangely unreal, but it was a relief to know that the Navy had skilfully brought us safely ashore to the friendly, land-based torch signals of the advance party. We were undetected and at the planned landing point east of the village of Bol.

Intelligence had earlier reported that there were no Germans in the village but, as Brac was an enemy-held island, the moment was not without its tension. It seemed an age since the vessel's engines had been slowed down to the muffled purr necessary to glide us discreetly ashore.

The other assorted craft on either side of us appeared ghostly and sinister, as their superstructure occasionally glinted in the moonlight, yet they added a 'safety in numbers' sense of security to the occasion. As new recruits to raiding operations we found it all very reassuring.

So the bedlam, when it did shatter the peace without warning, was a shock not solely reserved for our group of nine, but I would imagine that our inexperience ensured that we suffered most from it. Landing ramps on LCIs require motors to power their lowering and raising – motors which are mounted on deck – and which must be among the highest decibel-rated cacophonies that exist. By switching them on, the naval ratings had broadcast our arrival, not only to the enemy anywhere on Brac but, I thought at the time, to anyone within the whole group of Dalmatian Islands. Our fury at the stupidity of this din, neutralising all the previous good work, was soothed only by the relief and realisation that our first fear-induced thoughts were wrong. We were not sitting ducks for a fusillade of hostile enemy gunfire. The commotion and the tension it had produced had one beneficial effect: with the ramps resting securely on the beach, disembarkation and unloading were completed with an alacrity I would never have thought possible. The common resolve was to leave the source of that noise as distant as possible in the minimum time.

The Navy lads worked like Trojans in helping us unload our gear, so that within half an hour LCI 289 was fading into the blackness of night at half-speed astern, having discharged its duty to land a couple of hundred of us ashore. The whole raiding force began to sort itself out. Once the various organised groups had filed off silently to their respective tasks, the beach bore no witness to the previous half-hour's intense activity. Silence reigned again. Bol might well have been a deserted village: no sign of life emanated from its few houses, probably due to a prudent evacuation which was doubtless prompted by the advance party's warning of the hostilities to come.

Our role had been explained to us on the LCI. On the face of it we had an almost passive part in an operation destined to be intensely hostile in its ambition to engage the Germans already on the island, and to draw more from the mainland within the following few days. The Battery of eight 25-pounder guns of the 111th Field (Artillery) Regiment was to be sited near to the landing beach on the fringe of the village, to give shelling support to the attacking force of Commandos and Partisans during their approach to the four strategically held, German-fortified positions situated mainly on the heights to the north.

Our Brownings were to be employed in an anti-aircraft role in the defence of the 25-pounders. In the positioning of our weapons each gun-commander was given a surprising degree of freedom of choice for the site within a generous area of hillside, allocated by our officers after their deliberations (mainly on avoiding 'bunching') once the Artillery had affirmed their advance party's assessments of the most suitable site for their guns.

A strange sense of detachment had already affected us. Seeing the Commandos and Partisans disappear into the blackness of the village and then, a short while later, listening to the sounds of their broken-step marching gradually recede into the night, settled over us a naked silence of isolation which was at once tense and expectantly stimulating.

Brac is a vaguely plum shaped island approximately twenty miles long, lying roughly in a west to east direction, while its maximum width is about five miles. Its northern coastline runs roughly parallel with the Yugoslav mainland – a mere mile or two away. This afforded the easy supply of the island from the enemy-held mainland.

Like the other islands of Dalmatia, Brac is rocky. While its heights (at a peak of 2500 feet) would not normally qualify as mountains, their unusually steep sides rising from deeply troughed valleys make it a difficult landscape to traverse. Nature had therefore favoured the occupying forces on Brac. Activity on almost any part of the coast could be observed from at least one of the heights.

The Germans had learned from the growing number of guerrilla raids and ambushes that a blanket occupation of so rugged a territory was a sheer (in both senses) impracticability. The consolidation of commanding physical features which protected supply points had, therefore, become the pattern for the defence of the islands from 1943.

Thoughts of the inevitable frontal assaults on such fortified high points on Brac – even if the element of darkness aided our surprise – rapidly moderated my enthusiasm for personal involvement in such attacks and consoled my initial disappointment at our defensive, anti-aircraft role. Such anxiety grew within a few minutes of the gradual disappearance into the darkness of the last of the Partisans. With their objectives known to be four or five dark, difficult, foot-slogging miles away, why was the sound of a distant small-arms battle disturbing the night's tranquillity? Our officers didn't know. They could confirm only my guess that the sound came from the north-west.

The mystery remained with me for 43 years. Only Michael McConville's excellently researched book 'Small War in the Balkans' provided the essential explanation, while it reflected war's usual state of confusion. We had been wrong to imagine that our landing had been among the first on Brac. On the previous night a Company of the Highland Light Infantry (HLI), with sixty or so Partisans, had landed four miles west of Bol from Partisan schooners.

Their specific objective was the urgent liquidation of the German Observation Post (OP) on the highest peak of the island, at Nidova Gora. From there, fire from island and mainland based enemy artillery could be directed to any part of Brac. That the gallant Scots failed to achieve their objective is no reflection on their valiant endeavour or courage. It was an early instance of Partisan obstinacy, muddle and casual disregard for detail.

Firstly, the schooner's skipper had refused to take the Scots to their agreed landing place. They thereby faced a difficult, overland climbing trek of five or six gruelling miles. The chance of an attack on the first night was thereby lost. Secondly, their Brac-based colleagues had provided totally misleading and inadequate information about the OP's defences, upon which it was necessary to rely since daylight reconnaissance would have been suicidal in open exposure to the peak.

So their second night's attack (the noise we heard) was heavily repulsed with such devastating casualties inflicted on the HLI, particularly their officers and NCO's that they had to withdraw with their wounded, make their way back to the coast for re-embarkation and return to Vis. The first of the Brac calamities had taken place.

If the HLI attack on Nidova Gora had surprised Jerry he would, within an hour or so, be aware of the Partisan force that had landed in the south-east supported by the RSR's 75mm mountain guns. There rapid total success was soon achieved by the invaders. That noise was understandable. We knew about those landings, scheduled for a trifle ahead of ours.

Any inference that the south of the island was low-lying became a manifestly relative term when we set out to select our gun sites. Steep foothills rose immediately from the narrow, metalled road which serviced Bol, where it skirted the beach. With the 25-pounders satisfactorily installed in a sparse copse at the roadside on the fringe of the village, we crossed the road and began our ascent in search of a suitable site. By then there was little moonlight.

We stumbled and grumbled our sweating way up the hillside, trying to share equally the burden of the Browning – its absurd and grotesquely unmanagable steel anti-aircraft pedestal, its 0.5 inch ammunition and a couple of Bren guns – together with our own personal small-arms, ammunition (both boxed and in magazines) and all the other myriad items of equipment and impedimenta, including rations and water for an estimated forty-eight hour stay. We progressed slowly on a potato-race formula, alternating loads as we climbed, dumped, descended, reloaded and dumped at progressively higher stations. After an hour or so we rested while Archie and I went on alone to 'recce' a suitable site, so as to avoid any unnecessary carrying by the rest. It did not take us long to decide on what appeared to be an ideal position. Archie went down for the others.

Despite the darkness, by the time they had arrived I had deduced that the site was admirable for another reason. It was a flat area of terracing on the hillside that had obviously been cultivated in the not-too-distant past for vines, probably until the German occupation of the island in 1943. Digging-in with our entrenching tools was therefore going to be relatively easy and indeed several personal trenches had been dug and the gun-pit itself almost half finished when daylight came. I had been particularly careful to ensure that the 'grafting' was shared equally to avoid any allegations of favouring my own crew members.

Spike's reputation for work aversion meant that I had to be seen to supervise him in order to reassure the others that I was not going to tolerate any of his 'skiving' on our first operation. In truth, the work was carried out with a missionary zeal and in a fine spirit of comradeship and amity.

Before dawn, at precisely 05:05, the enemy gave an indication of their awareness of our presence on the island. Heavy artillary on the mainland – 105mm guns, we correctly guessed – began to shell. The target area, being a rare ideal island landing point, would obviously have been previously registered by their OP for just such an eventuality. Sparse and desultorily at first, the shells dropped over a wide area – indicating a speculative covering of a territory most likely to accommodate south-coast landing facilities. It was so speculative as to endanger us on the hillside as much as the 25-pounders, but so fortunately dispersed as to avoid any casualties or damage.

My smug satisfaction with the night's work was short-lived. The coming of daylight brought ego-shattering dismay. It was immediately apparent that the site was virtually useless! With mountains behind, I knew I could rule out any air attacks from that direction, so my siting had reckoned on providing protection from any other angle within a 180 degree arc. But daylight had immediately revealed that although there was a perfectly uninterrupted view out to sea in front and up the coastline for a mile or more to our left (the east), an erratic protrusion of rock on the hillside to the right gave a severely limited arc of fire on that side. Perched as we were, directly above the artillery guns, the sickening thought dawned that I could give them no cover from attacks from the west until the aircraft reached a point almost vertically above the guns. Much too late! I knew I had to change the site and, as I clambered higher up a now much steeper hillside in search of somewhere practical, I knew too that, whatever my nickname might have been, my new one was 'mud' – at best. It was not only the hot morning sun which had my ears burning.

By 08:00 I had selected a new site which, though admirable for our purpose, meant scrambling almost as high again as our night-time hoist, over a steeper, rockier slope. I had chosen the nearest area of suitably level terracing I could find. Like the previous position, it once had another use: a beekeeper's decrepit hives still littered the western edge of the site. The arc of visibility which then presented itself was perfect and I felt much more satisfied about our value to the artillery boys. I felt much less satisfied at the prospect of breaking the news of the hard slog ahead to my gun team, but a diversion – a timely, fortuitous boost to morale – cushioned the initial impact of my command to the crew to commence the resiting.

At 09:00 the 25-pounders opened up. It was the start of a series of daylong barrages on the enemy-held heights, which brought cheers of delight and encouragement from us all. It also brought an almost immediate response from the German 105s, once their gunners realised that Bol was harbouring such a menacing firepower. Jagged chunks of shrapnel whirred and whined around us before clattering against the surrounding rock, often creating secondary shrapnel from the chippings of stone. It was quite a frightening experience as the bombardment continued through the day – and the odds of a direct hit against us increased. Fortunately neither happened, though each of us experienced being covered with soil and the feel of tinkling, spent chippings against our helmets and clothing.

Each cloud, they say, has a silver lining. If the one which had enveloped me since my decision to move the Browning might only have received an electro-plating, it quickly dispersed completely in the popularity of any move which would take us further away from the 25-pounders which were the enemy's main target. Furthermore, one of our elusive officers made his only visit to the site that morning and decided that we should "move higher up the hill, for your own safety." At that time it seemed an even better reason than the mere triviality of the more efficient fulfilment of the duty we had been sent to perform – the protection of the 25-pounders.

It took all day to complete the move and install ourselves in an effective, dug-in position ready for action. Almost every carrying journey was interrupted by the need to hit the ground and take cover. Obligingly, the Germans sent over no hostile aircraft that day: their duelling courtesy obviously noting that we were not quite ready. It would be an ungrateful omission not to record that the team worked wonderfully well in completing the move and digging-in.

The new site could offer neither cover nor camouflage. The trees had long since given up fighting for a living and moved much further down the hill. Worst still, we were mainly on broken rock and, as we laboured to dig-in, I wished a score of times that day that we had brought with us some of the plastic explosives which had transformed our dug-out construction task on Vis from the impossible to just manageable.

I decided to give the gun pit priority and to limit the personal slit trenches to only three, on the principle that if we were subject to a strafing attack by planes, half of us could be expected to be on the gun anyway. We could review the situation on the morrow when we were less tired. Being further away from the artillery and the beach also meant we were less in the intended area of fire of the German 105s.

The decision to limit the number of trenches was a popular one with the men. A tense and sleepless night, to say nothing of their physical exertions, had left us all thoroughly exhausted. It was a decision which incidentally revealed one of Spike's unusual qualities. I certainly had not been aware of it before, but it did not take long for all of us to discover that he had the gift of uncannily acute hearing. By the time most of us heard the whine of a shell coming, we invariably found that Spike had beaten us to it and was already in the limited trench space. He revealed that he could actually hear – or 'feel' – the enemy guns as they fired some miles away. Although he could not be convinced of the uniqueness of his gift and we found it almost unbelievable, accepting his invitation to test him settled the point. He would declare "Now!" when he sensed the gun had fired: we would count the number of seconds the shell had taken to arrive and, as sure as fate, each subsequent shell would be amongst us in the same time that the 'test' shell had taken. If Spike warned us, we could anticipate the arrival of every shell. If…

It became a cat and mouse game which he came to enjoy so intensely that I remember thinking how incongruous it was that lethal Jerry shells produced some of the best examples of the infectious Spike guffaw. With possession of a slit-trench space being subject to the 'nine-tenths of the law' principle, he could leave his plunge into the trench until the last possible second. With the rest of us scrambling for the safety of any remaining protection, one could hear above the explosion the howls of laughter from a submerged Spike. Only once did the job rebound on him. It was while Bert was relieving himself at the edge of the site that Spike hurriedly plunged into the end trench, where the ever-alert Bert, still unfinished, completed the function on top of him. The shelling, which continued throughout the day, was our only reminder that we were at war. We had no radio, field telephone or any other scientific means of communication with anyone else in this wide world.

I had been concerned for some time about the welfare of the 25-pounder crews who, although firing intermittently from 09:00 onwards, had obviously been the serious target of the German 105s from early morning. From our 'grandstand' position, I judged that the vast number of shells we observed falling amongst them must have wreaked havoc. Archie answered my call for a volunteer to go down and investigate. I was pleased to accept his offer, as I knew I could rely on him to obtain as much useful information as possible about the whole operation from the gunners' radio contact. As we were almost out of water, I got him to take down both two-gallon cans, together with as many of our personal water bottles as he could manage. The midsummer Adriatic heat and our extreme physical exertions had greatly increased our desire for the intake of liquids. It was not a return climb any of us relished in the heat of the day. Incidentally, I noted that my general appeal for a volunteer had suddenly rendered Spike's hearing quite defective! He was not very much enamoured of the gun, or with taking his half-hour stint of watch, but that was a typical Spike reaction which contained no real substance. On this occasion I could tolerate his attitude: each of us knew that we would hear aircraft before seeing any. The novelty of scanning everything through the binoculars soon wore off: there was little one could see of Bol except a few rooftops. The 25-pounders were completely hidden by the trees, so that no movement was discernable. The unusually attractive beach before us, stretching out of sight a mile away to the left, looked very inviting. Perhaps, as much as anything, due to the scarcity of good beaches in Dalmatia – but without a soul on it, the view barely justified a second military look. Only the spasmodic and sometimes erratically dispersed shell fire kept us awake and alert.

Archie's news was remarkably uplifting. In spite of the volume of shells falling among them, none of the guns had been hit and only two of the gunners had suffered slight shrapnel wounds, neither of which were incapacitated. The news of the raid was also encouraging. The force of Partisans, supported by four of the RSR's 75mm gun howitzers – which had attacked the east of the island from their Bol landing point – had surprised the Germans and liquidated all resistance there, killing about 130 and taking over 100 prisoners, as well as capturing several heavy guns. The Commandos attacking the four well defended, heavily mined, important heights to the north of Bol had met much tougher opposition, but were poised for an all-out assault later in the day. Despite heavy casualties, the Partisans had taken the OP height which, it seemed, had been more than softened by the HLI. attack on the previous night and the praiseworthy accuracy of the 25-pounders' bombardment.

It was early evening when we heard the sound of the aircraft. The adrenalin began to flow at the prospect of having a stake in the events of the day. There was no need to tell anyone to 'stand-to' in the gun pit, as each one wanted to apply the finger to the trigger – particularly Spike. Ironically, the planes turned out to be our own Spitfires. The anticlimax proved too much for Spike, who seemed to resent the Royal Air Force trying to do our job for us. He swore frightening oaths at everyone from High Command to the pilots themselves. That the planes could be heard machine-gunning brought no comfort to Spike: he was actually disappointed that they were ours! Perhaps shell-sensing was not his only mystical quality. It was much later when the rest of us learnt that the Spitfires had attacked 43rd Marine Commando (as well as enemy targets, it is to be hoped). Spike became an absolute misery. He would have demoralised us completely had it not been for a Heaven-sent diversion.

Bert was relaxing as only he could. Puffing away at the pipe from which he was inseparable, he reclined on his back on a smooth slab of rock conveniently sloping at an angle of about 30 degrees. The palms and interlocked fingers of both hands supported the back of his head: a picture of restful, recumbent relaxation. His open but unseeing eyes pointed towards the tranquil sea as he probably meditated, as he usually did in such near-comas, on what the Stock Exchange was doing in that long-detached world which he had not seen for over four years. As a stockbroker, Bert was not particularly entranced with Spike's limited range of conversation at any time, but at that precise moment he was beginning to convey his resentment at the inanity of Spike's intrusion into his mental leisure. I was never quite sure whether Spike knew how much he aggravated Bert, but listening from a distance I could sense that Bert was reaching the point where, to say the least, he was wondering why that nuisance figure who stood before him had singled him out for his attention.

"Did you know, Bert, that there are some bloody great snakes on these islands?" Spike enquired.

"Of course," Bert snapped, hoping to show the disdainful indifference which would terminate the encroaching subject.

"Are you fond of snakes, Bert?" persisted Spike.

Slowly and deliberately, Bert removed the pipe from his mouth and eased himself up on his elbows. Glowering straight at Spike, he snarled aggressively, "No! I detest the buggers!"

That Spike did not react at the tone of the response surprised me, though having been only half listening I could have missed a point or two and, anyway, I felt relieved that no trouble had ensued. However, I felt compelled to look around for some indication on his face of how he had taken it. The absence of a snappy Cockney response was only half as surprising as the whimsical expression he wore, which I remember likening to Stan Laurel's when he would sheepishly scratch his head with extended fingers stretching down from a hand held directly above. It also surprised Bert, and I suspect worried him, as Spike's bland expression remained unchanged for several minutes. What was he up to? Bert's erstwhile dreamy expression turned to a quizzical one and, as his curiosity got the better of him, one could sense that he had changed his mind about having delivered the conversation closure. With a discernibly false attempt at reconciliation, he enquired:

"Why do you ask a bloody silly question like that, Spike?" It was the stand-up comic's feed line for which Spike had obviously been waiting.

"I was on'y finkin'," he mused with uncharacteristically slow deliberation, "if I 'ated the bastards so much, I wouldn't be lyin' dahn there wiv a bloody great big one eighteen bleedin' inches from me 'ead!"

Bert was the oldest member of the crew: though far from indolent, inactivity came easy to him – the archetypal dour, undemonstrative Scotsman. He had survived the rigorous parachute training in Palestine and completed his jumps through sheer guts and determination, but would find no shame in admitting that he was not a particularly swift or athletic mover. Yet the fastest camera lens and film in existence would not have caught anything other than a blurred image of him that day, in his transition from reclining on the rock to a rapid descent of 50 yards or so of rugged hillside.

When he stopped and looked back, his gaunt facial expression conveyed a mixture of fear and suspicion. I could soon eradicate that suspicion. Spike was not leg pulling – except to the extent that he had deliberately delayed his warning – for I had seen that five foot long reptile, startled by Bert's sudden movement, slither away with almost equal speed and certainly much less noise and disturbance. To me it was a monster and, as I watched it disappear, I prayed that the commotion had driven it a long distance from the site, as we would soon be bedding down for the night. Relief tempered Bert's fury at Spike, whose wholesome laughter at the incident proved so infectious that it dissolved us all into a state of near-helplessness.

We had been so absorbed in the snake incident that it seemed almost to have monopolised the short twilight period. Darkness had fallen with Mediterranean swiftness, making the sound of small-arms and mortar fire seem nearer than it actually was. The German artillery had not bothered us for an hour or so, and the fact that our 25-pounders had stopped firing led us to believe that their daylight-established targets had been overrun by our own troops, necessitating the morrow's light for our OP to define, bracket-on and register new targets.

We were probably the safest troops on the island, but the imagined nearness of the rattle of small-arms fire neutralised our fatigue so that, even after an hour of look-out duty (I had extended the daytime half-hour purposely to facilitate our having more satisfying off-duty sleep) few of us rested well in our sleeping bags. I confess that in my case, the snake had more than a little to do with it too.

Day Three on Brac – June 3rd 1944

I suppose the lack of sleep partially accounted for our early morning irritability with each other, but the dawning futility of our role was beginning to prove anticlimactic too and was, I suspect, the main reason for everyone's grumpiness. We were still wallowing in miserable self pity when the enemy planes arrived, taking us completely unawares and finding us totally unprepared. The cynicism with which we treated the Spitfires probably contributed to our lethargy but the two Messerschmitts which tootled along the coastline almost level with our eyes, directly across our front from left to right, seemed to cast a mesmeric spell over us. Their low altitude and the screening of the hills meant that their sound barely heralded their approach. They had appeared and disappeared before any one of us could shout – as we did simultaneously – "They're Jerries!"

My disappointment at not 'having a go' found consolation only in the realisation that the pilots' behaviour indicated that they were unaware of the presence of the 25-pounders or ourselves. It seemed like a very leisurely morning spin for them, their slowness leaving a puzzling question mark in my mind. Reconnaissance would have demanded greater height. If they had suspected our presence in Bol, a course further out to sea – enabling the pilots to observe to their right – would have been more likely, as in their current flight path, they would have been unable to see anything directly beneath them.

What made us seethe all the more was the ideal target they would have presented for the Browning. A range of not more than 700-800 yards, an almost level trajectory and their slow air speed were factors, which, if presented to us in target practice, would have been regarded as unrealistic simulation. I was speechless, and I knew from each of our expressions how much lower it had dragged our spirits. Spike must have suffered the same but he seemed to recover before anyone, a fact I attributed to a possible feeling of guilt at his then-fabled hearing having seemingly let us down. "They'll be back," he joked with consoling and transmitting optimism, "but this time we'll be bloody ready!"

It was Paddy who was on gun duty at the time and sensing Spike's enthusiasm, he needlessly fondled the butt and lethargically swivelled the Browning on the pedestal mounting – 'testing' for freedom of traverse and elevation as if he feared that Spike might snatch it from him if it were left momentarily unattended. The gun pit became overcrowded with unusually enthusiastic ammunition handlers moving loaded magazines from here to there without purpose, as if to justify their presence in the pit. I had to restrict them to two, plus Paddy, lest during any rapid traversing the preoccupied gunner might fall over one of them. But we each stood by too closely, silently praying for the planes to come back. Whilst I was at it, I thought it was the right opportunity for me to thank God for making me move from the first gun position: if the planes were to come back, this time from right to left, we would have been quite impotent had I not moved.

"They're here!" yelled Spike. I never quite understood how he heard them so much in advance of seeing them this time, but he was uncannily right. Paddy had astutely swung the gun in the anticipated direction of the planes' arrival and had very little adjustment to make when they appeared, and he didn't need any orders! The gun was chattering away with the zipping tracers, proving Paddy's excellent marksmanship. In the short time available, even if he had hit one of them – and we all felt he had – there was insufficient time to assess if any damage was caused before the planes disappeared around the foothills to our left.

In the immediate silence that followed the gun's noisy assault, we instinctively froze as we listened intently for the rewarding sounds of a crash or explosion. What we heard was least expected. I stupidly thought at first that the Browning was actually sizzling: how or why it could or should had no valid place in reason, but I could not suggest any other cause for this slight buzzing which quickly grew in volume. Then there was an almighty yell from Paddy, followed by one from Bert, then Tony, and, looking in their direction, I observed a phenomenon of human behaviour that was at once puzzling, alarming and hilarious. All three left the pit at speed and almost flew down the hill in obvious distress, bobbing and weaving and shaking their arms about their heads as they did so, like those barmy football spectators who spot the TV cameras on them. Spike, who at the time was about fifteen or so yards from the gun pit, inexplicably broke out in convulsive laughter which shook his whole frame and which was punctuated with a series of his usual "Bloody 'ells."

"Spike!" I roared with as much authoritative drama as I could put into my voice, "Spike! For God's sake, the gun! There's no one on the gun!" He knew that as well as I did. He was also as aware that the planes could come back now that Jerry knew where we were situated. But the comedy of the situation, which seemed to superimpose itself over the drama, was something that he was aware of well before I was. He slowly staggered, still seeming to be handicapped by laughter, towards the gun – obviously relegating it to something of relatively minor importance. He reached the pit no sooner than I did and for the first time observed my bewilderment. "It's the bees! It's the bloody bees, Wal!" he sniggered in explanation, collapsing on my shoulder in uncontrollable glee.

During these many years since the event, I have often wondered why it took me so long to grasp what had happened. Sure enough, as Spike said, it was 'the bees'. The hives, which I thought were empty and disused, were neither. The firing of the gun had disturbed the bees and they had set about the source of all that tumult – the gun crew. What range of circumstances might constitute desertion I am not sure, but I question whether military discipline has ever had to cope previously with dereliction of duty due, not to fear of the enemy or such things as climate, food or living conditions, but to a direct frontal attack from a swarm of bees. What I can vouch for is that any of those three would be prepared to face the enemy or a court martial, but on no account would they return to the gun until the belligerent bees had dispersed.

It was during a spell of Bert's lookout that one of Spike's more noteworthy exploits evolved. With some ten minutes remaining of his half-hour stint, though I confess to dozing a little, I thought I heard Spike ask Bert if he wanted to be relieved from duty. Astonished into full wakefulness, I looked in Bert's direction to see if he appeared noticeably unwell but saw only understandable amazement in his face. Everyone else was sitting upright by this time and wondering, as was I, if we had heard rightly: our reflected, collective surprise confirmed that we had. Now, I thought, watch Spike for the early sign of a smile which will herald a "Can't you take a joke?" jibe. But no, he seemed to mean it. Bert half-heartedly reminded him, "But you came off yourself only twenty minutes ago. I relieved YOU! You're not on for hours yet!" Spike was insistent. "Look Bert, you're the oldest one amongst us and frankly, you look as though you could do with some kip. The last few minutes won't 'urt me." Bert started to offer a feeble protest but Spike was in first. "Anyway," he cajoled, "I owe you a bleedin' favour from yesterday." And with that, a bewildered Bert stood down, obviously agreeing that Spike's snake prank should possess some bargaining value.

The rest of us glanced at each other in mystified disbelief. More surprising still, Spike grabbed the binoculars and zealously proceeded to scan the whole landscape with the enthusiasm of a Sandhurst cadet.

This was too much out of character: the work dodger looking for work? I was puzzled. It took a long time to dawn on me (and I blamed myself for not realising it sooner) that Spike had heard something – probably aircraft – and he was merely making sure that he would fire the gun this time, if any action resulted. Crafty! Crafty, as ever! I found it impossible to relax again as I wanted to be sure that when the sound of the planes reached me, there would be no delay in standing-to. But the planes did not come and, as the minutes ticked by, I smugly revelled in a fair degree of self-satisfaction at being able to boast to the other NCOs at having actually seen Spike volunteer for, and perform, a duty which he need not have done. Yet he continued to gaze through the binoculars avidly.

With five minutes of the shift outstanding, he showed obvious signs of restlessness due, I reasoned, to the realisation of his mistake. He called to Tony: "Better start getting ready Tony. You're on in five minutes and I don't do no bleedin' overtime." The words he directed to me were much less in character: "If it's all right with you Wally, I'll do the water run for you when I come off 'stag' (guard duty or watch). We must be gettin' short again." Mystery upon mystery! What on earth had happened to Spike? Could he really have developed a conscience? I knew from Archie's patent and well-voiced fatigue, resulting from the first water run the previous day, that there would be no point in asking for volunteers this time. It was going to be necessary to detail someone to do it and whoever the victim was, I knew I could expect moans and groans and appeals for justice. Yet here was Spike, sparing me that embarrassment by volunteering to do it himself.

I felt quite touched at his thoughtfulness and indulged in a spell of self-condemnation for – even momentarily – questioning his value to the team. As soon as Tony relieved him, Spike hopped out of the gun pit, grabbed the cans and bottles and was gone, galloping down the hillside like a mountain goat. Bert's "What the bloody hell's got into him?" echoed all our thoughts. When one considered the pace of his descent, it would not have been unreasonable to expect Spike back in three quarters of an hour. Archie had confirmed that the village's communal tap was a mere 200 yards from the 25-pounders directly below us. When he had not returned in two hours, I had been through all the emotions from resignation, frustration, irritation and anger through to genuine concern. Once again, Archie read my mind. "I'll go," he said, knowing exactly what was required, but he had scrambled down no more than a hundred yards or so before he stopped and poised like an animal sensing a predator. "Hear that?" he called. I couldn't hear a thing and told him so. "It's someone singing," he replied, using a quieter voice for the sensible dual purpose of aiding his own listening and of not giving away our position, should the voice or voices turn out to be hostile. I called back in matching undertone. "English, German or Partisan?" "Can't tell yet," Archie softly mouthed, "but it's away to the left front," Then it can't be Spike, I thought. He would have had no reason to have gone any other way than directly down or, if anything, to the right, nearer Bol.

With Archie lowering his voice even more, I also strained to hear and then laughed to myself because I half imagined that his next sentence was, "Did you ever see a dream walking?" I used to like the tune and its lyrics, and whatever words he had called out – due to my not properly hearing them – seemed to mischievously mould around that song title and its tune. Such things do happen to me. Before I could ask him to repeat it, and after experiencing a second or two of disbelief at the very idea of succumbing to auto-suggestion at such a time, I heard it myself: "...and the dream that was walking – and the dream that was talking – and the Heaven in my arms..." I not only heard it but saw it – Spike emerging from around a crag a hundred yards or so to the left, singing his heart out and waving about the water cans and bottles as though they were celebratory flags and bunting!

I had never been conscious of having heard Spike sing before. Nor did I imagine that the first time would be at the end of such a physically exhausting chore as he had just completed. Permitting myself a few private seconds of relief, I tore into him and demanded an explanation for his unnecessarily protracted absence, while at the same time noticing that my first supposition – that he was drunk – was entirely wrong. He was deliriously happy! Spike explained that he had first thought he had heard female voices soon after handing the gun over to Bert, but put it down to wishful thinking. After trying to dismiss the thought from his mind, the sensation persisted to such an extent that he decided to use the ploy of offering to 'relieve Bert' early to get at the binoculars. Scanning the skies and the hillside was a pure decoy to confuse us all but, in his occasional intensely directed views of the beach, he soon confirmed his first thoughts: that there were at least two female figures playing in and out of the sea down there. The mysterious magnanimity of his out-of-character offer to go for the water was thus explained. Yet even as the story unfolded, none of us could imagine any situation at such a time where two females could be playing on that beach!

Once down there he confirmed something else which he had hesitated to believe from the image of the binoculars: the girls – two of them – were completely naked. Their voices conveyed they were Yugoslav. He approached them overtly, as only Spike would, forsaking the cover of the shrubs and finding that his presence provoked no more than some even louder giggly conversation and a retreat into the sea. He decided to join them. I could imagine, without Spike's superfluous estimate, the alacrity with which his clothes came off! If, as Spike insisted, they each 'seemed anxious for a man's company', one can only imagine how the Gods could have arranged for the simultaneous presence, at that time and place, of one such as Spike – the comprehensive answer to a maiden's prayer. Two maidens at that! He claimed all three revelled in playful excursions into the sea. I suppose when we learned that the girls were Partisan nurses – he saw the Red Cross armbands on their uniform jackets when they dressed – who were enjoying a brief relief from tending the wounded at the first aid post in Bol, some of the story became credible. But what of the risks they ran of the penalty for violating Tito's sex embargo – if indeed they did? Spike insisted they knew that they could not be seen from the village. They might be heard, but surely that was a good sign for anyone at the first aid post: they were within hailing and responding distance. His theory was that it was likely to be the only welcome opportunity for a frolic presented to these girls during the whole war; and he was going to help ensure that they would not miss it. The naked bathing was perfectly understandable. One does not take swimming clothing on raids into enemy territory, assuming one even has any. We certainly hadn't any, yet it didn't stop our enjoyment of the Adriatic – and the Partisans' supplies of such luxuries were inferior to our own. Nude bathing did take place off Vis.

It has to be said that none of the crew believed Spike's story, but they had not known him as long as I had. Neither could they offer any alternative theory for his unusual absence. Even so, it should have occurred to them that something extraordinary must have happened to affect his demeanour so dramatically: he was in positive bliss, and I had witnessed that countenance several times before when he arrived back at camp late at night in places such as Cairo, Beirut and Aleppo.

With the excitement dying down I thought it was time to brew some tea, but I almost gave myself a knock-out uppercut to the chin with the two-gallon water can in the act of lifting it. I had anticipated it would be heavier. The damned vessel was empty! "Spike!" I stormed: "What the hell's happened to the water?" I'm sure the doubts in the minds of the others went through something of a change when Spike, embarrassed like I had never seen him before, blurted out. "Oh! Bloody 'ell! I forgot the WATER!" Before I could say any more, he had gone with the cans and bottles. Within half an hour, with all the vessels duly filled, came a heavily perspiring and breathless Spike.

At 17:45 war had the damned nerve to interrupt the proceedings again. Two Messerschmitts, taking exactly the same course as the earlier planes (if indeed they were not the same two), caught us one-legged again on the first run. As if to draw our fire, they had drifted further out to sea for the expected reverse run. Paddy had the good fortune to be on the gun again but the range appeared too far. No claims of a hit that time.

Day 4 on Brac – June 4th 1944

Although I slept lightly, I was not awakened by the disturbance which had prompted the noisy ritual challenge by Tony: "Halt! Who goes there?" He had heard the clattering footsteps coming up the hill for some time and, after eliminating mountain goats or sheep from his reasoning, decided he should combine the challenge with the certainty of arousing the rest of us. The stranger answered as 'friend' as quickly as his breathlessness would allow. He was a gunner from the 25-pounders, from which, aware of our isolation, he had been sent to warn us of a signal they had received – reporting a German counter-landing about a mile to the east of Bol.

The impression was that their forces would try to take back the Eastern part of Brac, which they had lost on Day Two, and neutralise Bol as a beachhead for re-embarking. It was 01:45 and we stood-to immediately, knowing that we represented the only small arms firepower on the south-east of the island: the only protection for the 25-pounders and, indeed, the Bol beachhead itself. Distant sounds of persistant small-arms fire, mortaring and shelling had indicated one hell of a battle preoccupying the offensive forces to the north.

I decided that the place for the Browning was much nearer the road. With armour-piercing cartridges inserted every fourth round in the ammunition feed-belt, it could deal effectively with most motor vehicles and even make things uncomfortable for lightly armoured vehicles at close range. Leaving one Bren gun on the 'beehive site' to help cope with any right-hook infiltration from above the road, the rest of us moved down the hill with the Browning. I sited the gun about 20 yards up the hillside above the road and about 400 yards from the village's first houses. Between these two guns, the rest of us took up a central controlling position with the other Bren, for rapid availability to whichever flank needed us first – or most.

We waited, straining eyes and ears, for the expected enemy approach on Bol. Here, I thought, is where we at last justify our presence. We waited throughout the whole night. When the enshrouding darkness eventually gave way to naked daylight, the absurdity of our position was embarrassing. Camouflage of our emergency sites at night was an unnecessary and superfluous precaution. In the revealing morning light we were as exposed as the proverbial sore thumb. Before doing anything about it, I decided to learn the latest information from the gunners' radio.

What I learned was another confirmation of the military truism that battles are usually won by the side in the least confusion. The message about the German landing had been found to be either rumour or misinformation within an hour of its issue. The only enemy on the island were still unyieldingly defending strongly held positions in the higher plateau zones (which incidentally had been reinforced). The commandos had suffered such casualties that further attacks were being abandoned.

The whole raiding force was making its way towards Bol and Planica (to the west) for embarkation onto the landing crafts, which had already been summoned and were now on their way to the island. Such was the general confusion that there has never been any doubt in my mind that, if we had stayed with the bees up the hill, we would have known nothing about 'pulling-out' until we had seen the Navy arrive. Everybody had forgotten about us. It came as no surprise to learn that faulty communications had proved to be the main reason for the raid's lack of success as an offensive operation. That it had achieved the objective of drawing attention from Tito was indisputable. The Partisan leader escaped and was soon to be with us on Vis.[12] Perhaps we had helped.

Bol soon became crowded with assembling troops and equipment, stretchered and walking wounded, bodies to be buried on Vis, loudly singing Partisans and inconvenient prisoners who, for obvious reasons, could not be left with the Partisans. At 09:00 the flotilla of landing craft appeared from around the hills. With none of the caution of two nights earlier they were soon beaching to take us on board. A commando officer confidently predicted that there would be no trouble from enemy artillery. He confirmed that the Germans in their fortified strong points in the mountains would be contained there by a rear-guard from No.2 Commando until our embarkation was complete.

He felt that any possible interference would come from the air and therefore he wanted the Browning aboard LCI 289 before anything or anybody else. Everyone seemed to be in loftier spirits than later information showed they were entitled to. We filed among the disorderly masses through the village towards 289's allotted landing point on the quayside. The greetings exchanged from all sides stemmed, I suspect, from expressions of relief at having survived the raid and a mutual recognition of each other's – always felt to be greater –- role in the operation. It made the nine of us feel very humble indeed.

The Partisans, right-hands clenched to their right temples, repeatedly called out their impassioned "Zdravo!" greeting to all and sundry, and in their rarer moments of emotional enthusiasm wished long life to the allied leaders with their usual 'Zivio Tito!', 'Zivio Stalin!', 'Zivio Churchill!' and 'Zivio Roosevelt!' – which one was expected to echo, but always in that order!

It was as we passed the houses displaying crudely adorned red crosses that Spike nudged me, pointing to the collection of Partisan medical staff and stretcher-bearers relaxing among their wounded, waiting to be loaded on board. The usual greetings were exchanged as generalities and I confess that I had quite forgotten the connection with Spike, until I noticed two of the girls making animated signs of recognition to each other. I knew too, that he had seen it. Whilst I was still mentally congratulating him on controlling any acknowledgement, lest it incriminated the girls, I heard the most amusing sound of the whole raid. The occasion certainly needed some humour. Above all the serious hubbub of assembly came the chorus of two female voices in unison: "Zivio Spike!" How they explained that to their colleagues I shall never know.

"Our troops had landed in Normandy! It was THE D-Day! Our jubilation was irrepressible."

Return to Vis

After taking on board about fifty commandos, our LCI was directed to Planica, a small beach to the west where it filled up with still-singing Partisans. By 14:00 the Brac raid was over so far as we were concerned and the LCI started the voyage back to Vis, which was completed without incident. It was 20:45 when we landed at Komiza. To add to our depression, resulting from the contrast between our wasteful contribution and the heroic stories of the Commandos' and Partisans' bitter yet purposeful fighting, and of heavy and notable casualties (some of whom we knew well), there was no transport to take us back to our Troop Headquarters at Podselje. So another night had to be spent sleeping in the open on the quayside, whilst all the other units: Commandos, Light Infantry, Artillery and even the Partisans seemed to have reception committees waiting for them.

The following day, after many telephone calls made for us by the Commandos, two jeeps eventually arrived to take us back to the plain. It was a depressing 'homecoming', not made any easier by rumours of a pending move from the village – unless it were to Italy for leave. Sleep was an urgent priority and, for once, authority's blind-eye discretion permitted the postponement of the weapon cleaning and personal sorting out (made necessary by our 'holiday' on Brac) for a few hours kip. Only the awaiting mail cheered me – an exciting and surprising assortment, including two from Anne… But, most surprising of all, there was a letter from the USA from the parents of Wayne Rush – an American railroad engineer I had met in Tobruk at Christmas 1942. Exhilarating news from Eddie in Italy and Dick Ellis in India completed that cheering collection of writings.

We fully expected the following day to be just as depressing as its predecessor, but that day's news was so momentous and heartening that all misery and discontent dissolved as sugar in tea. Our troops had landed in Normandy! It was THE D-Day! Our jubilation was irrepressible. Spike was in sheer ecstasy at the news, with the broad beam of his grin moderating only sufficiently to accommodate his occasional 'bloody 'ells'. He pumped the right hand he had astonishingly thrust in to mine in a gesture of mutual congratulation for which there was no conceivable justification, yet which managed to convey that this was an occasion which warranted celebration.

"What a coincidence Wal!" he laughed. "What a bleedin' coincidence!" I couldn't let him get away with that. "No, Spike," I corrected with as much knowing authoritative paternalism as I could display, "Our little raid on Brac was NOT a coincidence. I'm sure it was all part of the great master plan, to keep Jerry guessing, and involve him in as many places as possible. It was just our little part, Spike." "No! I don't mean that," laughed Spike. "I'm on about the two Milkas." I knew to whom he was referring, if not what. So many of the Partisan girls we had come across on Vis were called Milka that we tended to call them all 'Milkas', rather like the Australians called the girls 'Sheilas' and the Liverpudlians 'Judies'. Spike then related how, when he first entered the water, the giggling, chattering girls shyly turned their backs on him as they walked out to sea. He called out to them, 'Zdravo! Me Inglisi!' – which had no other effect than to provoke more laughter and animated conversation between the girls. Spike's next friendly comment might not have been quite what the girls expected, but possibly it emphasised to them that he wanted the relationship to progress. "Zivio Tito!" he called. Although the Yugoslav leader's health was hardly what he had on his mind at that moment, he hoped that it might confirm his friendliness. It had the desired effect. After a few words together, one of the girls turned around, returning the greeting and waving as she did so. Spike almost drooled as he described her to me. The other girl was still looking out to sea and very obviously laughing. She had to turn around some time, Spike reasoned, and if Tito worked why not try the rest? "Zivio Stalin!" Obviously there was no logical reason for this to bring the other girl into the social group, but it so happened that it was the time when she had decided to join in the fun. If Spike was enthusiastic about the first girl, his 'bloody 'ells' and 'smashers' left no doubt about the full-frontal, ravishing, naked beauty of the second, with overworked reference to our oft-used pun linking Milkas (although pronounced Meelka) with 'milkers'. "I 'ad to say it," explained Spike, "although I knew they couldn't understand a bloody word I said. You can tell your mate Joe Stalin that I'm in favour of the Second Front, too!" I understood the coincidence.

"It was at Ravnik's grotto lagoon that I came face to face with Marshal Tito in rather bizarre circumstances."

The Aftermath of Brac

Brac had been costly. I cannot find any records of how many casualties there were among the Partisans, so I can only guess. From the known ratio of British casualties to those actively involved, it is safe to assume that many of the 2,500 Partisans involved have their graves on Brac. The commandos lost nearly half of perhaps three hundred men who were involved in the main attacks on the heights – a proportion comparable with the Highland Light Infantry's losses. Similarly, their losses were relatively greater among the officers. History records the raid as a failure of communication. In basic terms, if 43 Commando had known what 40 Commando were up to at the critical attack time, a co-ordinated assault was almost certain to have been more rewarding, and the devastating German counter-attack less likely or successful. Instead, there are recorded instances of senior officers of 43 Commando not even having been aware of 40 Commando's wholesale involvement in the attack. The latter, having been belatedly summoned from Vis to arrive early on Day 2 as urgent reinforcements to supplement the frontal assault, were equally baffled about the lack of communication from their counterparts in 43 Commando.

The officer commanding the raid is said to have been wounded when leading an attack while playing "Will ye no' come back again?" on his bagpipes. While still stunned from his wounds he was taken prisoner. Doubtless the German marksman who stopped the noise was doubly decorated. My simple mind has never understood why we had to attack the heights. With the Germans marooned there, and their supply route to the northern port of Supertar effectively cut by the Partisan 'North Force', we could have withdrawn from the immediate area and bombed, mortared and shelled them out. No wonder Colonel Elliott objected to re-embarking his 25-pounder guns onto the landing craft whilst he 'still had plenty of ammunition left'.

"Perhaps, on reflection, I was over-enthusiastically indulging in estate agents' fiction in describing Ravnik as an island."

Ravnik

Wartime fatalism tended to dissipate the genuine sympathy we felt for the victims of the Brac enterprise all too soon. The sadness we each felt in our hearts for the casualties among our Partisan and commando neighbours would have been fleeting enough through sheer selfish relief at our own escapes. Furthermore, the uplifting impact of the momentous 'D' Day landings in Normandy, followed swiftly by our hearing that General Alexander's troops in Italy had taken Rome on 4 June, hastened the mind-diverting obliteration of the occasion's solemnity. A new phase of my life in Yugoslavia was unfolding.

Without prior warning, we were whisked away from Podselje before we could deliver any farewells, to be plonked on the tiny island of Ravnik – some half a mile from the south-east coast of Vis, opposite Rukavac. We were there to relieve three RSR Browning crews, the existence and deployment of which we had hitherto been unaware. If life on Vis could ever have been considered as normal, I suppose our sojourn at Podselje had reached a predictable regularity which sorely tempted the military leadership to 'change it' before we became too happy. Leaving our good friends in the village created less trauma than it would have done had we known that we would never be likely to see most of them again. That 'temporary' relieving role was destined to last for the whole of the remainder of my service in Yugoslavia. Perhaps a change was not such a bad thing.

The growth of the Vis garrison over three months was beginning to neutralise the proud, pioneering spirit with which we had been imbued in February and March, when British troops were rather thin on the ground and material support had not made any significant change to the landscape. Engineers from the Eighth Army in Italy, with their earthmoving equipment, had begun to increase the width and improve the surface of the roads, particularly on the treacherous descent into

Komiza, taking much of the risk out of vehicle transportation, the volume of which had increased almost beyond belief on the main Vis/Komiza road. A start had been made on a considerable extension of the air-strip by expert airfield construction engineers who, in truth, saw our meagre initial effort, on the northern side of the road below Podselje, relegated to a mere dispersal area. All of the reasonably level area south of the road, between it and at the foot of the southern enclosing hills had been cleared of vegetation, presaging the ultimate construction of a runway some 3000 metres long and 150 metres wide for the whole of its length. From such humble, if enterprising beginnings, Vis' airstrip would eventually witness over two hundred forced landings and save the lives of over 1000 Allied aircrew.[13] Whether we had a right to or not, we never ceased being rather self-satisfied with our small contribution to this success story, even if initially we had had football more in mind than the remote possibility of saving aircrews' lives. Today, the ultimate airstrip's boundaries are deliberately and conspicuously indicated by permanent marker posts wholly dominating the central plain within which the vines now grow again in peaceful profusion. But significantly, the memorial to Allied airmen stands on the opposite side of the road, where the football pitch was first cleared. SUBNOR – the Partisan equivalent to our British Legion – remembered!

Ammunition and stores dumps had been established around the island. They grew in size and number literally overnight from the disgorging holds of navy-escorted supply ships making their regular nocturnal dash from Italy with their variously useful cargoes. By then these included barrels of drinking water to augment the rapidly diminishing output from the island's wells, which had never before had to supply so swollen a population. Oh, yes! Vis was changing rapidly.

Perhaps, on reflection, I was over-enthusiastically indulging in estate agents' fiction in describing Ravnik as an island. Ravnik is a ROCK.[14] An uninhabited, barren, unyielding and inhospitable rock; it has an area equivalent to about three or four football pitches (I apologise for this unimaginative yardstick), its highest point is barely one hundred feet but its all-round steep descent into the Adriatic affords but two rather precarious landing ledges on opposite sides of the island – one on the side facing Rukavac, which we invariably used for its obvious nearness and shelter, the other on the seaward side. Stepping ashore from a heaving supply dinghy in a rough sea (which was not as rare an occurrence as one might imagine for the Adriatic) called for a deft agility and sense of timing acquired the hard way – after several lesson-learning duckings, invariably involving nasty contacts with unwelcoming rock. Landing our supplies presented even greater difficulties.

The strategic value of Ravnik was instantly apparent. Situated conveniently at the entrance to the inlet serving Rukavac, it dominated the approach route of any force seeking to seize the only beaching alternative to Komiza or Vis Town. Our gun emplacements, mainly on the island's seaward side, were deployed to make things unpleasant for seaborne invaders and any supporting aircraft. A platoon of the Highland Light Infantry was Ravnik's only other defence. The immediate prospect was a disconcerting one, given that the threat of a German invasion was still on the cards. The previous occupants of the gun emplacements' had done little towards personal protection, concealment or comfort. The gun pits were too shallow and openly conspicuous: the 'residential' dug outs – a hundred or so yards from each gun – were austere, skimped, littered and uncamouflaged. However, the explosives which we instantly requisitioned were supplied with surprising promptness and, even more astonishingly, without question. Within a week we had protection up to chest level in the gun pits and something resembling order, living space and relative comfort in four-foot deep accommodation dugouts. When heightened by two feet of crudely erected dry-stone wall around the periphery, a dugout permitted a near uprightness of posture beneath its re-roofed lid of timber-supported corrugated iron. Look-out gaps in the wall and the final draping of the whole with scrub-speckled camouflage netting, added pleasing assurances of security to the atmosphere of 'home'. Our base was completed outside by the construction of a basic field kitchen. We felt quite proud of our 'koocha'.

This rash of unbridled, and wholly unbidden, activity should not be construed as a highly principled gesture towards disciplined orderliness or military zeal. Spontaneous industry was applied towards resisting a menace which owed no allegiance to the Axis powers. An unexpected menace! This menace was not even mentioned by any member of the crews we had relieved, on their undisguisedly joyous departure. The menace did not manifest itself until nightfall. Ravnik, we learnt when twilight merged into obscuring darkness, was infested with thousands of rats.

What they lived on was not readily apparent; where they disappeared to during daylight was equally unfathomable, but Ravnik obviously presented no barriers to their prolific breeding. After dark they paved the ground with a ceaselessly mobile carpet which dictated the imperative need for feet to be booted when necessarily moving about the island at night. Treading on or brushing against the repulsive creatures was a nauseating inevitability, more particularly because of our 'golden' rule of always using indirect meanderings through the scrub between guns and dugouts lest we established well-trodden footpaths, discernable in daytime to enemy observation planes.

Though none of us would ever admit it at the time, Ravnik's rodents were assuredly responsible for the heaviest consumption of alcohol of any previous period of our lives. Like the flies in Egypt and the bees on Brac, nature had again provided more discomfort to us than the Germans had. In unspoken, understanding sympathy with our servitude on the rock, our new Partisan friends at Rukavac ensured that a two-gallon can of vino was available for us each day. No barter charge was ever demanded, but we tried to be as generous as we could with cigarettes. Two gallons – at least – a day may not appear to be much between eighteen of us, but its potency was unquestionable. Sleep without it was well nigh impossible. Fortified with it the squeaking, shuffling rodent traffic through the dugout in search of food, and their inquisitive but happily unsuccessful, clawing attempts to scale our mosquito nets were merely subliminal sensations. What this 'Dutch' courage did for our military vigilance at night I shamefully squirm to think, but the absence of officers and, more importantly, the enemy, ensured that it was never put to the test during nearly three months of our shared occupancy of Ravnik with the rats.

Why then, given the discomfort, isolation and tentativeness of service on the rock, is it so easy to recall this period with a tenderness almost akin to romantic nostalgia? There were quite a few reasons. Without disregarding the importance of our responsibilities, we were able to enjoy a freedom from even the relaxed discipline which prevailed at Podselje. The island was ours. Our self-sufficient status was exemplified by the issue of a liberal cushion-stock of fourteen days' supply of rations and water, to provide for any emergency which might maroon us from Vis. Communication with Vis consisted of a Don 5 telephone link, a two-man dinghy with oars and an unofficial, but totally reliable link with Rukavac via an outboard-powered dory, operated by a loveable old sea-faring character called Marco, who guaranteed a daily service. The Don 5 hardly ever rang. We were conveniently ignored – and we didn't mind that at all. The novelty of a soldier's life without a timetable, save for each individual's two-hour 'stag' on the gun and consensus mealtimes, had a lot of appeal. Our independence fostered a healthy interdependence strangely reminiscent of service in the desert.

Our evening booze sessions were very deliberate affairs, held in turn at one of the three dugouts. They began about an hour before sunset, so that by the time the rats were bold enough to make their appearance we were nicely inured and uninhibitedly deep into our repertoire of songs. We learnt a lot about each other from the songs we sang.

Whatever our deprivations, it should not need emphasising that we were on an island in the Adriatic in midsummer. Idyllic swimming in deep, crystal clear, invitingly warm water was but a dive away. Dreamy, hot summer days, often moderated by a cooling afternoon breeze, were the norm, so that during the daytime clothing became such a burdensome superfluity that only shorts were worn – not out of any sense of decorum but because they offered that useful carrying facility of pockets. That 'dive away' was, in truth, about fifty yards from the gun position, at a lagoon almost three-parts enclosed from the sea, the depths of which we could never reach. Yet every pebble could be clearly identified through the aquamarine shimmering pool of seawater. It was a sublime spot, facing, as it did, out to the soothing nothingness of azure, horizon and sea. Nature had scooped out of the lagoon's rocky surrounds a mammoth cave which held an even more breath-taking secret up its sleeve. Marco had soon pointed out the means of access to an inner cavern with a blue grotto which, he claimed, for sheer beauty challenged the more accessible and therefore better renowned one at Bisevo. Access was no simple matter; it was certainly unattainable by non-swimmers. The inner chamber, which constituted the grotto, could only be reached from the lagoon within the cave by swimming underwater for a couple of yards – a distance which would not normally daunt even an average swimmer, but to plunge oneself below the barely submerged, dividing rock which separated the two chambers called for courage from even the strongest of swimmers. What if I run out of breath before reaching the grotto chamber, with only rock above me? How do I know I can find the way back?

After my first frightening adventure into the unknown, I can testify that it was truly worth any risk there might have been. It was an uncanny experience that approached the mystical. I spent every spare minute at the cove, swimming as the fancy took me, but mainly writing reams of letters home in the inspirational solitude and rugged beauty of the place.

War was a lifetime away, awareness of which was resurrected only by the daily drone of squadrons of American bombers, routed directly overhead in formation. They merited a mere glance skywards in blasé confirmation of one's subconscious estimate of that day's total number, guessed from the collective volume of their noise. Most of their crew members would be praying to survive the return trip and add another digit towards their fifty missions, the number required for a home posting on the basis that they had done enough – while I stirred in involuntary, self-centred objection to the temporary distraction of their drone.

That one of the most utopian retreats of my life, situated in so remote a corner of the world that it is unlikely to be known to more than a mere handful of people today, even in this much-travelled era, should be the venue for my encounter with one of the war's greatest leaders – destined later to become one of the great international statesman of the century – can be nothing short of incongruous. Yet it was at Ravnik's grotto lagoon that I came face to face with Marshal Tito in rather bizarre circumstances.

Dozing between swims, I was suddenly alert and on my feet at the then distant sound of a boat's engine – a sound we had soon become attuned to listening for and adept at sensing through all other distractions (even sleep), like a mother's instant perception of her baby's merest whimper. I knew instantly that it was not the smooth, high-powered throb of a German 'E' Boat or one of our own Navy's MTBs or MLs, yet it was more powerful than the other, very occasional Partisan visitors to the lagoon from perhaps Rukavac or even Vis Town, or indeed the occasional vessel passing close to shore in transit by the southern route between Komiza and Vis Town. Because of the narrow opening to the cove, vision of an approaching boat was always sudden and, for those passing, brief.

The instant the boat appeared, I knew it was a situation out of the ordinary. Description of boats is not a forte of mine: I can remember likening it to a small engine powered trawler, displaying the Partisan red star on its hull and on the flag at its masthead. The first noticeable thing about the vessel was its crowded deck. Twenty or so people stood attentively gazing and animatedly gesturing towards the cave, as if absorbed in recognising points in the text of a guided tour. My presence too had also caused something of a stir – first evoking welcoming waves of friendship which I reciprocated, then smiles as the boat slowly edged nearer, followed soon by nudge-nudge sniggers, then downright raucous laughter. Cameras had appeared and I noticed that some of the vessel's passengers were female Partisans before I realised I had not a stitch of clothing on, as was our wont when swimming at Ravnik. I grabbed my towel, which I threw around me, having decided to beat a retreat from further embarrassment and perhaps some obscure charges of indecency from the several patently top-brass British officers on board, but not before I recognised the distinctive figure of the immaculately grey-uniformed Josef Broz Tito, clicking away with his camera. The event must deserve some place in the Guinness Book of Records or some other exclusive register of unusual occurrences. To have been photographed in the nude is rare enough for all but professional models, but has there been any other British serviceman (or any other nationality's for that matter) snapped in the raw by the great Marshal Tito? The answer must surely be in the negative. My theory had been correct. It was a conducted tour of inspection around the defences of Vis, for the benefit of the recently rescued Partisan leader who had made his escape from mainland encirclement a few days earlier (partly, we would like to think, due to the diversion of the Brac raid). He had been picked up from a secret air strip by a Russian-crewed Dakota and landed at Bari before being shipped to Vis.

In the boat party had been Brigadier Fitzroy Maclean whose picture, captioned 'Dalmatia' in Eastern Approaches, his definitive book on the Second World War as it affected Yugoslavia, is of the cave entrance at my lagoon retreat and shows the very slab of smooth, sloping rock of such fortuitous usefulness and pleasant memories. Tito immediately made himself 'at home' on Vis in a cave high on Mount Hum, the island's highest peak. His presence gave another boost to the island's increasing influence in the shaping of events and, by the nature of things, to our own sense of importance, too. It also heralded, however, a significant change of attitude by the Partisans towards their Allies, which seemed to imply that the Yugoslavs were once again in charge of their own island – and thus in control of their destiny.

I suppose it was not difficult to understand how the substantial material and manpower aid which we had poured into Yugoslavia – and which continued long afterwards – could have been interpreted as a means towards our own political ends. In Partisan reasoning, it ultimately suggested capitalism and the restitution of the Yugoslav monarchy. There was no doubt, however, that while we thereafter maintained our own personal friendships among the Partisans on Vis, their collective relationship noticeably hardened, coincident with a greater outward display of gratitude to, and sympathy for, the Soviet Union, which by comparison had done nothing for them.

To the relatively politically naïve Allies, the almost concessionary honour they granted to the Russian crew to keep the British-arranged appointment, to pick up Tito from a secretly controlled British runway in Yugoslavia in a American lease-lend Dakota, turned out to be one of the major diplomatic clangers of the war. Was it not the Soviet Union which had saved their leader? To the Partisans there was but one answer. If I had then thought that the Partisans' 'five columns' might have been clever enough then to glean certain information, now published in Harold MacMillan's War Diaries, I might have had some sympathy with their suspicions. On 10 June 1944 (MacMillan states) a telegram to him from Churchill suggested that King Peter of Yugoslavia, who was already then in Italy with Dr. Ivan Subasic – a former Governor of Croatia – to 'form a government', should be persuaded to land at Vis to take possession of his kingdom. A veritable red rag to a red star! Fortunately, MacMillan, who was then the British Government's ministerial representative in the Italian theatre of war, watered down the message sufficiently to allow him time to convey the folly of such a course of action and to suggest an acceptable alternative.

I think that either the fame of our immodestly, though admittedly excellent, work on the gun emplacements, or a compelling curiosity to confirm who the naked defenders of Ravnik were, must have prompted the authorities to take a greater interest in the rock. Within a week of Tito's visit, we had the first of three inspections in rapid succession. Our own Captain Collins came on 13 June and seemed pleased with what he saw. On 19 June the new Commander of Land Forces, Adriatic – the newly introduced composite description of all troops then engaged in special activities around the Adriatic coastal countries – Brigadier General Davy, braved the short crossing from Rukavac, accompanied by numerous retinue. Their crossing to the island was turbulent, as a result of the previous night's violent electrical storm – a storm which had put out of action the Don 5 telephone that could have warned us of the visit.

Captain Collins came over again four days later, inspecting everything minutely. He left with effusive expressions of satisfaction, yet I felt he hadn't found what he was looking for. Mind you, I had my answer ready for the question which I think he could not bring himself to ask: "Who was the naked soldier on duty at the grotto on 9 June?" Well, it was going to be another question really. "I don't know Sir. What nationality was he?" Still, I'm glad he didn't ask. I had no intention of confessing and I didn't fancy a naked identity parade.

June had been a marvellous month for mail. There were the almost daily outpourings of love from Anne, which the Army Post office always seemed to deliver in batches – necessitating chronological sorting first – but which it always made tantalising by the mysterious omission of one in a sequence, for delivery later in an unrelated consignment. A remark in one of them was indicative of the growing intensity and involvement of our relationship. "Mum has received another AG (air graph) from you and a letter from YOUR Mum. Everything seems to be happening nicely..." Impatience at this frustration is typified in an air letter she sent on that historic 6 June 1944. "The Second Front has started AT LAST!" I'll bet General Eisenhower had not even given a single thought to us. Many of my other correspondents also came up trumps.

"Such stupidity had by then become sufficiently commonplace as to barely disturb my eyebrows…"

Wounded in Action

I became very ill towards the end of June. The high temperature fever which was sapping my strength, I could only relate to an excruciatingly painful boil on my left buttock. That boil had stubbornly refused to 'head' over the period of a fortnight. Approaching the limit of my tolerance, I phoned across to ask if Ray Fishwick could come over to see me. He was dutifully at Rukavac early the next morning, having walked with his 'bag of tricks' from Podselje. Noting the Red Cross armband on the stranger at the jetty, Marco had him on Ravnik in minutes, tying up the dory before anxiously following Ray over the top of the island to find out the nature and severity of my 'injury'. During the ferrying, Ray had had no success in explaining to a genuinely anxious Marco what a boil was, so that the Partisan's snort of derision when he saw a mere inflamed swelling on my bottom was somewhat predictable and implied an unnecessary and wasted concern. A boil was kid's stuff to a Partisan. Ray opened up and worked on the boil, dosing me with all manner of tablets. Every day for the following week he came over and repeated the treatment to my, by then, agonised distress and almost total physical debility. He confessed to becoming more anxious at my fever each day. Malaria and evacuation to Vis for a second opinion was considered. Then his tweezers finally located and extracted a tiny fragment of stone, about thrice the size of a normal pinhead. It meant that we had been involved in the war on Brac after all. One of the many tiny particles of wall, chipped by shrapnel and showered over us amid the dust, had found a soft landing not discernibly holing my trousers. I had certainly not associated the onset of my 'boil' with Brac. My condition improved rapidly from then on, which was just as well because the crew's numbers were further depleted mid-way through my week of treatment – by Archie with a 'gammy' knee having to be stretchered back to Vis by Ray. I could immediately resume my stint of guard duty and by 1 July I was, to my intense delight, swimming again at the lagoon.

In retrospect, the month of July 1944 seems to have signalled the beginning of the end of my interest in meticulous diary keeping. I have to state 'seems to have' because I cannot recall any reason for terminating that almost automatic habit of my wartime years. It certainly does not signify that some other preoccupation had supplanted my interest, the pursuit of which I had previously found almost compelling. On the contrary, July 1944 must surely have been the laziest month of my life. Perhaps it was that very lethargy which led down a slippery slope of indifference. Maybe, as Ravnik provided the time and inspiration for so much writing to my many correspondents in seeking to shame them to respond, I felt there were enough chronicles of my exploits deposited around the world to render any further recording unnecessary. Let's face it, events were rather dull – even if it was enjoyable living in that very simple, stress free existence which detached my mind from war's happenings.

The transformation which had rapidly altered the physical face of Vis barely touched us on Ravnik, but the fresh attitude towards troop welfare, mainly pioneered by the enterprising Commanding Officer of 111th Field Regiment (RA), Colonel R. Elliott, prompted the necessary involvement of other units, including ours. This gradually permeated to Ravnik, and resulted in our isolation becoming less total. To our intense joy, it culminated in each of us in turn being given four days' leave to spend in Vis town or Komiza. We were also allowed a day off on Vis every week and, where our talent warranted it, selected for representative football matches and other sporting events.

Days off could work the opposite way too. Once Topper had discovered our cove on Ravnik, he longed for his weekly visit when he would enthral us with his daring (it seemed to us) dives from the very top of the cave, into the lagoon twenty or so feet below with such controlled artistry as to barely ripple the water on entry. His swimming speed was phenomenal and his stamina seemingly limitless, yet his modesty, in matching his inherent rather than trained skill at teaching, marked him as a natural instructor whose teaching was easily accepted and never forgotten. My swimming improved tremendously.

Rumours circulated early in July about the possibility of some leave in Italy. Although most of us had had no leave for almost a year, hardly anyone, no matter how optimistic, was very surprised when the rumours were squashed almost as quickly as they had started. In all honesty, the practicability of such a logistic exercise, with shipping space so valuable at the time, was hardly believable. My four days' leave on Vis was a unique experience of spending a holiday without it costing a penny. If payment for everything in cigarettes destroys that claim as a myth – for barter implies an economic consideration – I repeat that, since my cigarettes were collected from my free weekly issue of a tin of fifty, my resources lost nothing, except perhaps for a notional value attached to the alternative choice of 'spending' them otherwise. But on what?

A society without a currency is certainly a strange one. Although rooms were easily obtainable, a Spartan rest house had been established in a large dwelling in the alleys behind the sea front of Vis Town. There, a couple of elderly Yugoslav women provided clean, basic accommodation and worked miracles with the Army rations with which they were provided. I don't think it held many attractions for many folk other than ourselves, with our hermitic existences on Ravnik, but a few of the men from Podselje and other sites in the centre of the island found undoubted pleasure in ready access to the sea, in addition to an escape from discipline and guard duty.

I spent my time almost equally between Vis and Komiza, each day discovering better places to swim from. One day I walked up to Podselje and found Topper on his day free from duty. We hitched to Komiza, swam and we delighted, even in the midsummer heat, in exploiting the new amenity of an army mobile cinema unit. We watched 'Stormy Weather' that day, and followed up the next day in Vis Town by seeing Ginger Rogers in 'Once upon a Honeymoon'. The miracles of modern science had reached Vis! Before returning to Ravnik, I chanced on a brief renewal of acquaintance with one of the American Rangers whom I had met on one of my first visits to Vis Town. His reception was so effusive that we enthusiastically swapped addresses but never communicated with him. Ships that pass in the night!

Excitement wasn't needed to make my break from Ravnik's isolation a most pleasing change. The change itself was enough. The excitement materialised on my return on Sunday morning, 30 July. I observed immediately that the Browning had been made ready for transportation. With ammunition, and other small arms and miscellaneous kit already assembled, it had to be shipped across to Rukavac for (the story went) a raid that night. Not exactly accurate, but what was 24 hours, when the cheering essence of the story was true?

It took the best part of the morning to ferry our bits and pieces across to the village shore. To compound the pleasure at receiving confirmation that my Browning and I were on the operation (it actually transpired that eight guns were), it became obvious that the 25-pounders of the 111th Field Regiment of the Royal Artillery were also substantially involved.

It was only slightly dampening that I was again to lead a mixed crew, no member of which I knew very well. Such stupidity had by then become sufficiently commonplace as to barely disturb my eyebrows, whilst the prospect of the involvement of the efficient 111th Field Regiment radiated such optimism as to reduce the composition of my crew to a low order of importance. The whole day was spent in helping the gunners, with the Partisans, to load up the artillery pieces and their ammunition onto the landing craft, which we learnt were to move off the following evening.

Before bedding down in our sleeping bags, we had been unstintingly treated to copious quantities of free vino from the cellars of Rukavac's few houses. Marco invited his personal Ravnik friends to the privacy of his cellar and supplies of his own speciality drink, which we had encountered but once before – a fortified type of wine known as Prosiec, which I confirmed was delicious and potent. It was a highly commendable way to start a raid.

The Raid on Korcula

Mention the Korcula operation to anyone who took part and you will almost certainly observe a wry smile that slowly turns into a grin, which calls for explanation. It was that sort of a job. Unique, bold, surprising and downright mysterious (to the enemy), it also succeeded in harmoniously welding Partisan and British forces in every aspect from initial suggestion, to planning and execution without the suffering of either a single casualty or, above all, any subsequent reprisal. It was to enjoy a cheerful little place in the war diary. The Yugoslavs on Korcula were still smiling about it when I visited them in 1987 under slightly different circumstances – a holiday as guests of SUBNOR, the Partisan's 'old comrades' association.

The objectives were simple enough: to cause as much damage, and as many casualties as possible among the German garrisons on the island of Korcula and in the mainland town of Orebic. The island of Korcula (pronounced Korchula) and Orebic (Orebich), on the long Peljesac peninsula of the mainland, are separated by a deep, narrow channel of the Adriatic sea no more than half a mile wide, a channel which was extremely important to the Germans. It facilitated passage of vital supply shipping which served all occupied coastal Yugoslavia and Western Greece.

If denied use of the channel, alternative routes meant detours into the mid-Adriatic around the Dalmatian group of islands. That would expose vessels for hours to the British Navy's preying MTBs and MLs and to Allied aircraft based in Italy. So, in justification of the strategic importance of Korcula and Orebic, substantial German garrisons were necessarily maintained at both places, providing appetising targets to the local Partisans who were not remotely satisfied with their occasional, successful ambushes of German infantry patrols. Eventually, their frustration reached the receptive ears of Colonel Elliott, the adventurous

Commanding Officer of 111th Field Regiment, whose cheeky plan owed nothing to conventional artillery theory and utilisation.

Throughout most of July, undetected exhaustive recces were made by Colonel Elliott's junior officers, following a week long guided tour which he himself had made, all surreptitiously conducted with enthusiastic thoroughness by local Partisans who possessed intimate knowledge of the topography and of the enemy's dispositions. If the Partisans and Colonel Elliott were enthusiastic, the Navy – or more specifically, Lieutenant Commander Morgan Giles – became positively effervescent.

His novel proposal for the use of a decoy conveyed a touch of the man's humour, so typically (and topically) exemplified by his own distortion of the initials of his formal command S.N.O.VIS (Senior Naval Officer, Vis) to SNOW WHITE, with the almost inevitable outcome that his junior officers became 'THE DWARVES'. His suggested contribution was accepted with genial alacrity by the raid's other planners, and it became the explanation for most of the 'Korcula Smiles'. The raid's basic prerequisite for success was the undetected landing at night of eight 25-pounders on a beach on Korcula, within range of all the targets recommended by the Partisans (and confirmed by Colonel Elliott). With that achieved, the guns would blast away from first light until they ran out of ammunition, or enemy retaliation made the place too unhealthy – whichever came the sooner. They would then return to the landing craft and hurry back to Vis. For the operation to be successful and keep casualties to a minimum, the element of surprise was of paramount importance. Rapid saturation of enemy gun-position targets was necessary to keep down the heads of would-be retaliatory German gunners, whose known pieces of artillery within range well outnumbered and out-calibred our eight 25-pounders. SNOW WHITE eccentrically assumed (and how right he was!) that the Germans would be so shocked at the immense firepower suddenly dealing out deadly devastation among them, without their being aware of any landings, that they would think that they were being subjected to a naval bombardment. Why not help them to think that? If they did, wouldn't our gunners be safer? Retaliatory shelling would surely be directed at the puzzlingly out-of-range warship(s). There was then a shortage of big-gun warships in the Adriatic, so Lt. Commander Morgan-Giles therefore 'made a warship'.

With the enterprise and ingenuity expected of a Mardi Gras Carnival float team, a group of zealous Royal Engineers dressed an LCI with timber and canvas to reasonably suggest, in distanced, profiled silhouette, that it might be a British naval destroyer, its 'guns' sprouting at the appropriate angles.[15] But wouldn't the illusion be woefully incomplete if those 'guns' were not seen to fire? Simple! A few captured 75mm artillery pieces were assembled on board with a plentiful supply of blanks. Rough synchronisation, via radio, with the firing of the 25-pounders would complete the illusion, wouldn't it? It was a happy bonus which the unorthodoxy of the scheme deserved.

Korcula Day 1 - 31 July 1944

Not even the predictable acrimony resulting from the random jumbling of crews could dampen my exhilaration at being purposefully at sea again. We had left Rukavac at dusk on one of four ramped cargo lighters (RCL 11), the principal cargo of each being two 25-pounders, 700 rounds of their ammunition and thirty-odd men. Our Brownings were mounted for air-defence of the vessels – two to each RCL – and the opportunity was soon taken to test them at sea while the noise of their firing would still be associated with the Allied garrison of Vis and not the destination island.

Even so, such care had gone into the planning of the raid that not very many of us knew the identity of the island's destination. Had we been informed so, we would have been more baffled than the enemy – or have had suspicions aroused about the adequacy of our seamen's navigational skills – to find ourselves approaching welcoming torch-signals being flashed from (we were then informed) the island of Lagosta – not Korcula – just before dawn on Tuesday, 1 August 1944. It transpired to be another reassuring indication of the meticulous preparations for the success of the operation.

Korcula Day 2 - 1 August 1944

The Navy had found a splendid hideaway in a cove at Lagosta, in which I suspected rightly they had concealed themselves on previous occasions. The whole flotilla found near-total camouflage among the bay's delightful surrounding of rare trees more typical of the Caribbean. Not even a reconnaissance plane would have detected us lying-up for the whole of that otherwise gloriously revealing sunny day. Lagosta lies some 35 miles south-east of Vis and only about 7 miles from Korcula. Its use was to be twofold.

Firstly, in the unlikely event of the enemy having detected the fleet's progress whilst at sea, its course towards Lagosta would hardly be likely to alert the suspicions of the Germans on Korcula. Secondly, it provided a nearer base to Korcula for the reception and treatment of any casualties and could also act as an intermediate staging supply point. Lagosta has always been an enigma to me. If it was enemy-held then why was it never raided? And how could we use one of its coves as a base? Mysterious Lagosta abounded in colourful rumours which I thought I might have had confirmed or denied by the Partisans I met in 1987, but the seal – real or imaginary – remained as tight as an oyster shell. The best received – if not wholly believed – yarn was that Lagosta's only war-time inhabitants were some scores of Italian women, political prisoners of war, harbouring no serious ambitions about escaping from the Yugoslav guardians of their open camp until the balance of the military and political Adriatic conflict had been settled and their fate determined. It went further – the rumour I mean.

The Royal Navy had accidentally discovered the protection afforded by one of Lagosta's many delightful coves one dawn when frantically seeking a concealing haven from all-exposing daylight after a successful but over-extended night's foray in enemy waters. 'Exigencies of the service' had subsequently demanded frequent nocturnal calls to the island by sailors bearing gifts of then precious soap and chocolate with other goodies from Italy, to the mutual advantage of long-marooned female prisoners and love-lorn British sailors. Fanciful I know, but maybe on the basis of 'no smoke without fire' there could have been a modicum of truth. Like the song says: "...for you know what sailors are".

I suppose the air of mystery that surrounds Lagosta thrives on the fact that until 1988, when it was eventually opened to visitors, it was out of bounds to foreigners for security reasons. Between the two World Wars it was an Italian possession, and was handed over to the Yugoslav State in May 1945 when its Venetian name was changed to Lastova. We lounged and swam that gloriously sunny day, finding work only in cleaning the Browning so often that it could hardly have been hotter when fired. My diary tells me how much I detested my make-shift gun crew, but the smoothing effect of time suggests that I must have been unreasonably intolerant or, at best, impatient. Day two ended with the convoy stealthily slipping away in to the darkness from the protection of gorgeous Lagosta's sheltering anchorage.

Korcula Day 3 – 2 August 1944

No secret had been made of the fact that the landing on Korcula – even if unopposed – would be difficult for the artillery gunners. Such were the peculiarities of the draught of RCLs, that their landing ramp ends would, when fully lowered, still remain some thirty inches above ground.

Steel channels – not unlike those we had used in the desert to mount the six-pounders on a carrying portee – had been especially made to aid the run-off of the 25-pounders into minimal water on the beach. Winches would assist their manhandled reloading. Such measures appeared to me to be commendable in overcoming foreseen technical difficulties, but they did pose the question as to why we used RCLs instead of LCTs or other open-front landing craft capable of progressing further onto a beach. Perhaps they were all that were available.

To niggle at such apparent shortcomings, for which there must have been good reason, became churlish in light of the spirit in which unloading took place. Driven as fast as it would crunch onto the sandy beach, RCL 11 opened its mouth and signalled the start of one of the most proudly cohesive team efforts I have ever witnessed – or perhaps I should say been part of – because 'witnessing' in the dark was more an audible and sensory experience than a visual one. I often wonder whether we would have worked so hard if the artillery gunners themselves had not been so fervent in overcoming the physical difficulties presented by waist-deep water. They were ferocious in attacking the problem, the gun crew's silent teamwork illuminating the gloom of the hour. Practice near Ravnik – at Milna – had been invaluable, and its lessons heeded: wooden gun platforms of seven square feet, tried there, were shipped to Korcula with the guns, floated ashore and used with acknowledged favour by the gunners.

After helping that spirited discharge of the RCL's cargo, I was detailed to take my gun and crew ashore to the right of the lined-up 25-pounders, ready to play our part in forming a defensive perimeter. This was provided primarily by a thoroughly organised Battalion of Partisan assault troops from Skis. Their disciplined acceptance (possessed of much-reccied familiarity with the beach and its environs) of their placing was encouraging, as was their enthusiastic reception by their delighted Korcula-based compatriots whose anticipation of our arrival must have been very trying. A few of the Brownings were left on board the RCLs in their anti-aircraft role, which in the end proved to be as much a sinecure as mine was.

At exactly 05:53 the tranquillity of dawn was shattered by the opening salvo from the 25-pounders. (The gunners of the 111th were 'annoyed' – they were eight minutes late in starting!) Although we expected the tumult, we were nevertheless astonished at the sudden intensity of its volume and reverberations around the slight basin of the bay, so carefully chosen for concealment of the gun-flashes, among the many other considerations. What those poor enemy wretches, aslumber in their camp on the 'football field' transit-camp target at Orebic, experienced when the lethal product of the din detonated amongst them takes some imagining. Target No.1, chosen for its effect on personnel rather than on tangible structural, transport or shipping targets, had been well and truly hit on the nose.

For almost three hours those eight artillery pieces barked their obedience to their Command Post's insatiable fire orders. Already possessed of many previously registered targets, they also received radio reports from five strategically placed observation posts, each clamouring to have their own identified targets prioritised. So exhaustive a range of targets had been identified through prior painstaking reconnaissance and registration, and so few and slight were the correcting instructions found necessary and executed, that the Germans must have imagined a fleet was bombarding them, let alone a 'destroyer'. It made it almost comical to watch the occasional, pathetic token bursts of smoke emitting from the cruising 'destroyer' as it plied monotonously to and fro, matching only about one in five of the shots issuing from the eight hostile beach guns. Talk about confusing the enemy – no wonder we smiled.

It soon attracted some sparse and inaccurate response from the enemy's heavy artillery. Our five observation posts had such a comprehensive field of view, however, that the instant a fire-burst was detected, precise instructions could be transmitted to the 25-pounders and the offending weapon knocked out or – as it transpired – the completely demoralised enemy would be seen to abandon their gun. Fifty tons of 25-pounder ammunition had been manhandled ashore: not many of those shells were brought back when the decision was taken to terminate the operation, which I think was between 08:00 and 09:00. The droll touch was the collection and loading of every empty shell case onto the RCLs. Not a single trace of our occupancy of that beach was to remain: boots disturbed and redistributed the sand which might otherwise indicate the presence of an invader. The only thing that had been forgotten when the raid was planned was a rake.

The hours of hard work had been endured uncomplainingly in the collective exuberance derived from the cheek of the expedition. Reclining on the unyielding, steel decks of our homeward-sailing vessel, we joked in an atmosphere of released tension, until the rocking-chair effect of mechanical propulsion at sea supplemented sheer genuine exhaustion and induced the inappropriate sleep of the innocent. Rukavac was the next thing I knew in the darkness of evening. No need for the Lagosta haven on the way home, apparently. It was just as well: the inhabitants might have been expecting virile sailors. The aimless, languishing leisure of Ravnik was just too much of an anticlimax after the rewarding sense of effectiveness generated by the Korcula job. The immediate return to our rocky seclusion might have been more widely accepted if we had been told something of the raid's success. I had to wait forty-odd years to find out about that.

Efficient in everything it did, the 111th Field Regiment's war diary (now available at the National Archives in Kew) glories in its detail of the reports of the havoc which their guns had inflicted on German strongholds and morale on Korcula and at Orebic. As if such details needed confirmation, the file includes a translation of a report lodged by the Partisans' 26th Division. In fact, I commend this version even more since it is compiled from local Partisan and civilian observations, and is less likely to be moderated by traditional British humility:

The quick shelling of the enemy positions on Peljesac (the mainland peninsula) and Korcula on 2 August at dawn took the enemy completely by surprise. Enemy soldiers ran about panic-stricken. They looked for shelter in the civilian air raid shelters and carried no arms. Their morale seemed completely shattered and they shouted "We are all prisoners and the war is over." They abandoned all their positions except one at the top of the hill and another in the harbour, mounting anti-aircraft machine guns. The harbour master, a German, said the German soldiers were completely demoralised and that the best thing to do was to go back to Germany.

The report continued by detailing the various targets on which direct hits had been observed, including the Navy HQ, the stores of 14 Company, cookhouses of 13 and 14 Company, workshops, the Fortress, the Korcula cemetery ammunition dump (and one senses a pained disappointment in '...no explosion, but ammunition boxes scattered about') and all the main roads were well covered by the shelling. The enemy must have collected themselves somewhat by later that day, for the report tells us that a patrol of about 50 soldiers were sent to the beach at Lumbarda, where they stayed until 19:00 – obviously mystified. Then a whole company arrived and stayed until dawn. The same deployment was used the following day, when the target proved just too tempting for the author of the report. With two other Partisan men and a girl, they ambushed the company's vanguard of 20 men, killing five Germans and wounding four while putting the rest of the Company to flight. The enemy left behind them a light machine gun, a machine pistol, a rifle, a pistol and a pair of binoculars. One can detect the 'stable door' cynicism of the report's next sentence: "Two hours later the enemy started to shell the village." Apparently, they did have one gun left.

The Partisans' Korcula correspondent could hardly comment on the effect of the shell falls on the Peljesac peninsula. The 111th's ubiquitous coverage of OPs, however, confirmed for posterity, the success of that aspect of the attack. The famous 'football field' bombardment did more for morale than material damage. The almost simultaneous onslaught on German heavy artillery gun positions did both. The guns that were not previously known about were silenced within minutes of having revealed their positions, the Orebic sited guns being caught by a heavy 25-pounder concentration while they were actually firing. To explode and burn this position the ammunition dump was blown up, and this continued for an hour. The RAF support played its part admirably. Bomb-carrying Spitfires spotted the prearranged marker smoke-shells, which the artillery had deftly plonked on an enemy gun site, with two bombs finishing off the job with equally clinical precision.

To add insult to injury, shells carrying propaganda leaflets produced by the Psychological Warfare Branch (PWB) were deposited on selected targets. It would be nice to think that this was the final, disheartening factor in impressing upon Korcula's German garrison the futility of their position at that stage of the Balkan War, and restrained them from exercising reprisals against the local people. That restraint was excused by the Germans in their publicised statement that the raid was the work of British Navy Commandos. We all have our uses.

In such a successful joint operation, one could hardly expect many tales of individual derring-do to emerge, but I would disappoint myself if I failed to mention the Partisan 'brains' (and not a little brawn) behind the operation. Comrade Prsona's name appears frequently in the reports. He organised the many advance reconnaissance parties, recommended the OP sites, was the reception agent on the beach and organised the highly individual evacuations of the five OP parties after the day of the operation with daring enterprise.

"Perhaps we had not influenced the outcome of the war very much in Yugoslavia, but we had done something out of the ordinary."

Return to Ravnik

That the personal diary I kept for those years (which just happened to bridge a war's duration) should become a 'war diary' never ceases to surprise me. Consequently, I derive rather smug satisfaction when apparently innocuous entries (and weren't they all such, at the time?) find themselves linked with moments of some historical importance. Tuesday 15 August 1944 is one such day. As a rarity, allow me to quote the whole entry appearing on that day's page, which measures but 3¼ inches x 2½ inches. The very trivia of its miscellanea may, perversely, prove to be of some interest:

"Today I receive yet another AL [Air letter] from Anne – and a letter from Ed's brother. Reply by AL to Anne, send one also to home, hoping they arrive before her holiday.[16] AB 64 turns up.[17] The weather is still super-hot and no signs of a crack-up. Archie goes to Vis for 4 days. It looks as if some important guy arrived this evening... 2 DCs and escort?"

The last two lines of the day's entries, posing unanswered questions as they do, are the ones whose historical significance I only discovered decades later in a book borrowed by chance from a public library. The 'important guy', it transpires, was Tito – returning with his retinue from his historic first meeting (on 12 August) with Prime Minister Churchill, in Italy at Caserta. The 'DCs' mentioned refer to two specimens of that wonderful transport plane of the era, the American Douglas Dakota, numbered in gradually modified sequence as DC3s, DC4s, etc. I had probably been watching DC3s. Undoubtedly the meeting was momentous, since it led to the tenuous acceptance of some delicate compromise proposals for the immediate post-war international recognition of a Yugoslav government, without wholly discarding a role for King Peter – at least until elections could be held.

It was not merely our exile on Ravnik which had denied us the news that Tito was in Italy. Certainly, secrecy of such an important movement was necessary and to be commended, and it is comforting to know that it worked, but frankly I don't imagine that we even cared then – and surely, barely understood – the significance of such an encounter. Whatever else it achieved, it certainly confirmed the admiration each statesman had for the other.

Another epoch-making happening of 15 August, about which we were then ignorant, was the commencement of operation 'Anvil' – the substantial British and American landings in the south of France. Ah! Yes: that accounts for the shortage of suitable landing craft for Korcula and the inventive enterprise needed to produce a do-it-yourself 'destroyer'. How heartening it was that almost all the war news was then about Allied offensives; on every front the enemy was being gradually pushed back.

It was strange that I would hear from Eddie's brother James that day too. Since Eddie had disappeared into the blue with the Long Range Desert Group almost a year earlier, and I had been despatched in my own militarily secretive way, it had been difficult to keep directly in touch. Yet by using our families as news agencies, a tenuous contact which bordered on the incredible was achieved. James was easily able to confirm that Eddie was still in Italy and had had some hair-raising experiences whilst operating behind enemy lines as a radio-communicating observer of German troop movements.

While still indulging in envious gloom at his exciting contribution to the war effort, I set off with Jimmy Irvine for our day off, which we had decided to spend in Komiza. In the torrid heat of a mid-August Adriatic day we went to the mobile 'flicks' unit. They were showing, to my chagrin, 'Once upon a Honeymoon' – which I had already seen during my previous day out at Komiza with Topper a few weeks earlier. Obviously, it was the only film can on the island. Still, Ginger Rogers was smashing – so with therapeutic escapology in mind, what price glamour? I imagined that I was still immersed in a whirl of celluloid fantasy when I walked out of the 'cinema' and almost literally bumped into Eddie. Eddie Keeley on Vis? Can't be! But he was there, true enough. What's more, he was at that moment engaged in the process of asking, among the beige berets, for my whereabouts. Telepathy or mere coincidence?

With the LRDG's role in Italy being temporarily completed, its attachment to our Balkan enterprise (then known collectively as Land

Forces Adriatic) was a logical side step. Eddie's business on Vis, or rather his officer's, was to arrange a seaborne passage with the Partisans for a small group of LRDG to Yugoslavia's occupied mainland, and their clandestine infiltration for observation of enemy aircraft strength and activity at the German-held airfield near Mostar. He was not expected to be around Vis for long, so over throat-lubricating, tongue-loosening vino we launched into an extensive, garbled gossip about our respective experiences during the previous twelve months. When he was summarily called away by a colleague to join the briefing, I merely had time to promise to try and see him again the next day – which I did.

Ignoring all my responsibilities, I left the gun in charge of Bert early the next morning, Archie being away on his four day scrounge at Vis town after a seemingly successful surgical operation on his knee. I rowed myself across to Rukavac, walked the mile or so to the Komiza/Vis road and easily hitched a lift into Komiza. I was glad I had acted so briskly. Within half an hour of finding him – a feat of brilliant, 'Sheerluck Jones' deduction, there being few bars in Komiza – he was whisked away to some craft or other for more useful purposes. It would be exactly a year before I would see him again.

Detached from substantial associations with the Partisans, as we were on Ravnik, we were rather late in becoming aware of the cooling of their attitude towards the British in the mid-to-late summer of 1944. Obviously concerted, and thus even more obviously dictated, it probably had its roots in their interpretation – planted or merely speculated upon – of Churchill's 'interference' in negotiations involving the constitution of Yugoslavia's first post-war government. To those of our colleagues on Vis, the sudden change was considered more sad than annoying. The demeanour of kindly, hospitable and grateful people may change overnight but I would take some convincing that their hearts would. Unmistakeably, Joseph Stalin had been at work. On the face of it, nothing in the relationship had changed but, when socialising dramatically ceased, the spectre of the watching eye had to be suspected – arousing fear among the Partisans and among us, sadness at their duplicity. So, the unexpected news that RSR were leaving Vis on 21 August to return to Italy, affected the Ravnik hermits rather less dramatically than it did those of our British colleagues on the main island.

Whatever Ravnik's drawbacks might have been, they were mainly natural ones for which we could justifiably blame no one: on Vis the deliberate, alienating processes which were imposed so suddenly must have disconcerted everyone and intensified, more than the welcome prospect of some leave in Italy, the desire to get to hell away from these apparently ungrateful people. Whether the decision to depart was thus a diplomatic one or merely marked the end of our likely military usefulness in the Dalmatian islands, we shall never know. For me, unexpectedly confronted with the prospect, Italy immediately became a dream of rapturous anticipation. At the same time I reflected on exactly six months of a quite extraordinary slice of life, mingling hardship, adventure and real pleasure which I knew I would neither forget nor regret. Cliché or not, mixed feelings abounded.

That travelling hopefully is better than arriving, and that anticipation is usually better than realisation are quotations with which I have long been in general agreement. However, our arrival at Vis easily yielded a flood of memories of different experiences, which I knew I would treasure as we sailed away from the quay at Komiza that day – even allowing for an inherent emotion I always experience at departures by sea. Perhaps, if I had ever been seasick, dread would have supplanted the romance. Nevertheless, there is no denying the nostalgia in my diary entry for that day, which also quite incidentally and innocently includes a prophecy, now partially realised:

> "This is the day, six months exactly after landing at Komiza, we leave Ravnik and board once more – for Italy. I could write a book about my impressions of my contacts with the Partisans. It's been an education and I feel a little regret at leaving here despite wanting leave so much. Spend night off Komiza."[18]

Memories? What about the football matches against the Partisans, when their band, which always attended, would play (with instruments probably supplied by the British) 'Partisani Nasa' whenever they scored and 'Tipperary' when we did. I recall the day, when scuttling down the hillside from Podselje to the pitch after duty, hoping to catch some of the game, I met Roko on the way up. "What's the score, Roko?" I asked. "Ah! Yes, football!" he cottoned on, "'Partisani Nasa', t'ree," he emphasised with three fingers, "'Lang, lang way to Tipperary', two." Then there was the day I was playing in one of those matches and was knocked unconscious in a collision with one of the more massive of those usually large-framed Slavs. I regained consciousness after only a few seconds, and almost wished I hadn't. Charlie Winch had apparently dashed onto the pitch to 'sort out the dirty bastard' and almost precipitated an international incident in the mêlée that ensued in restraining him.

What about the day when I plunged into the Ravnik dugout in a state of obviously infectious agitation after a dash up from the lagoon, and impatiently pleaded "Quick, a hand-grenade someone!" When 'someone' smartly obliged, exited as quickly as possible and returned to the cove totally unaware of the commotion I had innocently left behind me among the somnolent crew. The grenade's explosion coincided with the alert and heavily armed crew's peeping from behind the rock that formed the grotto's roof. "Where are they?" one asked tentatively from their cover. "They're floating on the top of the water, dead," I replied. "What, Jerries?" "No, fish of course!" I snorted with pained irritation at their ignorant failure to understand my enterprising contribution towards varying the diet, after spotting the shoal of potential dinners in the crystal-clear waters of the lagoon. Their annoyance at the false call-out was assuaged only partially by my provision of a couple of days' fish menu.

Could I ever forget the stoicism of Marco's personally assumed, nightly responsibility for landing Charlie Grant on the ledge at Ravnik from the dory? Never! Charlie was one of Jimmy's crew – loyal, dependable, industrious, sentimental and steadfastly faithful to the young wife he had married immediately prior to his embarking overseas, almost four and a half years earlier. Enforced separation had demoralised Charlie more than anyone I have ever known: his only solace – and thankfully his only vice – was booze. He would volunteer each late afternoon to row across to Rukavac with the two gallon can for refilling with vino, and in so doing create a 'duty' which did not exist. He would complete his self-sacrificing mission by getting tanked up on shore simply (he contended) so that no inroads need be made by him into the two gallons for the evening consumption of the rest of us.

That we could easily have kept a greater supply of vino on Ravnik escaped nobody's attention except Charlie's. A delightful charade!

Similarly, he was the only one who failed to notice that his imbibing at Rukavac barely affected his instinctive dipping-in during our evening boozing sessions. Charlie could not swim. Consequently, the chug-chug of the dory's approach meant one of us meeting Marco to help fish a drunken, mis-stepping Charlie out of the sea – always (it must be said in his favour) with the treasured can held above his head out of the water, as if in recognition of its greater importance to Ravnik's defenders than human life itself. Dear old Marco entered into the spirit of things, playing his part manfully in the pantomime by resignedly towing our rowing boat back to Ravnik and tying it up for us after Charlie's rescue.

It seemed like a hundred such incidents were remembered that evening as our craft lay-off in Komiza's cosily enclosed bay. Perhaps we had not influenced the outcome of the war very much in Yugoslavia, but we had done something out of the ordinary. And wasn't it boredom, rather than bravado, which had dictated our volunteering to be there anyway? We sailed for Italy early the next morning – significant in itself. The Navy and the Air Force obviously felt sufficiently in command of the situation in the Adriatic for daylight crossings to Italy to be confidently embarked upon.

Return to Italy

Hardly anywhere in my writings so far have I given much credit to the officers of the RSR. It came almost as a shock, therefore, to read in the diary entry for the day we returned to Bari (22 August 1944) my effusive praise of our Troop Commander, Lieutenant Watson, for the smoothness of the organisation of our reception and transportation to billets near Mola-di-Bari, a small fishing village about 15 miles south of the city. Rare praise can only come of rare justification.

There could be no complaints about our accommodation, either. In that still, torrid summer of 1944, Mola was an unspectacular seaside village, typical of many on the Southern Italian eastern coastline, in an endless, flat, featureless landscape. Only a relatively new, partially enclosing, protective sea-wall jetty of dazzling bleached white distinguished its seaboard from scores of other such villages, half suggesting a parochial affluence starkly belied by its immediately contiguous, drab, shuttered dwellings, meagre shops and unmetalled streets and roads. The only good road was the Bari/Brindisi coastal highway which partially split the village.

Mola's only signs of prosperity lay, almost secretly, not near the sea but inland, off the road serving the small town of Rutigliano (which we would come to know better). This road split the village the other way – at right angles to the coast – then crossed the railway line which also roughly marked Mola's closely built-up limits. Here, beyond the level crossing, among acres upon acres of ornamental and mixed orchard trees, were a number of expensive individual villas. They were sat in spacious gardens off anonymous dusty lanes which all looked confusingly alike. In such villas, requisitioned unfurnished, we were billeted. Their illusion of seclusion, enhanced by the region's total absence of any high land to provide a view of the whole area, negated any pretence of military uniformity. That created untold problems of administration, centralised feeding and security, but it provided a brief period of such comfort as to suggest a calculated measure of reward for the deprivations we had endured over the previous six months.

In further praise of our officers, it also has to be stated that their promise of leave was immediately fulfilled. In a state of stunned bewilderment all but a short-straw minority (left behind to guard the villas) found themselves the very next day in a remarkably well established Eighth Army rest camp (Camp A) on the coast in Bari's northern outskirts.

It was our first real chance to enjoy Italy – and enjoy it we did, although it was the near total freedom from the shackles of duty within a reasonably civilised environment which provided as much pleasure as the facilities 'laid on' by the camp itself. It has to be admitted that Bari also offered its 'real' cinemas and a variety of entertainments provided by ENSA, among other acceptable venues, the Petruzzelli Theatre (Opera House) – happily untouched by war's ravages. It had even escaped unscathed during the infamous German air raid on the city on 2 December 1943, which was said to be second only to Pearl Harbour in its intensity and effectiveness as a raid on harbour installations.

Forces' canteens offered acceptable day-long menus of meals and snacks in conditions of cleanliness and comfort which, after six months of hard-tack living, we probably appreciated more than most of the teeming thousands of British and American troops who then seemed to populate the city. Bari's tranquil atmosphere was in stark contrast with the deadly warfare being enacted a mere hundred or so miles to the north.

More than anything, that leave was most memorable for its cementing of friendships. Unshackled from the arbitrarily imposed attachment of 'gun crew', 'troop', or 'battery', friendships flourished based on some kind of natural affinity. Topper, Jimmy, Archie and I gravitated towards each other without conscious effort on anyone's part. Photographs taken on that leave rarely show us singly: common interests, tastes, humour and aversions developed into a give-and-take accord to be grateful for such a group. It must have been an absorbingly enjoyable leave because diary entries for those seven days are scant, although the very first day displays some sorting of priorities: "...find out where the ice cream is sold..." (Yes! An Army camp, not a school outing!)

Apart from a noted visit to Molfetta on the second day, which rated 'very disappointing', nothing appears until Day 5 when there is recorded a visit to Bari's imposing sports stadium to see a USO-arranged exhibition 'fight' (among other genuine contests) by the then-reigning heavyweight boxing champion of the world, Joe Louis. He dutifully toyed with several unfortunate would-be heroes in turn, before despatching each of them to the canvas with a crisply unleashed blow delivered with the apparent physical effort required in the use of a fly swat. Noteworthy it might have been at the time, but rather nauseating in its conception – never mind its execution – in retrospect. I suppose we attended just to be able to say we had seen a world champion; perhaps more of the thousands of troops enjoyed it for what it was. Maybe too, Joe Louis' obscure victims that day gloried forever after in their own humiliation – if they could still reason.

Our sporting enjoyment came the next day when all four of us were selected for a camp football side to play a DOG (don't ask me today what that means) side. Our team selector was the camp sports organiser who had obviously seen us kicking around together during the week. The face seemed familiar, but the accent clinched it – Stan Cullis, the Wolverhampton and England football international. Even his playing ability failed to prevent our 4-2 defeat but I learnt more about football in those ninty minutes than I had in a lifetime. His repeated exhortation to 'use it, lad!' is such a valuable, if elementarily, dictum as to make one wonder why, even today in British professional football, the aimless, speculative (and invariably fruitless) boot upfield still has its disciples.

Further evidence of total enjoyment is my diary's only entry for the final day of my leave. There is a suggestion of guilt in "Lazy day. Write, at last, to Anne." Back at Mola, it seems I had even more cause to feel the guilt of neglect. "Huge mail awaits me on return. Countless air letters from Anne and a 20 pager including photo of Joan's (her sister's) wedding."

Not all of that day's mail bore welcome tidings. Tony (Big Mac) McCollah's letter plunged me into the depths of depression with the news of Joe James being killed in action. Apparently, a loitering German night-fighter had picked up Joe's bomber as it was about to land after a raid (a fairly typical military ploy of the time) and demolished it, killing all the crew. Even today, I can still recall that remorseful news which was soon to be followed by the report of a similar fate befalling Malcolm Simpson. It stirred, in me, a bitterness which thereafter replaced (what I had not formerly realised to be) a thirst for boredom-relieving excitement rather than the resolve for the merciless, purposeful prosecution of the war, which it should have been.

The fateful selection of those two, of all people, to be the first of my friends to go seemed a fiendish injustice. Joe and Malcolm possessed all the qualifications for the 'cream of British Youth': talented, personable, conscientious, considerate, and of unlimited potential. They would have been wholeheartedly dedicated to the cause, which they believed to be just and honourable, yet I feel sure that they were incapable of nurturing hate in their hearts for anyone. It took me a long time to slightly modify my fury with the sobering thought that they had been in the death distributing business themselves. Who knows what number of innocent Germans they themselves had disposed of in the cause of duty and without hate in their hearts? They certainly would never have known – and I cannot imagine that it would have influenced them one jot if they had, for duty would have ranked high in their commitment to life.

It would have been recklessly optimistic to have hoped that the relative luxury afforded by Mola's dispersed villas could have been anything other than a transient, gratuitous diversion from routine army life, particularly for what was supposed to be an elite, hairy-chested, combative unit. Duties there were more notional than real; training programmes almost impracticable (your place or mine?); parades were a virtual impossibility. Of course, it was necessary to go through the motions, presumably to placate people in high places who (I imagined) scrutinised the daily Battery Orders, but apart from guard duties, nothing very inconvenient disturbed us at Mola.

In terms of the training I neither recorded, nor do I remember, anything except for some enterprising venture into 'familiarisation' with pack mules. Only too well can I confirm the beast's best known characteristic. I learnt, also, that if one can overcome its resistance to doing anything, then there remains the problem of stopping it from doing everything it wants to do. My bitter experience centres on a plan for each of us to practise loading and then riding one of them around the lanes. It took an hour to attach a balanced load of small arms and ammunition 'securely' to my specimen, whose eventual state of inertia (sufficient to allow that to happen, after its earlier effortless rejection of the loads) fooled me into believing I had mastered the brute. Once I had been hoisted onto its back, it displayed a fleetness of foot seldom associated with the species, resulting in my association with it for less than five seconds. Bren guns, sten guns and ammunition cases didn't last much longer, despite the care taken in their attachment.

Muffin was last seen heading towards Rome, freed from the burden of military equipment and employment. I assumed my responsibility for the security of the weaponry to be greater than that for the animal, and I have grim memories of searches in ditches and hedges for what I took to be equipment more likely to frustrate the enemy. Having neither love nor use for the mule, it is little wonder that I cannot remember what became of it but I imagine, since I was never charged with the careless loss of WD property (i.e. one mule) that someone faltered in checking the number of beasts we finished up with when compared with the number of those issued to us. Mules may sway the issue as to which side wins a battle: if so I will wager that the winners would be the side that had not used them. I affirmed that view a month or so later when we tried to use them in an earnest and practical way.

Notable among few other memories of Mola were the almost embarrassing, daily visits to our villa by two young brothers of the family whose home it really was. They would have been twelve or thirteen years old. It was difficult not to feel uneasy at having been the unwilling cause, if not the instrument, of Vito and Pietro and their parents and sisters becoming temporarily displaced persons. There was certainly no discernable hostility or bitterness about the boys. An initial cycle ride of curiosity turned into regular neighbourliness, which we doubtless encouraged, hoping that they would one day fulfil their promise to bring with them their teenage sisters when they showed us the best places to swim. The absence of legendary cheek and rascality in the Italian boys was as refreshing as was their intense desire to polish up their English.

My only other vivid memory of Mola was of my introduction to the passion of local participants in an Italian version of our 'Spoof' game, played across pavement-café tables, surrounded by an excitable, noisy gallery of men, young and old, awaiting their turn to challenge the champion of the hour. So far as I could tell, the point of the game was for the 'guesser' to try and guess the number of fingers his opponent would extend as he revealed a hand hidden behind his back. The 'guesser' called out his forecast simultaneously with his opponent's hand being thrust forward and slapped on the table. It was a pastime the Italians loved and one in which a considerable amount of gambling took place, hence the passion and the bedlam.

The Mola-di-Bari 'holiday' lasted for only three weeks. 'Serious training' was the stated purpose of our move on 10 September to a camp near a small town called San Nicandro, near San Severo, some eighty miles north of Bari and about thirty miles from the Mediterranean Allied Air Force's massive concentration of air fields around Foggia. The blank pages of my pocket diary concerning that period are as informative as the memory that naturally rejects everything it considers not worthy of storage. It is sufficient to say that there was rigorous and intensive training to an extent that I did not want to remember, although it soon materialised as being less aimless and pointless than I had then imagined. Those two weeks at San Nicandra were, it transpired, the preparation for our next operation, whereas I can honestly recall the period for but two matters. Firstly, our circle of close friendship had then increased to five with the welcome addition of Steve (Bernard Stephenson), and I can put a date to that due to the second reason, although I apologise for harping on about banality. The local ice-cream was memorably delicious, prompting, in the absence of opportunity for any other leisure pursuit, competitions to see who could eat the most, which Steve invariably won. It made a change from Vermouth and Spumanti.

Albania

After an ominously swift recall of the Battery to Mola-di-Bari, there was hardly time to store our kit before being hastened away, with bare operational arms and equipment and one day's compo rations, to Monopoli. There we boarded a Landing Craft bound, in some haste it seemed, for enemy-occupied Albania.

The whole of No. 2 Commando was involved with a rare combination of support from the RSR, comprising of 'C' Battery's .50 inch Browning machine guns, one troop of 'E' Battery's 75mm howitzer guns and a detachment of 'D' Battery's 4.2 inch mortars, under the overall command of No. 2 Commando, led by Brigadier TBL Churchill.[19]

A purposeful, composite role appeared to have been found for our Cinderella regiment at long last. We had been told nothing of the raid's objectives, cynically considering ourselves quite privileged to have been told the country of our destination. It was not a bit like the cloak and dagger operations one sees depicted in war films, where maps (and sometimes even photographs and scale models) are pored over and objectives and alternatives discussed. If our officers knew more than we did they kept it to themselves, but I doubt if their information extended beyond the expected duration of the raid – 48 hours.

It transpired that Albania was then only sparsely occupied by the Germans. The Albanian Partisans had control over vast areas of their country and certainly of most of its coastline, although I felt that the contracting ambitions forced on the enemy in the Balkans in late 1944, and the sterile military value of mountain ranges, had more to do with that state of affairs than the dubious, warring fervour of those Albanian Partisans I came across. However, the Germans had comfortably sustained a vital escape corridor for their substantial garrison on Corfu across the Northern Straits of Kerika (Corfu), where Siebel ferries regularly plied their relatively unmolested way to Sarande, the nearest mainland port of any consequence to the island, and thence along a strongly controlled road to the nearby small town of Delvine. From there, well established supply routes led to and through Greece.

Not surprisingly, Sarande's strategic position presented a very tempting target to Land Forces Adriatic HQ, after local intelligence had reported that the Partisans had been sounding out prospects of possible Allied support in their imminent, ambitious attempt to capture the town themselves. Borsh (then Albania's only other enemy-occupied part, some twenty miles north of Sarande) presented the only other feasible exit for Corfu's German garrison. However, the strength of the enemy strongholds in Borsh, Delvine and Sarande were almost unknown quantities, so a reconnaissance party from No. 2 Commando had been landed on the night of 19/20 September at a beach about five miles north of Sarande, charged with a directive to reconnoitre and report its valuable information by radio to Special Service Brigade's HQ in Italy. I have not been able to satisfy myself that it ever did.

Our hurried, false alarm embarkation onto the landing craft at Monopoli on 21 September was followed almost immediately by shambling disembarkation at the news that sailing had been cancelled. This, compounded with the next day's equally frantic departure in tumultuous seas on a 'now or never' command, bore more hallmarks of irrepressible impetuosity than the reasoned outcome of sound, intelligence-based planning.

We reached Albania with no apparent news from the advance party, and with 90% of the raiding party on our LCI debilitated by seasickness. I knew the beckoning torch beam flashes which pierced the ebony blackness of the night with their 'friendly' signals were not as welcoming as an enthusiastic potential invader, as I knew they ought to have been. At 23:45 on 22 September 1944 the Navy, as ever precisely on course and remarkably on time considering the turbulent crossing of the Adriatic, gently nosed the LCI ashore. The landing beach, operationally named 'Sugar' Beach really was one of a rare, granulated, sugary textured sand, such that the vessel could safely crunch its bow deeply ashore leaving the ends of its promptly lowered landing ramps in but a few inches of water. No enemy in sight! The reception party went into a huddle for a hasty conference with the officers who had landed. Even in the darkness, we could sense the closeting enclosure of the beach by sheer, towering mountains on either side of the cove which was barely 250 yards wide, whilst the unknown depth of the valley they bounded, could be anybody's guess. The LCIs navy crew, and fewer than a dozen of us (including myself) who had not suffered the ravages of seasickness, half carried the harmless, ineffective – and wholly indifferent – remainder of the 'raiders' ashore, and laid them in serried lines beyond a low ridge of sand as if for identification and subsequent burial. Grim as the situation was, a scenario suggested itself akin to the Great Plague, yet imbued with sufficient farce as to have begged a Gilbertian libretto. An enemy patrol of mere platoon size could have effectively polished off the whole two hundred or so of us in an instant, with only meagre resistance offered. No Errol Flynn stuff here: no virile, hairy-chested charging, yelling invaders. Death, if one seriously heeded the pathetic wishes of the limp seasick victims, would have been a merciful answer to their prayers, half suggesting that they should temporarily be disarmed. Fortunately, there remained sufficient hours of darkness during which even the worst affected would recover sufficiently to recognise the importance of clearing the beach of personnel and stores to less conspicuous, sheltering positions, hugging the rocky, confining sides of the cove. The landing craft disappeared into the night, leaving me with an awesome sensation of isolated finality.

What next? With no evidence of enemy presence, nobody seemed sure. The essence of the saga of the 'recce' party's adventures gradually filtered down the line to the rank and file, the general tenor of which was that prior military intelligence of the situation had been too rosily presented and was basically out of date. The only encouraging news was that Borsh had already been evacuated by the Germans, though the resulting redeployment of the town's troops had swollen the garrisons of Sarande to about 600 men, plus the unknown but continually increasing number of enemy evacuees from Corfu. Delvine's numbers had risen to 1200 and the strengthened German control of the road corridor between both places had been supplemented with a further 600 men. By far the most revealing – and dismaying – aspect of the advance party's discoveries was the formidable physical difficulty encountered in negotiating a passage in strength up the valley, from the beach to any point from which the attack on Sarande had been expected to be launched.

After five years of war, we were still learning that maps and aerial photography do not wholly reveal all of the secrets of topography, even to experts. (I have recently learnt that Brigadier Churchill was himself an acknowledged authority on the interpretation of aerial photography.) And what of our good old military maxim, quoted to boredom: 'Time spent on reconnaissance is seldom wasted?' What is the sense of reconnaissance if, before its intelligence can be imparted, we barge in flat footed, ignorant of, or at best indifferent to its findings?

Daylight confirmed only too realistically that the steeply ascending, densely wooded valley (immediately denominated 'Commando Valley') represented the only avenue of progress to anywhere by land from the beach. It meandered its steeply ascending way through the mountains so that one could see barely 400 yards ahead, as each cleft between the towering peaks merged into the wooded landscape, bewilderingly 'scrambling' one's sense of direction.

The absence of news regarding the raid's objectives, and the extent to which the advance party's knowledge had influenced them (as it obviously had) plunged us into demoralising depths of futility, eased only minimally by the assumption that the enemy was probably unaware of our congested presence on the beach. The gloom was further aggravated by the immediate revelation by our 75mm gunners that their weapons were useless at Sugar Beach, since their fire, even with supercharging, could not lob over the too-near, lofty peaks of the enveloping mountains.

Someone wisely decided that we should evacuate the vulnerable, limited confines of the beach and take up positions a few hundred yards up the valley. This proved to be a leisurely move, which used up the best part of the day, but sparked off competition for the rare, reasonably level spaces on which to bed down that night. Each of us inwardly nurtured the hope that bedding down in Albania might not materialise, that maybe the raid had been aborted and that darkness would produce LCIs requisitioned to lift us off Sugar Beach and deliver us back to Italy. No such luck!

When the naval vessels did arrive at around midnight, it was to deliver further stores, the time consuming unloading of which ironically ensured that we did not need to speculate very much about where to sleep in Albania that night, but when? Consolingly, it did mean that we would eat on the morrow. More significant was the passenger the Navy took back with them to Italy: records show that Brigadier Churchill had decided to confer at LFA HQ on the destiny of the 'raid' in the light of the newly-revealed difficulties.

Ben Travers could not have schemed a better farce than that which ensued. While Brigadier Churchill sailed to Italy to confer with Brigadier Davy, the Commander of the LFA was himself sailing to Albania to meet Brigadier Churchill. It was 25 September before they met on Sugar Beach. Snap! The content of their talks we shall probably never know, but I hope they were not too influenced by the contempt in which Brigadier Churchill held his superior (as outspokenly revealed in his book Commando Crusade).[20] We soon knew the consequences, however. Certainly a 'raid' as such had been abandoned, but the Albania 'campaign' to rid the country of Germans was on.

The raiding force was to be substantially reinforced. Operation 'Mercerised' had become Operation 'Houndforces'. The attack on Sarande would begin when sufficient supplies for its execution had been manhandled up the formidable valley to the heights above the town – perhaps in a week.

Nature – perhaps even more than the enemy – was to prove that forecast to be one of supreme optimism. With uncharacteristic efficiency, reinforcements arrived on the night of 24/25 September. They compromised No. 40 Marine Commando – who were fast becoming experts at short-notice expeditions – the nucleus of the headquarters of 2 SS Brigade, and another Troop of RSR's 75mm guns. The impotence of the 75mm guns on Sugar Beach had also been commendably, if belatedly, recognised and thus their prompt and unhindered movement by sea to another beach near Borsh ('Nan' Beach) had been effected during the night. There, contact was made with the Partisans and, most importantly, with the Borsh/Sarande road.

On day three, the enemy shelling of Sugar Beach and Commando Valley started. We learned that the shells came from guns on Corfu, and the accurate placing of their shots at first suggested directed fire instructions from an enemy OP on the mountain tops surrounding the valley, but none was ever found despite the diligence of searching patrols. That the secluded target area had been previously registered by the Germans on Corfu seemed too far-fetched a theory to contemplate: there were hundreds of similar coves along that rugged coastline. How could they have known in advance where we would land? A teasing mystery... nevertheless, there seemed little doubt that not only was our presence in Albania known about, but the exact location of our landing place was precisely targeted. Strangely enough, this reduced the effectiveness of the bombardment. The unadjusted predictability of the shells over the following week, though inflicted at mischievously irregular times of day and night, meant that we could avoid being near the fall areas throughout the duration of the barrages, which were of an infrequency that suggested cautious conservation of a limited supply of ammunition.

Our smug perceptions of the artillery onslaught, as an inconvenience rather than a danger, was soon abruptly altered, when after a few days it became clear that the enemy's 105mm guns at Delvine had joined the action and could at will lob shells on Sugar Beach or at any random point in Commando Valley.

The situation became decidedly uncomfortable – but as we were supposed to be trekking up the valley towards battle positions above Sarande in the following few days, the general tolerance was quite remarkable, and was aided by the comparatively few casualties suffered from the shelling. The rain, which coincided with the start of the Corfu barrage, at first presented minor additional discomfort. 'A drop of rain never hurt anyone...' A drop? After eight days of continual downpour – of monsoon proportions – the weather had become a more significant influence on the outcome of the operation than the strength of the enemy.[21]

The difficulty of moving troops burdened with heavy loads over such terrain had already been recognised: by 1 October the situation, aggravated by endless torrential rain, had become almost impossible. All attempts at transferring stores to staging posts up the valley were abandoned when an increasing number of men had to be returned to Sugar Beach, requiring medial treatment for exposure, exhaustion and trench-foot. The prevalence of trench foot was admitted with chastening apology. It was almost a matter of shame that such a condition could immobilise a modern fighting force within a week, providing convincing testimony to the suffering, fortitude and tolerance of First World War victims, who had had to wallow about in such conditions for months on end and considered such deprivations the very least of their problems. Imagine the white pulpiness of skin after lengthy immersion in water, which we have all experienced, then try to visualise that skin adhering to one's socks and coming away with the garment's removal. It was a sight sickening to observe, let alone be afflicted by. Why I was not a victim is beyond my understanding.

Mules, sent from Italy to alleviate the transportation problem, merely created new difficulties. Trying to lead four reluctant animal feet over jagged, uneven and continually ascending ground multiplied the barriers to progress in the valley, whilst the feeding of the brutes added another dimension to the catalogue of problems encountered.[22] In character, most of those obstinate creatures refused to work: many died from exhaustion, the stench from their bloated bodies announcing their location well before they were sighted on the hillsides. The use of mules was soon abandoned.

The official war diary of those days makes interesting reading: "But the rain continued. Frantic messages to Italy produced sufficient Italian groundsheets for each man to get one. Even when these groundsheets, together with dry clothes and new boots, had been carried up the hills to the troops, the soldiers could not get dry in the periods between guard and other duties." The situation was indeed critical – and a conference of medical and commanding officers on 2 October revealed that, at the most, only one third of the troops in the force were fit to fight. 130 men had already been evacuated to Italy, and some 200 more, with feet too swollen with trench-foot to allow them to wear boots, were being kept in tents on Sugar Beach under the care of the doctors.

My memories of that period are of utter despair, mingled with a continuous nagging fear that inevitably one of the enemy's shells would find an intended destination or that I would succumb to the dreaded trench foot. Sleep was almost impossible: imperative as it was, it took some desperation to actually lie down on soggy, wet ground or on rivulet-streaming rock.

And yet, I remember with amusement and pride the hours we spent singing as we huddled together, as if to convince ourselves that there really was safety and consolation in numbers. The challenge was that these vocal sessions should be of the non-stop, and non-repetitive formula of Ravnik days so that, during the rendering of one song, each of us would be searching the resources of his own repertoire to be able to launch into the next, if not without actual delay, certainly before we ran out of the deliberately protracted codas of 'shirt tail' last line reprises or 'vamp till ready', 'da, da, da, da's.' I hope it's not too mawkish or too juvenile to state that it was great fun. It went on for hours. Another useful and popular time consumer was a round-robin word building game which required no writing. It was a game that used to exercise the minds of my pre-war circle of friends on our evening promenades in Liverpool's Walton Hall Avenue.

In the stalemate of the military situation, and misery of the awful conditions, the game was an absorbing diversion which occupied minds not only for the time while it was actually being played, but also during work day duties when, due to the competition it inspired, it was not unusual to be nudged and winked at with the issue of a whispered threat of expectancy like, "I've thought of a good one for tonight." The wide differences in the literacy of the vastly varied members of the unit seemed not to affect unduly one's chance to shine at the game, hence its surprising popularity.

An enterprising naval officer, Lieutenant Commander Usherwood RN, came up with a brilliant suggestion for a partial alleviation of the grim and worsening problems of exposure, which by then were considered to be almost insuperable. What about bringing over from Italy three or four otherwise idle LCIs for use as floating hospital/recovery stations at Sugar Beach? With the Corfu guns then significantly silenced, and those at Delvine beginning to engage more in the artillery duels then at Shen Vassil, his offer was gladly accepted. As soon as his 'convalescent homes' arrived on the scene, men in their hundreds were called in from beach, mountain and valley to spend 24 hours or so enjoying the comparative luxury of a bed, a shower, hot meals, facilities for washing and drying clothes, and general recuperative escape from the rigours of the quite extraordinary climatic conditions. For reasons that I cannot recall, I did not get a chance to enjoy this brilliantly innovative diversion but there was no doubting its beneficial effects in the improvement of troop morale.

By 6 October (a day significant for another, but totally unconnected personal reason to be revealed later) the weather had considerably improved. Further reinforcements had arrived, including 'Queen' Battery of the 111th Field Artillery Regiment (our reliable friends of the Vis days), and the preparations for the attack on Sarande went ahead. The news was almost worth a cheer. Whatever lay ahead, the prospects of a breakaway from the deprivations and sheer boredom of Sugar Beach and Commando Valley elevated spirits tremendously.

The Ambush

I had the questionable privilege of gaining some prior experience in how physically arduous that breakout from Commando Valley would be. It came from a totally unexpected call to duty at the end of September. At long last some enterprising soul felt it was time to put to the test the .50 inch Browning machine gun's oft-lauded potential. An artillery observation officer, high in his eyrie in the mountains, had earmarked a profitable ambush site; an obliquely angled bridge over a stream on the vital cross-plain road linking Sarande with Delvine. He had observed heavily-laden troop-carrying trucks regularly plying between the two towns, even at night, and to his credit had managed to convey to our leaders how ridiculous it was to allow their unmolested movement while our own deadly armed combat troops were idly killing nothing but time in the valley.

Why my gun was chosen for the single Browning patrol was something I did not speculate upon unduly, but I know the others did. With an officer in charge (whose name I honestly cannot recall) six of us began the trek into the 'the unknown' at about midday, carrying the bare necessities required for maximum destruction and essential self-preservation. Our directions were scant – an understandable vagueness due to the recognised but scarcely proven difficulties of traversing the formidable, almost uncharted, winding valley. We first climbed its long obstructed, upward slope; then we dropped down the much steeper, but shorter, gradient to the extensive plains below. There, the first noticeable landmark would be the Borsh/Sarande road which, although no longer enemy controlled, was very probably in the view of his artillery observation posts as much as it was our own.

So the plan was to try to arrive at the road just prior to dusk and, by keeping to the valley stream, pass under the road bridge at that point. The tricky part then was to use the fading daylight to traverse the mile or so across the plain towards the target bridge on the Sarande/Delvine road, using whatever cover could be found. The Autumn sun seemed determined to atone for its inopportune holiday of the previous weeks by probing through the branches of the trees which we had optimistically hoped to use for cooling shade, as well as for visual screening from any enemy observers as we laboriously slogged up the valley. Every muscle and sinew strained to its limit: every pore exuded moisture so that sweat sodden winter battledress added near intolerable weight to the already burdensome load. We interchanged equitably the carrying of the Browning and its fiendishly awkward tripod mounting, a Bren gun, our own small arms, and what we all agreed to be too much ammunition for each weapon. Raid rations (which at that time of the war were happily scientifically dehydrated, or 'compo-ed') and water might have added relatively little to our toil, but the anxiety brought on thoughts of failure to arrive in sight of the plains before the onset of darkness masked the view of our target and its approaches contributed heavily to the 'sweat'.

The cheeky purposefulness of the project proved to be the inspiration which harnessed our hidden reserves of strength and resolve, finding us overlooking the all-revealing panorama of the plains even before the sun had set. Better than any map or aerial photograph could portray it, there – striped across the carpet of green which dominated the foreground – were the two important roads: Borsh/Sarande and Sarande/Delvine. The angled bridge on the latter was conspicuous by the way it disrupted the smooth symmetry of the landscape less than a mile away across the plain.

Urgency and possible danger then made their demands on our already dwindling physical and mental resources, as we contemplated the extent to which our images might be appearing through the prisms of enemy binoculars. Our clattering, unsubtle descent to the Borsh/Sarande road was due, however, more to gravity and enthusiasm than to discretion – surely revealing our arrival at the first point of decision, the Borsh/Sarande road bridge over the Valley stream. Thankfully, intelligence reports seemed to have been correct: all enemy interest in that road had been forsaken in the interests of reinforcing control of the vital Sarande/Delvine escape route into Greece, on which our road target was situated. Now, how to get there?

Recent rainfalls had so much swollen the stream that our original plans to walk its course under the road bridge were immediately abandoned. Caution nevertheless dictated that to cross the road we should scuttle singly and as briskly as possible at one minute intervals, and reassemble at the other side under the cover of foliage to confer on the next stage of our route.

Reaching a consensus was not too difficult, although I feel sure it was exhaustion rather than audacity which prompted the decision to abandon the protection of the sunken stream course in favour of taking pot luck, in the then sunless glow of evening, by conspicuously trekking along the reasonably surfaced road for a quarter of a mile in the direction of Sarande, before smartly breaking off to the left into the fringe of an almost unbelievably convenient field of maize.

During our descent of the hillside we had noticed that the huge field at that point filled the whole area between the Borsh/Sarande road and our objective on the Sarande/Delvine road, and seemed to offer the only likelihood of cover for any approach to the bridge. One can imagine what manner of 'bloody fools' the artillery OP men would be calling us, as they doubtless watched us through their binoculars with obvious incredulity, but the gamble paid off with dividends. None of us could have guessed that the maize would be seven or eight feet high, so that we were completely hidden to any but the keenest forewarned observer, once we had entered that maze of maize, so to speak.

The relief generated by this almost total concealment adequately compensated for the irritation of the scrapes and scratches inflicted by the sharp, protruding, autumnally brittle leaves as we thrust and crackled our way enthusiastically through the cultivated 'jungle'. The pleasing pace of our progress was, in fact, hindered more by the sloshy, 'paddyfield' conditions underfoot (further testimony to the recent 'monsoon' rainfall) than by the bristly plants. The crop ended abruptly about 150 yards from the bridge. No doubt the enemy had made a gesture towards limiting the concealment of would-be attackers by clearing away the plants from that small area – a self-defeating ploy which afforded us both ideally sited cover and an uncluttered field of fire.

Our approach to the fringe of the crop was nevertheless negotiated with much more caution than our earlier barging, even if our hearts were beating more noticeably. Without disturbing a leaf, we peered out at our target, seeking in vain for sight or sound of its supposed defenders. The bridge itself seemed to sneer a silent response of anticlimax as twilight raced to dusk, then dusk to darkness.

In an atmosphere of cumulatively deflating disenchantment, we mounted the belt-loaded Browning onto its tripod on the firmest surface available, setting aim at the centre of the road where it crossed the bridge with only the gun's slender barrel protruding from the screening of the maize crop, rather like the inconspicuousness of a submarine's periscope. Then began the tiresome wait in the dark: the marking of time and yearning for something – we knew not what - to run into the Browning's range.

Everything else in that sketchily planned day had evolved so favourably. The dread of nothing happening tended to blunt our enthusiasm, as did the discomfort resulting from our superficial scratches, wet feet and the rapid chilling effect of the cool night air on our perspiration-soaked clothing. The situation revived in me grim recollections of the futility engendered by tiresome winter's night manoeuvres in the snow covered Cotswold Hills in 1941. Surely an officer-umpire, wearing a broad white armband, would soon miraculously appear declaring, "Right! Browning No. 6. You've been knocked-out and you're all dead. Back to billets with you!"

Then our keenly primed ears discerned the sound of a distant vehicle, hushed at first but unmistakably approaching. Early doubts, which we thought were the result of wishful thinking, were not altogether dismissed until the heavily-masked, dim, swaying side-lights came into view, tracing the vehicle's negotiation of the slight bends in the road as it approached from Delvine.

Sound is a notoriously fast traveller at night; consequently we had ample time to prepare ourselves for the vehicle's arrival and for its anticipated, enforced gear change to the walking pace necessary for the sharply angled change of direction demanded by the road where it crossed the bridge. Amidst such tension, our officer's command came as something of a shock, as much in its contrast from his hitherto unobtrusive exercise of authority, as from its dismaying content: "Leave it! Let it go!" For the first time on the venture he had discarded what had obviously been his pose as 'one of the boys' and, while the command startled us by its rare assertiveness, it instantly registered as a dulling restraint on the 'let it rip' wishes of the rest of us. A hesitant – almost truculent – compliance posed the unspoken question, which he adroitly 'collected' and deftly answered with such wisdom as to earn for himself our unanimous and later, well voiced respect. "It's only a car!" He whispered the explanation as if he were addressing a cavalryman of the pre-internal combustion engine era. He then expanded immediately with its significance. "We want bigger spoils than that," he reasoned. "At the most, we'd only get four of them in a car – maybe only one." Our praise for the wisdom of his judgement might have waned if the target we had been hoping for had not appeared within the hour.

The unmistakeable droning and throbbing of the powerful engine of a lorry, approaching from Sarande, suggested the imminent arrival of the 'bigger spoils'. That the lorry was laden with troops was confirmed by the ludicrously misplaced strains of many unsuspecting male voices raised in pleasant harmony. I could almost appreciate its quality. What was it about the canopied rear of a troop-laden vehicle which (rather like a bathroom does for each one of us) induced in all troops a desire, if not a compulsion, to sing?

I clearly remember a momentary, sickly sensation of 'not cricket' about the ambush, just before the Browning spat out its alternate tracer and armour piercing, half inch projectiles of death and destruction. Only the slightest of swivels had been necessary to direct the fusillade accurately between the two faintly glimmering, red rearlights of the then almost stationary vehicle before they ceased even to glimmer.

I had expected an explosion, followed by a fire, but neither came. In the desert, one rifle shot into the petrol tank of a clapped out vehicle was usually sufficient to ignite the firework display which our pitifully aimless minds then demanded. Such a spectacular detonation and a crackling blaze would, oddly enough, have made this occasion seem less callous. The reverberation of the blast and the roar of an impact induced conflagration would have masked the haunting, terror stricken cries of the victims and ensured that death would have ended earlier the mass moaning and groaning which came from that wheeled tomb, in the incongruous stillness of the night. There was not much doubt about the vehicle's destruction. God only knows about its passengers.

I am aware that in any gang killing, each member is just as guilty as the one who actually performs the deed. Perhaps that is the explanation for my uncharacteristic lapse of memory about not only the name of our leader, but also whose finger squeezed the trigger and the identity of any of my colleagues on the ambush. "Right! Let's get the hell out of here." There was no doubt about the authority of that command, nor delay in its execution.

Leaving behind only the unused Browning ammunition, which constituted the heaviest burden, we rapidly draped ourselves with our respective loads and actually ran with invigorated zeal in the general direction in which we had come. This time it was so dark that initially we were perversely glad of the guiding 'feeler' sensation of the sharply scraping leaves as they lead pathways through the rigid uniformity of the rows of maize. 'Initially', I stated. We had barely traversed a hundred yards into the planted thicket when suddenly the whole night sky was brilliantly illuminated by the seemingly miraculous appearance of several incandescent flares hanging above us. As soon as we had recovered from our startlement, we were able to turn our heads to the heavens above and express our heartfelt thanks to anyone listening up there. Without the flares we would doubtless have been floundering, widely separated, and in the plantation for hours. Their guidance actually helped our successful mass escape to the Sarande/Borsh road without pursuit. Then we were able to make an unhindered march in total darkness along the road towards the eastern entrance to Commando Valley.

The significance of the flares? To our surprise, they confirmed the observation post's opinion that the bridge had been defended, with the enemy cleverly concealed from our view. A few widely dispersed mortar shells were plonked speculatively into the maize but none came even remotely near enough to cause us any anxiety whatsoever. Once in the shrouding concealment of Commando Valley, we halted and consumed our compo rations with a relish born of satisfaction and relief. Without much serious hope of success, we tried to sleep and predictably failed. When the interminably awaited dawn provided enough light for us to tackle the dangerous scramble, we pushed on back to base at Sugar Beach.

For a moment we were heros, envied by our comrades, but we thought their news was more important than our own. The attack on Sarande – assuming that the logistical problems of carrying all the weapons and equipment up and over the mountain range could be surmounted in the time allowed – would go ahead on 9 October.

The Attack on Sarande

D-Day for the attack on Sarande was fixed for 9 October 1944, with H-Hour's timing to be decided just before dawn on that day. The RSR's Brownings were to be seconded to No. 2 Commando, whose allocated task in the overall plan of things was to capture the German artillery positions in the north-west section of the town. Our attack would coincide with simultaneous assaults on the town itself by 40 Royal Marine Commando (from the west) and with seaborne landings south of the town by the newly arrived Royal Air Force Parachute Levies. The Partisans' role was to be mainly one of thwarting the feeding of German reinforcements or other counterattacks from the Delvine area and controlling the roads east of Sarande. Barrages from the 111th Field Regiment's 25-pounders, the RSR's 75mm guns and the 4.2-in mortars had been detailed as a prelude to the attack.

To assist in the softening-up process, the Royal Navy and Royal Air Force had been asked to supplement the bombardment with any firepower they could spare from Italy. A comic touch was included in the plan, too, in the rather off-the-cuff and prospectively bizarre 'firework display' which a New Zealand officer of the Royal Engineers had successfully pleaded to be able to contribute, as a diversion.

The movements of the troops from Commando Valley to their allotted assembly points (No. 2 Commando to Point 586 and 40 Royal Marine Commando to Point 122) presented a dreaded logistical undertaking and was calculated to take the whole of D-Day minus One – and it did. That is, it did take all day and it did present a massive, exhausting, movement problem.

My own memories of that day – uncomplicated as they are by any apprehension which might have arisen had I had prior knowledge of any of the battle plans – are dominated by the horror of the sweating fatigue of a clambering, crabbing, load-carrying ascent. This was performed with the truculently abusive, yet doggedly obedient resignation so typical of British troops, inwardly determined to get the job over and done with as soon as possible. Uncomplaining complicity would have been uncharacteristic – almost alarming!

The rigours of our ambush trek of a few days earlier had proved to be a useful apprenticeship, if only in providing us with a better notion of what to expect. However, traversing the valley had been child's play when compared with that day long, back breaking slog up the mountainside to reach the plateau before sunset. Over the previous week, conscientious attempts to reconnoitre routes throughout the territory had been made by patrols experienced in such roles, but we encountered frequent signs that they had been forced to double back from dead ends or obstructed routes through the undergrowth.

The only fixed feature of the whole operation was the distinctive, map-referenced objective itself. Progress towards it became nothing less than a trial and error, compass-aided exploration of the merciless terrain, with vehement cursing accompanying every misroute or impassable obstacle encountered, and with rebelliously voted rest periods coming closer and closer together in time as the mountain's summit was approached.

Arrival at the top was something of an anticlimax. Foolishly, we had imagined that the whole panorama of Sarande and its bay would have been laid out below us, but the width of the mountain range and its intervening foothills screened us from a premature sighting of the campaign's ultimate goal. An instant measure of compensation came from easy identification of the rocks marking Point 586, our rendezvous where groups of Commandos were already gathering. The view was made even more pleasing by its slightly downhill route from our peak. We were there, unburdened, speculating and resting within minutes. The sun, still fairly high in the sky, was warm enough to gradually neutralise the comparative cool of the summit, aiding the drying process of our sweat soaked clothing before the chilling process had chance to start.

From the formal strategic planning which then ensued among the officers, I soon became sickeningly aware – that once again – no positive role was to be given to the Brownings. There were hints that they'd call us if we were needed but in truth, it was a further affirmation that either the Commandos considered the Brownings unsuitable for such enterprises or that nobody in command knew how best to use their formidable firepower. I knew the lads were feeling as sick about it as I was – and equally as helpless, though ever hopeful.

During the last hour of daylight we were to follow the Commandos down the Sarande side of the mountain to Point 469, a hollowed cleft in the hills within close attacking range of the first of the enemy's two strongpoints to the north-west of the town. We learned from that 469, No. 2 Commando would launch its assault at 04:30 the next day, after the artillery and ships had ceased fire. 40 RM Commando's attack on Point 261 and the Levies' landings at what had been tagged 'Parachute Beach' would go in at the same time. So far as we knew, the element of surprise was still an asset in our favour, but from what followed one could be forgiven for thinking that I was trying my best to put our luck to the test.

At our first rest after Point 586 on the downward journey, I set about my usual task of supervising the fair load distribution. It wasn't until I came to allocate the Bren gun that I realised that we didn't have it with us. The fool I had given it to at 586 had 'forgotten' to pick it up. Although being burdened with a share of Browning ammunition he confessed that he 'thought he'd got off lightly this time!', attributing his easy burden to the fact that for the first time we were starting to descend. Worse still, he claimed, "I'd never be able to find my way back to Point 586".

I had some sympathy with him. Only the observant would have been able to retrace our trackless route; a thicko who forgot a Bren gun had very little prospect.

I discussed it with Archie and, confident of finding Point 586 myself (and rightly blaming myself anyway), I left him in charge of the crew to follow the Commandos, asking Jimmy Irvine to keep an eye on my crew as well as his own. I then lumbered my load, with relish, onto the idiot and scuttled back up the gradual incline, in light that was just beginning to fade. Fortunately, I had very little difficulty in tracing the route and, glowing in the glory of my personal achievement, was approaching recognisable signs of the site, when I was startled to see a Commando looming towards me – carrying the Bren.

"Oh! You found it then?" I asked, and answered, the obvious in the same sentence.

"Found what?" he queried, and I mentally cursed him for playing comic games at such a time.

"The Bren," I spat out.

"Never lost it," he half laughed.

"No, but I did," I said. "One of our lads left it on the ground when we last rested near here."

"What the hell are you talking about?" he sneered, then suddenly spotting a couple of stripes on my arm, modified his tone slightly to add

"Corp. I've had it all day – I'm a rear guard."

Curtly, I explained 'what the hell' I was talking about and I think he, not unreasonably, started to disbelieve me.

We decided to walk together the hundred or so yards back to our former resting site and there in it stood my Bren gun challenging anyone to have genuinely 'forgotten' it, yet unnoticed by the nearby Troop of No. 2 Commando left at Point 586 in reserve. The Commandos, lad to whom I had taken an instant objection suddenly became the most likeable of characters as we laughed with, and apologised to, each other over the coincidental circumstances of our meeting. Then, for the first time, I observed he was a Royal Marine Commando and not from No. 2 Army Commando, in whose sector we were. It was soon established that he was lost. That accounted for his missing Point 586 and its plain-as-a-pikestaff Bren. Any hope of getting himself to a mountain away to our right before dark was simply out of the question. He agreed with my suggestion that he should stay with me and attach himself to No. 2 for the morning attack – once we had rejoined them – that then being the most urgent and worrying task in that half light.

From that point on, I knew I was relying solely on my usually dependable sense of direction. Previously recognisable landmarks had disappeared through my wanderings. In reasonable confidence we strode off. Then, like a bolt from the blue, the ground shook under our feet as in a violent explosion, and half threw us – and half caused us to instinctively throw ourselves – to the ground. After shrapnel and splintered stones tinkled to earth around us, and the settling dust coated us to look like flour millers, a tentative enquiry came from 'Yorkie' (whom I had instantly been able to establish, as he was a native of Yorkshire).

"You okay?"

"Yes! You?"

"Yeah. What the bloody hell was that?"

Instinct suggested it was a mine, but reason soon ruled out that theory: our contact with a mine would not have left us as whole as we were – and what would be the point of anyone mining remote areas of mountain? We also dismissed mortars from the possibilities – one could never fail to hear the dreaded whine heralding a mortar bomb's descent. Surely the same would apply to artillery, wouldn't it? Well, it would of course – unless it was a flat trajectory weapon, like an anti-tank gun, or a conventional artillery piece, like a German 88mm, being used to fire directly at a target over open sights. In such cases there is no prior warning of a direct hit.

The mystery unsolved, we started to march again, nervously laughing so much that we almost forgot our respective Brens in the excitement of our encounter. Crash! It had happened again! The impact was just as close to us, yet we had then travelled fifty or so yards from the first explosion. Flat on the ground amidst the clattering debris, we gazed at each other in total bewilderment, before rising and hastening our redirected steps towards what we hoped might be a safe distance from whatever menace was seeking us. When the third explosion came, again with unnerving proximity, we knew we were in someone's sights. This one was closer: we ended up clutching each other in our attempts to burrow deep into cover – any cover – that there might be. I was thoroughly scared. It seemed quite uncanny that, in the wilderness of those barren mountains, two people could be seen by anybody, let alone be targeted in such gloom. Yet we were, and not just by small arms snipers. This was big stuff.

Before the fifth shot arrived we had each observed in the murkiness of twilight the tell-tale muzzle flash in the distance. It was at this instant, as we grovelled in Mother Earth, that Yorkie uttered one of those fitting sentences which one never forgets: "Bloody hell! I know there's a war on, but if those buggers aren't careful they'll kill somebody." They came very near to it. But that muzzle flash at little more than 1000 yards range had indicated the direct line of fire we were in, and we were able to skulk off the skyline (an elementary military rule which we had foolishly disregarded). We followed a screening fold in the hillside, to once again pick up my notion of the trail of my RSR colleagues and No. 2

Commando in the very last glimmer of natural light. We tried to move silently. Lessons had been learned the hard way in Yugoslavia in the misuse of 'creepers' in such territory, but our alternative, more robust, sensible boots were rather self-announcing among the loose particles of rock. We stopped regularly to listen.

At last, at one of these hush-sessions, we convinced ourselves that we could hear voices and stole forward as if entering a church mid-service until, to our intense relief, we were able to recognise that the language was English and we found ourselves among lads from No. 2 Commando, who were settling down to get as much rest as possible to alleviate their fatigue and to cope with a 03:30 reveille for the fateful attack. Some RSR were gathered nearby and, locating my crew, I handed over the wretched Bren gun to the idiot with a graphic explanation of what the mysterious artillery firing had been all about. My friend Yorkie attached himself to his other green beret colleagues and I never saw him again.

It seemed that we had gathered in a natural, high-sided bowl in the hills, about 200 yards long and around 50 yards at its widest, with a natural entrance at each end. One end had been our point of entry and the other was to be the exit for the morning attack on the elevated German strong-point guarding, it transpired, a battery of four artillery pieces. Amazingly, they were British 25-pounders which had probably been captured from our troops in Greece a couple of years earlier. The revelation next day that it had been these British 25-pounders which had stonked us the night before made my discomfort doubly embarrassing.

Sleep, it was clear, was going to be at a premium, despite our fatigue. Although we still had no prearranged role to play in the morrow's plans for the attack on the hill guarding the 25-pounders, the night was hardly devoid of anxiety – if only about the fortunes of the Commandos. It was bitterly cold, although we could only have been a mere couple of hundred feet above sea level at that point. One blanket and a groundsheet, the most non-fighting gear we had been allowed to bring, were clearly inadequate in spite of our remaining fully clothed. We each mooched around the area, seeking to park our bodies in the softest spot which would afford the best shelter from the slight, chill wind. In the darkness I became aware of the vague outlines of a roughly constructed shepherd's hovel and, when I mentioned it, I was told that there was 'somebody already in it'. "Somebody?" I strained to keep my objection to the whisper demanded of the situation. "That could almost take three!" I snorted, as I picked up my blanket and groundsheet to make sure I was going to be one of them.

"Can you shove over mate?" I enquired as I crawled inside, in tones that one might well use to plead for a share of someone's umbrella in a downpour at a bus stop. He did. Mumbling something about there not being much room, he nevertheless rolled further from the crude hovel's entrance, and to all appearances was asleep again. I was soon joined by my mate, whom I had clearly converted to the idea that three would fit. They did – just. The warmth generated by those three bodies reminded me of the sleeping arrangements on cold desert nights, when the 6-pounder anti-tank gun crew would struggle together for warmth within the fuggy confines of the vehicle's canvas canopy, removed from the portee for that purpose each night.

Sleep was fitful – tension would not permit it to be otherwise – but my memory of that night was rendered unforgettable by what happened later. I could have been in only a shallow sleep to have been alerted by the slightly crunching, approaching footsteps, followed by the near alarmist whisper of, "Mr Coyle? – Mr Coyle, Sir?"

"Yes?" The body was awake, alert and answering.

"Mr Coyle, Sir: it's half past three, Sir."

"Mr..." the Commando knocker-up had started again but broke off as he, at the same time as his officer, realised that there was something wrong with the situation. I'd kipped with a Commando Officer.

"Who are these people, Martin?" enquired an obvious Lt. Coyle. I decided that it was my place to explain.

"We're RSR, Sir." I spluttered in my embarrassment. "I'm sorry, Sir. I didn't realise – I thought – well! In the dark – I had no idea – I couldn't."

I rambled on in stuttering apology. I believe he had seen the funny side of the situation.

"Oh! Forget it," he chuckled, as I scrambled out to join my RSR mates. Then we mingled, though in an understandably detached way, with those tense, but businesslike Commandos who were within minutes of putting their lives at stake. I felt like a second in a boxer's corner.

Five minutes or so later Lt. Coyle would not have needed a knocker-up. Our artillery barrage had started, shattering the quiet of the imminent dawn and releasing the gripping tension, which enforced silence had fostered among us all. The encouragement of such firepower was immediately apparent. The echoing effect created by the mountain slopes made the reports of our guns seem to come from every direction. This was not too much of an exaggeration. The 111th Field Regiment's 25-pounders were firing from near Shen Vassil, one troop of RSR's 75mms were firing from Yoke Beach and the other troop from a gun site at the eastern end of Commando Valley, between Shen Vassil and Sarande. The Royal Navy had provided more heavy guns on specially designed landing craft (LCG's). From ground position at Sugar Beach they were firing salvoes not only on Sarande but also, as a diversion, on Delvine. When the RSR's mortars joined in too, heads began to pound. We gained in confidence and perhaps even began to hope that the enemy might consider the strength of the force which suddenly opposed him formidable enough to suggest surrender. Not Jerry!

The impact of the artillery fire which had been so accurately directed at No. 2 Commando's objective appeared to be so close to where we were that it sent a shiver of retrospective relief down my spine, and made me realise how justified our stealthy silence had been that night. Jimmy Irvine told me later that he had wandered off among the various groups in the darkness that night in search of news of what had happened to me. He was approaching one source of conversation when he suddenly identified the language as German. He turned on his heels and unhurriedly (he said, to avert alarm but contrary to his more instinctive impulses) walked back to our lines unchallenged.

No. 2 Commando's attack went in at 04:30, after the artillery and mortar barrage had lifted and following an incongruous, diversionary 'firework' display that was set off near the bridge, and which had been our ambush target a few days earlier. This was the proud work of Lt. McNab, the New Zealand engineer. I think he had accumulated an assortment of everything that flashed and went bang, and contrived to link them with fuses. When they exploded they must have suggested so many secret weapons to the enemy that Jerry wastefully discharged an alarming number of salvoes from miscellaneous weaponry in Lt. McNab's direction. Amazingly, he and his half dozen volunteer helpers escaped completely unscathed and very amused.

Left behind in the hollow with the Commando's small reserve group and casualty-clearing medical staff, I felt like some useless supernumerary, unsuccessfully trying to assure my colleagues that we would probably soon be called. At first the clatter of small arms fire was intense. Then, as the morning wore on, it became more sporadic and suggested that a stalemate was developing. As the wounded began to appear we fell over ourselves in our desire to try to help, and the departure of their replacements left us amidst the inevitably confused reports on 'how things were going'.

From soundly entrenched defensive positions around their 25-pounder site, the Germans were able to hold out until just before midday, inflicting many casualties on the Commandos, particularly in the final assault up the last few steep yards of the hillside. It was here that their commander, Captain Parsons, had been killed when within a few yards of the 25-pounder. He was a man who had earned our admiration when he had briefly talked to us all in comradely, encouraging terms a few hours earlier at Point 586. Unless my memory is playing tricks on me, I held the notion that he was then a sick man running a high temperature when he addressed us, but dismissive of the Medical Officer's plea that he should not take part in the battle. Saddened as I was at this blow, I felt even greater remorse at the news that, within a few minutes of assuming Captain Parsons' role, Lieutenant Coyle had been killed instantly when leading the final assault. I was sensitive to the thought that I had been so close to the man in his final hours and this was not made any easier when his men confirmed his admirable qualities as a leader and popularity as 'one of the lads'. 'The lads' took their inspiration from their fallen leaders and, fired with passion, soon finished the job.

I had had one useful part to play in the attack. The Commandos were held up at one stage by a stubbornly resistant machine gun crew cleverly enclosed in an almost perpendicular hillside foxhole, presumably with some side access. After unsuccessfully employing everything else, including mortars, in trying to destroy it, the Commandos called for some ideas from the RSR's machine gunners. They gave my crew the job. The long range of a Browning enabled me to site the gun beyond the effective range of the enemy's small arms and align it on the seemingly impenetrable foxhole with only exit firing slits at which to aim. The Browning's ammunition belt could be fed with three types of .50 inch calibre bullet – a tracer, a normal projectile and an armour piercing shot in whatever sequence one chose. The gun was amazingly accurate up to 1000 yards but recoil, that inevitable 'kick' from the minor discharge of any shot, does tend to move the gun about, so I decided to forsake its automatic capability (as a machine gun) and so restrict the movement which results from a rapid multiplicity of recoils. Accuracy, not firepower, was called for. I changed the sequence of the belt load, making the first three guiding tracers, aimed the gun on one of the slits, fired a single shot, observed its hit point and made the necessary correction. The third tracer was not necessary. The cheering around us, which resulted from the second one disappearing into the slit, confirmed the accuracy of the aim adjustment.

Even so, I thought, a spent projectile might not create many problems inside unless luck would have it that it hit a human first. However, I knew that the armour piercing round which followed it would perform a skidding, circuit of death within the enemy foxhole, with alarming unpredictable ricochets which would frighten the life out of any of the occupants. Six more single shots, including two further armour piercing missiles, accurately discharged into the slits were enough. The two German gunners appeared with hands aloft from the side of their defensive position, and that major hitch was removed from the scene. I do not think that the Brownings fired any other shots in the whole operation: all that humping of heavy machine-guns and weighty ammunition was merely for the single figure shots. Thank God, they had been useful shots.

All firing had stopped in our sector by midday, with the four 25-pounders and dozens of prisoners securely in No. 2 Commando's hands. It was then safe for all of us to leave our covert positions in the 'bowl' and assemble on the surprisingly exposed, elevated, natural platform of the gun site. I cannot ascertain the total number of Commando casualties that resulted from taking those guns, but my instant thought on arrival at the site was how exposed and conspicuous it was – an ideal target for an RAF fighter bomber to have blasted it out of existence. My mind went back to Brac. There I had questioned the wisdom of a costly, frontal storming of such otherwise easily defendable positions, when their very isolation rendered them such easy targets from the air.

The second most impressive feature of the site was its grandstand outlook over most of Sarande and the bay, affording for the first time a glimpse of Corfu.

From a completely safe position we could observe the progress of No. 40 Royal Marine Commando's attack from the west into Sarande, as if merely watching a film. As a soldier, I have never felt so well informed.

No. 40 RM Commando had captured their first objective, Point 261 by 08:30, supported (I am pleased they acknowledged) by RSR's 4.2 inch mortars. In the process the marines mopped up the enemy's beaches, which we had battle-labelled Zebra Beach and Italian Beach, effectively bypassing the mines. It was not to be an easy passage for the lads of No. 40 commando.

Point 261 was the subject of a heavy counter-attack which, although repulsed, resulted in every officer in one commando troop becoming a casualty. The records show that it was an RSR officer who assumed command, so there was another little feather in the cap of our much maligned regiment. Moving into the western outskirts of the town, the commandos again encountered strong opposition from enemy positions located in the relative protection of the town's buildings, the most troublesome of which appeared to be the hospital.

A heart-rendingly difficult decision had to be made. The bombardment called for artillery and mortars to be plonked on and around the hospital. From our Spion Kop viewpoint we could watch in complete immunity while literally cheering our enthusiasm and support. The house-to-house fighting qualities of the Commandos eventually wore down the enemy's resistance, and the town's garrison surrendered at about 16:30.

To complete the story, the RAF Levies who had landed at dawn – unopposed at Parachute Beach, south of the town – captured Point 264 in total surprise and had its 30 dispirited defenders 'in the bag' by 10:30, effectively controlling the eastern part of the town and its road link to Delvine and onwards, thus sealing the link with the Partisans.

The battle for the town of Sarande was over, but there were some Germans who were either unaware of the garrison's surrender or were perhaps of a more defiant calibre than their captive comrades. They had installed themselves in two so-called 'flak' towers situated about 800 to 1000 yards to the north-west of the 25-pounders' site, to which they were linked by a slightly ascending promontory. Detached as they were from the town, such monstrosities (as the towers truly were) could surely have been constructed only for defensive use and gave added credence to my theory, which Jerry obviously supported, that the 25-pounders' site presented an obvious target for an air attack.

The Albanian Partisans had reported that they came under fierce small arms fire from the towers whenever they tried to take them. Again, I thought, why try to take them? That is, until accurate sniping fire began from the towers, confirming the more obstinate attitude of this small group of Germans and demolishing our smug illusions of immunity in this campaign. There were far too many exit fire slots in the towers for an equally effective repeat of the Browning exercise which had been successfully employed earlier that day. Then someone thought of what should have been obvious. Couldn't we fire the 25-pounders over open sights and, bit by bit, demolish the towers, picking off their occupants as they fled? An infectious air of enthusiasm pervaded the atmosphere in which we trundled the guns round to face the towers. I don't imagine that anyone could have enjoyed the prospect more than I did, having experienced the wrong end of those guns the previous evening. Yorkie would have loved it.

Now, who knows how to fire 25-pounders? Oddly enough, so much collective military ignorance could never before have been assembled at one spot, but after pooling our limited knowledge and supplementing it with guesswork, we eventually fired a shot and then set about the more difficult task of aiming. Gun sights, which had not been destroyed, looked too confusing, so it was decided that we would train a gun on the target by the elementary expedient of opening the breach block and lining-up by looking through the gun's barrel. Deceased Woolwich gunnery instructors were, doubtless, turning in their graves as we banged away in joyous amateur abandon in a hit and miss, gradual demolition of the towers. There was ammunition galore. As the towers began to disintegrate, white garments were seen to be waved from the tower on the left and, holding fire long enough to allow for the surrender of the tower's occupants, we were rather caught off guard in allowing some of the Partisans to advance to collect half a dozen or so surrendering prisoners.

A fusillade of small arms fire promptly erupted from the other, less damaged tower, resulting in two of the Partisans being hit. In a rage at our own naïvety, I feel sure that we all hoped that there were not going to be any of the enemy offering to surrender from the second tower. Nor did they when the same stage of demolition as the first tower had been reached. Its unyielding occupants attempted to make a fighting escape from the imminent danger of the blasted masonry cascading around them. So far as my Bren gunner was concerned, it needed only the merest nod of command (like that of a hardened Sotherby's bidder) to guarantee that my trail back to Point 586 for the Bren had, after all, been well worth the trouble. Mind you, it was not the only weapon that fired. In other RSR troops, Brens and small arms fire from Commandos and Partisans had 'made sure' too, but I had had my own moment of personal satisfaction from a rare fit of vengeful temper.

One practical aspect had bothered me ever since our departure from Commando Valley. What arrangements were in place to ensure that the wounded were shipped out of the battle zone for proper treatment? Carrying them back to Sugar Beach was an unthinkable task, so Sarande had to be captured to guarantee access to the ships which would take them to hospitals in Italy. Unimaginable traumas must have been endured by those unfortunate enough already to be in need of hospital treatment while awaiting the outcome of the battle. In our winding descent of the poorly maintained road into the town we could, at least, be helpful and assist with bringing them into town.

We had been wearing the same clothes, without removal, for 17 days. Filthy, verminous, bearded and bedraggled, our awesome appearance was not too greatly out of place, however, in the sheer drabness of Sarande. The instant mediocrity and uncanny desolation of the place made it perhaps the most easily forgotten town I had encountered in my travels. As a seaside resort, Sarande lay claim to a charm untypical of most Albanian towns, not much of which registered with me, so that I cherished little desire to see much else of Albania. Yet it is only for this reason that I would like to see it again.

The few shops were tiny, austere and unadorned. Most had had their contents strewn and trampled in the hurried but selective looting of anything of obvious value. Apparently not all the German troops had been caught napping, and some had had time (or warning!) in which to collect a few souvenirs, and bolt along the road to Delvine before the Partisans could seal it off. The Germans could not be blamed for the general cheerlessness of the town, however, nor for the sombre uniformity of its dwellings, which were more reminiscent of those of a mining town than a resort. The contrasting sparkle of Dalmatia's islands came easily to mind.

Nevertheless, four walls and a roof offered agreeable prospects of shelter and sleep, and perhaps even facilities for a measure of cleaning-up. In undisciplined, wandering groups we eyed the relative merits of several terraces, while discharging with a surprisingly workaday aplomb our truly exceptional duties of supervising the now docile groups of loitering prisoners, whose 'homes' they had been until only a few hours earlier.

It was while I was approaching one of the houses to make a closer inspection that one of a group of Germans became wildly animated. "Minen! Achtung minen!" he called, as he advanced in agitation from the group, gesticulating towards the house. The alarm which could be read in the man's face would have been sufficient warning by itself to tell me that the house was booby trapped; the obvious displeasure of his colleagues at his gesture was confirmation enough. When Lt. McNab was called he soon established that the houses were veritable death traps. My nod of gratitude in the direction of my saviour yielded the most fleeting of smiles from the sad, but otherwise featureless face of an obviously out-of-step, middle aged German trooper.

A school in the town centre was subsequently allocated as our billet for the night and it enabled us to enjoy the deeply beneficial slumber (subject only to a two hour 'stag' duty) we had craved for weeks, even if it was prematurely curtailed early the next morning by the ubiquitous Lt. McNab. Acting on evidence he had unearthed on prisoners' conflicting information (but unanimous alarm) and on pure hunch, the redoubtable Kiwi decided that Sarande was in great danger of being blown up.

The German POWs were sure that huge, time-fused charges had been placed about the town but they did not know where. The 'Kiwi' himself had found many empty boxes for timed fuses, whose labels were sufficient for him to deduce that a major explosion might be expected around late afternoon. Orders for the evacuation of the town gave so much evident relief to the prisoners that only the timing of the blast was in doubt. While many troops moved back to the foothills, we were among those whose boarding of the LCIs was brought forward for shipping back to base at Sugar Beach.

We were a mile off shore, awaiting further developments upon the cheering news relayed from the RAF that white flags of surrender had been detected flying from the German garrisons on Corfu, when the spectacular explosions took place in Sarande. The concussive effect of the blast was felt even at sea: the relief we each experienced at our fortunate escape reduced us to silence, immersed as we were in our own thoughts of how much we owed to Lt. McNab. He had thoroughly deserved the commendation which earned him the Military Cross. It seemed as if half of the town's buildings had been blasted to rubble. I had no regrets at not having the opportunity to inspect and check that estimate: I had seen the last of Sarande – well, perhaps not quite.

"One man begged me to go with him to his aged mother (or was it grandmother?) who was too frail to manage the 300–400 yards to the hotel, but who desperately wanted to see the British before she died."

Corfu

When the LCI moved off, it was soon apparent that it was not heading for Sugar Beach but more surely out to sea. Before joyful speculation could take hold – that we might possibly be returning directly to Italy – it was announced that the Skipper had received instructions to proceed to Corfu Town, where Corfuites had assumed control of their own town again. A mile or two along the coast to the north of the town, a group of about seventy Germans were reported to be anxious to surrender to British troops.

What followed the nosing of the LCI's bow into the harbour and its tying up, to the accompanying cheers and tears of hundreds of the town's anxiously awaiting population, still continues to amaze me. Expecting, as did the natives of Corfu, that the LCI would disgorge its couple of hundred Commandos onto the quay, I was as astonished as I was pleased to learn that only six RSR men were to be landed to accompany a Commando officer in accepting the surrender of the Germans. The LCI was to proceed first to Sugar Beach to offload, then to return to Sarande to collect as many prisoners as possible for POW camps in Italy.

Even now I cannot decide if my selection as one of the six RSR men was by way of reward or punishment, but to be singled out along with Jimmy, Topper, Archie, Bert, Roger and Charlie Grant made me think that someone 'up there' was at last arranging that we, the closest of friends, would take part in something together. Our role was to collect the prisoners by Greek boat and return them to a quayside hotel, which had been their headquarters, guard them there overnight, then await an early morning LCI that would take the whole contingent to Brindisi.

When Corfu's natives recovered from their near disbelief at witnessing the LCI casting off as quickly as it had tied up, and then disappearing into the late afternoon sun, they directed their concentrated joy on the six of us. I find it difficult to describe the emotion of being feted: I suppose 'pop' stars and the like become inured to such mass adulation, but as a unique experience in one's life the memory is at once embossed, yet through the sheer intensity of its impact, also confused. I found that people just wanted to touch us; and if touching, for females, meant kissing them, we knew it meant no more than the transient expression of joy and gratitude. History was being made and physical contact probably helped ensure it would never be forgotten. But for us, there was first some work to be done – work which I viewed with a little apprehension. Who really knew that seventy Germans were impassively standing-by, waiting to be caged for the rest of the war?

My concern increased as we boarded the Greek schooner which then set sail to the up-coast rendezvous with a mere handful of crew, an English-German speaking Greek and our own Commando officer. Our massed armament consisted of a Sten gun each. I lost all sense of time in my excitement and could not say how long had elapsed before the Greek gave the warning that our goal would be in view around the next headland.

The loud chugging of our engine would have broadcast our approach for thousands of yards in such inappropriately tranquil conditions, but even so the sight which was gradually revealed, as the vessel teasingly inched its way around the headland, will live vividly in my memory for the rest of my days. The Germans were lined up in perfect order on the cove's beach and, the instant we came in sight barely fifty yards away from them, an order was barked, which for one tense moment I thought could be a fire order, but they sprang smartly to attention, then stood motionless and, seemingly, emotionless.

It did not take more than an instant to discern in front of the German troops an orderly array of weapons, sufficient to have blasted us to a watery grave in a trice. There was an odd pervading poignancy about the spectacle which affected me, I feel sure, much more than would the sight of a defeated, dejected, disorderly rabble. I cannot say truthfully that I admired them, but in my mind I compared them to the touching stories I had heard of British units marching proudly and defiantly in disciplined order onto the jetty at Dunkirk in 1940. I could more readily understand why the German was such a menacing foe, invested with such pride and arrogance. It was almost as if they were saying 'You didn't beat us – we merely gave up.'

The schooner tied up at a fragile jetty; we landed; the officers exchanged salutes, but not handshakes. Then, at our officer's command through the words of the Greek interpreter, the senior of two German officers (equivalent in rank to a Colonel) commanded the men to break ranks, load themselves and the weapons aboard the vessel. The whole fateful event was completed within a few minutes and we sailed with the crowded prisoners who gradually lost their composure at the approaching confrontation with the hostile population they knew awaited them at Corfu Town. We were still edgily concerned at the rather ludicrous imbalance of the military situation, should the Germans decide to change their minds.

As the vessel came to reveal the hundreds waiting on the quay, the Germans knew that, for the first time in their war, we were to be allies. Our difficulty was not going to be to guard the Germans from escaping, but to protect them from vengeful Corfuites, who had plenty of scores to settle with their former imperious, occupying overlords. We were hopelessly outnumbered. Fortunately, there were two elements of salvation. Firstly, the hotel was but a step from the quay – a mere fifty yards of gauntlet-run, and secondly, our Greek negotiator had enough rational friends in the crowd whom he succeeded in persuading of our difficulties in the situation. An insulating corridor of sympathisers enabled us to marshal the conscience-ridden, scurrying prisoners into the refuge of the hotel without too much incident, in admirable discharge of our paramount duty as custodians of the Germans' safe conduct.

Our officer and the Greek interpreter arranged for the locking of all entrances into the hotel except the main one, so that we could guard the prisoners more easily. In truth, as darkness fell Corfu's mood changed to jubilation and festivity, with everyone anxious to speak to us in their universally understandable English, a friendliness steeped in gratitude and a genuine, intense desire to show it in any way possible. From civic dignitaries to humble labourers, they queued to pay their respects; and always with handshakes, kisses, the hand on the shoulder, the touching – as if testing the event's reality or perhaps even to boast, "I've touched a British soldier!"

One man begged me to go with him to his aged mother (or was it grandmother?) who was too frail to manage the 300-400 yards to the hotel, but who desperately wanted to see the British before she died.

There were so many requests of this nature that we agreed to maintain half of us on guard while the others slipped away for 30 minutes or so. The proffered luxury of a bath had been added to this public relations commitment, which none of us refused or hurried. The best treat of all – yes! Even better than the few drinks – was the appearance of a barber at the hotel to administer shaves and haircuts en situ. That we were each left with pencil thin moustaches was mildly comical at the time, but marked the start of long lasting, top lip adornments for a few of us.

The delicate old lady I went to see must have been in fragile health, but my approach was heralded by an 'outriding', break away mass of excitable, noisily chattering youngsters, who surrounded me in Hamelin fashion as I walked with my new-found friend, George Arcudis. Already tearful at the mere thought of the meeting she was standing at a doorway at the top of a flight of stairs in what I seem to remember was an apartment block. Traditionally clothed in black from head to foot, her deeply wrinkled, leathery face cracked in a meagerly toothed smile as she grasped me and clung on like a limpet with emotionally charged strength. It made me think for the first time not of my temporarily exalted position as a representative of the victors, but of the relief of these people from the unspeakable horrors which had been inflicted by the vanquished Germans and their Italian predecessors.

As we left, George interpreted that his mother now felt fulfilled and would die happy. She passed the usual greetings that all mothers do – love and prayers for my parents, with the wish that I would soon be home with them. George hoped I would soon come back to Corfu after the war, however, and fished out a family group photograph I could take with me, writing his address on the reverse to confirm the earnestness of his invitation. I still have the photograph but have not yet been back. I fear I have left it too late now: the thousands of young Britons who had beaten me to it in the 60s, 70s and 80s have sullied with shame the impressions which George might hitherto have nurtured of our nation's sons since that historic October evening of 1944.

The next morning, an LCI duly sailed in to the Corfu Town quay. She was already partially laden with German prisoners from Sarande, but with reserve space remaining to accommodate the near 70 of our contingent of captives and their escort for the voyage across the Adriatic to the Italian port of Brindisi. There's organisation for you! (Oh ye of little faith!)

Any hostility the people of Corfu felt towards their former oppressors was temporarily masked by their jubilation at suddenly finding themselves liberated. In a curiously mixed atmosphere of carnival and pathos, they demonstrated their heartfelt gratitude and relief to the Navy and ourselves, while the vessel slowly edged away from the densely crowded quayside. The alarming political vacuum so dramatically created on the island was to be filled by the arrival later that day, of a considerable force of 40 RM Commando from Sarande. Their presence on Corfu for the following three months smoothed the orderly re-establishment of local government.

I remember the voyage to Italy for just two incidents. Firstly, I recall well the answer given to a casual question I asked of the young English speaking German (allowed above deck because of his usefulness as a ready communicator of our instructions). I was puzzled by the apparent happiness of his imprisoned countrymen, which the sound of their continual, joyful singing from below deck seemed to suggest. I should have guessed the reason.

"For us the war is over: we really are happy!"

"You still have to face dangers for as long as the war lasts," I replied.

I suppose it made some sort of sense, and it reminded me of an incident involving the German sidecar passenger of a motorcycle combination which had been thrown off the Sarande/Delvine road by the burst of one of our artillery shells. His driver had been killed but he, unharmed, had enthusiastically surrendered to one of our RSR groups, asking for his thanks to be conveyed to the gunners for providing him with the opportunity to desert unobserved.

The second memory of that voyage still causes me to feel guilt and apprehension about the way I descended below deck to relieve the prisoners of their hand weapons and, more significantly in personal terms, snaffle their watches. I cannot imagine how I had allowed myself to be deputed for such a task, which necessarily arose from the humiliating realisation that, due to our inexperience in dealing with such matters, we had forgotten to search the blighters earlier. Commando guards of other groups aboard were strutting the decks sporting wristwatches, Luger pistols and the like. Only their competitive inquisitiveness about 'how did you get on for loot?' exposed the startling possibility that our little gang of captives might well be a bristling armoury of weaponry, easily capable of hijacking the vessel, let alone an untapped source of untold wealth.

Fortunately, their hand weapons were surrendered willingly, indeed in such a state of jocularity at my stable door action as to cause me acute embarrassment. I was glad not to have been able to understand the banter. My demand for their watches provoked however, a rippling undertone of dissenting murmurs which for a moment or so added alarm to my chagrin. To my surprise, the interpreter came to my rescue by admirably putting my case to his countrymen. Watches, I had told him, (more tongue-in-cheek than from knowledge) would be impounded the instant the prisoners arrived at a POW camp, as their possible use in direction finding could be used in escape attempts. I had just begun to ask myself, "What do I do, if they each say 'No!'?" when the interpreter intervened to spare my blushes, while at the same time revealing a prospective talent as a diplomat of the future. He explained to the men that they would soon be separated from their watches anyway, so wouldn't it be fairer to part with them as spoils of war to men who had treated them well, and who were fighting men like themselves rather than base, idling, opportunist vultures?

I collected about a dozen assorted timepieces with which I proudly returned on deck, without, I hoped, revealing either distaste for the mission nor, worse still, my ever present fear at having meekly to report, "They won't give them to me." I distributed the watches among my clamouring mates, whilst surreptitiously retaining two which I considered to be the best of the bunch. As rightful retribution for my shameful greed, justice was duly done to ensure that I derived almost no satisfaction from either of those two wrist watches – which were incidentally the first I had ever possessed. One I could never get to work, so I presented it with feigned magnanimity to someone who thought he could. The other was lost a few months later in circumstances so bizarre as to convince me that God was reminding me of his Commandments and that he didn't think much of my excuse about the possibility of using a watch as a substitute compass. No good comes from ill-gotten gains. Well, so they say, 'they' usually being those who do benefit from ill-gotten gains.

Brindisi, symbolising as it did then a return to flesh-pot civilisation, held out reasonable hopes of a clean up, a nosh up and perhaps even a booze up, but none of the escorts were allowed to even step ashore from the LCI before it was smartly turned around for the return voyage to Albania. We had been relieved of the prisoners by a group of specialist POW guards who had emerged from a waiting convoy of trucks, and soon managed to affirm that my forecast of the treatment that the prisoners would 'enjoy' in camp would soon quell their desire to sing, unless – a very remote proviso for Nazi Germans – it was to sing 'the blues'.

During the return voyage across the Adriatic, the grim news was imparted that the first call was to be at Sugar Beach, where we would disembark to join the miserable majority of our 'Houndforce' colleagues in tented camps on the beach and along the valley. When habitable billets were available in profusion at Sarande it was obviously absurd to return any part of the force to the claustrophobic remoteness of Sugar Beach, with its attendant supply difficulties and morale sapping purposelessness. The explanation offered was the anxious possibility of further explosive charges lurking undiscovered in the town.

What we did not know then was that the bitter acrimony which existed between the campaign's leader, Brigadier Tom Churchill of 2 Commando, and his immediate supervisor – the new boss of Land Forces Adriatic (LFA) – Brigadier Davy, had openly erupted. Briefly, Davy wanted the Force to pursue the Germans into inland Albania and thence, if necessary, into Greece and Yugoslavia. Brigadier Churchill dissented arguing about the exhaustion of his troops and the absence of transport vehicles. Although he was duly relieved of his command, his reasoning must have made some impact for no other commander was found to do it. While the argument had raged, the troops slummed it out on beach or valley, not knowing whether the next move was to be the misery of a deeper probe into Albania or the prospective joy of a sail back 'home' to our Italian base at Mola.

Fate, which had been so kind to me in the past, showed no sign of desertion and promptly rescued me from that awful scenario by arranging for my further exceptional treatment, although Archie was included this time.

After only a couple of days at Sugar Beach, Archie and I simultaneously developed similar symptoms of illness: sustained raging temperature (104°F), blinding headache, sweating fever, the absence of interest in food and a general apathy towards living or dying. The summoned Commando medical officer was swift and emphatic in his diagnosis – malaria! Evacuated by sea, initially to No. 11 Casualty Clearing Station (CCS) at Sarande, we were soon stretchered, side by side aboard an LCI heading across the Adriatic, again, for Brindisi with the familiarity of season ticket holders. As awful as I felt, the agreeable prospect of a hospital bed – well, any bed for that matter after a month of snatched naps – suggested blissful compensations, despite malaria's discomforts. I was not disappointed.

Brindisi's major hospital, then commandeered by the Allies and labelled the 22nd British General Hospital, provided not only the dream-like comfort of a sheeted bed but the reassurance of clean and clinical conditions. The angelic ministrations from haloed nurses soon (inappropriately, you would have thought had you seen them) reduced the fever, and signalled a willing return of interest in a world which I had wholly disowned during the previous 'lost' few days of near coma. In one of my gradually extending periods of lucid consciousness, I anxiously asked about the whereabouts of my Bergen pack, the surprisingly prompt production of which augmented my recovery, not least from the obvious immediate relief at finding it had not been tampered with.

The diaries, which should never have been with me on such a mission (but I had never trusted anyone in a Quartermaster's Store since Gosforth), were there safe and sound. Hidden among the pack's obligatory contents were my new acquisitions of 'captured loot', an American Browning 'flat' .38 inch pistol and, the treasure of the moment for me, a palm-of-the-hand, Italian Beretta .22 inch automatic, with a small quantity of ammunition for each. It was odd to think that neither of the weapons, collected from the captives on the LCI, were of German origin, although the Browning was probably one of the 319,000 manufactured for the Nazi Forces by Belgium's forced labour workers at the Fabrique Nationale's factory at Liege. The Belgians had bought the licence to produce them from the Americans before the war. I never did acquire a specimen of the much coveted Luger pistol.

Medical testing and sampling over several days yielded no evidence of malaria in either of us, a result of no surprise to me. The rest, the amenable conditions and the wholesome sustenance, had worked such wonders, that when our condition had been officially attributed to exhaustion, I knew from the way I then felt that nothing much ailed me. Nevertheless, Archie and I were allowed to enjoy almost two glorious weeks of luxury and gluttony before being returned to unit on 28 October 1944 to find that the other RSR 'Houndforce' troops had returned from Sugar Beach ten days earlier. Our timing had been perfect. We had missed the irksome process of a military move from our Mola-di-Bari luxury accommodation to school billets in the small town of Rutigliano, about six miles away inland. The Albanian venture was over, regarded as a qualified military success. With better prior reconnaissance and with less taxing weather, there is little doubt that more of the Germans evacuating Corfu would have been nabbed. I cannot find any figures regarding the number of Germans killed or wounded in the operation but we took more than a thousand of them out of the war as prisoners, including a final figure of 250 from Corfu itself. British casualties were reported as six officers and nine other ranks killed and five officers and 53 other ranks wounded: quite remarkably light figures for an attacking force.

By the end of October 1944, the whole of the Sarande/Delvine area had been handed over to the Albanian Partisans. Our job was done. Aside from the slightly unusual nature of the originally planned operation and its Topsyish development, it is only in considerable retrospect that the rarity of our experience can be appreciated. Very, very few Britons were to be welcomed into that barren country over the following fifty years.

"Our eyes met in mutual recognition... A German!... He was the one who had restrained me from entering the booby trapped house at Sarande!... he knew me then. He beamed..."

A Small Italian Town

In the more discerning assessment of values which old age brings, Rutigliano was a typically small, charming and intimate Southern Italian town, which easily finds itself on a list of places I would love to see again. In the youthful minds of myself and my contemporaries in 1944, however, it was 'dead' and 'miles from anywhere'. As communal billets go, ours at Rutigliano were excellent. Again, we were in school premises (what in God's name did kids do for education during the war?) which might conceivably have been purpose built as barracks, arranged as it was as a quadrangle within which notions of barrack square, spit and polish parades and square bashing easily sprang to our unenterprising leaders' minds. Except for those of our batteries which were still helping Partisan guerrilla forces in occupied Greece (of whom we had heard nothing since we left Palestine a year earlier), the RSR was concentrated as a military unit for the first time since our initial training.

The understandable attempts to turn us back into conventional soldiers were met with the belligerence of mercenaries and prompted a shameful period of hostile indiscipline, assertive punishments and further friction to which, it seemed, only vino was the antidote – if it was not the cause. Not unnaturally, the acrimony became cumulative in incidence and intensity. The nearby camp of a US Army unit also poured its leisure time troops into the town and, whereas I never found any difficulty in harmoniously sharing the small town with them, their very presence acted as a matador's cloak to our own bred-to-brawl bull-heads. Drunkenness was rife and, despite the cheapness of an abundance of good local wine, the accumulated amounts of back pay from half a year's enforced thrift on Vis was in several instances soon exhausted. Their boozing then had to be funded from kit-flogging and pilfering. I remember one man who had sold his last blanket before he was carted away to be treated for alcoholism.

The guardian angel, who had always appeared to pluck me from the sites of such sordid happenings, did it again for me at Rutigliano. Perhaps six weeks on a wireless operator's training course at Salerno in an Italian mid-winter, soon to be followed by six weeks in hospital at Bari (receiving the drastic treatment necessary to remedy the dreaded amoebic dysentery), might not readily suggest salvation, but my memories of those twelve weeks are of happy diversions and pleasing relationships, which were also to be of fateful significance to the remainder of my army service.

Before these diversions, however, life at Rutigliano was enlightened only by 'liberty truck', off-duty evening outings in Bari and, as usual, when we were settled in one place the regular supply of mail from home. ENSA and its American forces counterpart USO strove to provide suitable entertainment in Bari, but there was never enough to satisfy the needs of the masses of Allied troops who spilled into the city's streets in the evening and at weekends. Certainly, 'star' attractions were sought and brought there, but I always missed anyone of fame or quality. Biographies of theatrical personalities suggest that Bari's showtime heydays coincided with our stay on Vis. I do recall a vivacious Hollywood starlet called Jinx Falkenberg whose main (probably only) claim to fame was a bit part in 'Cover Girl', and whose press agent did a marvellous job of publicising her further by having her walk the length of the inevitable queue which always formed hours before any theatrical performance in the city. "Chat with the lads," must have been her instructions.

She was not only beautiful, but brave.

I don't wish to carp about the paucity of entertainment in wartime Bari: after all, if more professional entertainers could have been induced to come to Italy, there would still have been the limiting factor of premises in which to perform. There was one considerable advantage for me in this. The city's opera house, the magnificent Petruzzelli Theatre, which was said to be one of the largest in Italy, occasionally presented grand opera productions for the troops. Thousands of watch-anything servicemen were introduced to a form of entertainment, indeed a culture, which they would never otherwise have dreamed of patronising.

It is true that for most the seed fell on stony ground, but the lavishness of the theatrical spectacle (yes! despite war-time austerity and the 'pillaging' reputation of Italy's former Axis partners) and the effect on the emotions of the stirring music of Puccini, Verdi and the like on its natural home ground, often made a profound initial impression. It implanted an interest in me, later to blossom into a rewarding sphere of theatrical enjoyment. But even my ignorance at that time could not approach that of two American servicemen, conversing behind me in the theatre whilst awaiting curtain-up on Madam Butterfly and speculating on whether grand opera was likely to prove an acceptable substitute for Glenn Miller.

"My sister went to an opera once." Long silence. "Did she like it?" Long silence, except for chewing noises. "Naw! Too much singin'."

Because demand easily outstripped supply for any cinema or theatre show in the city, queuing for admission started hours beforehand. Whenever we could be off-duty together, one or more of Topper, Jimmy, Archie and Steve would be with me, always whiling away the waiting time with the boredom-blunting tranquilisation of a passed around bottle of Spumanti which, when empty, was promptly replaced with another from an adjacent shop. On one notable occasion (it would be an absurd contradiction to call it 'memorable') it transpired that we had consumed the equivalent of a bottle of the stuff each.

Since popular shows attracted the bigger audiences, requiring earlier queuing and resulting in longer imbibing sessions, I have always been grateful that opera only attracted a minor interest. It proves that my initial attraction to the genre was only fractionally influenced by alcohol. A further attraction at Bari, at least for Steve and myself, was a jazz record club inaugurated in one of the canteens by a broadcaster from the Forces transmitting station, Radio Bari. We became very friendly with the chap who became quite well known, I think, in the post-war period.

A lot of football was played while we were at Rutigliano, with Jimmy, Topper and Archie being frequently selected (by Stan Cullis) for Bari area representative games. Less important inter-battery and inter-troop matches were played on a full sized, unyielding, grassless pitch in the centre of Rutigliano. The matches attracted the curiosity, if not the absorption, of many of the locals and guaranteed employment for our medical officer's orderlies in the treatment of abrasions and gravel rash. I played for Bari area only once. Perhaps I would not even have remembered that, for my performance was undistinguished, had it not been for a comical yet poignant coincidence. The match was played at the 98th British General Hospital, Bari's largest hospital – not only because it had suitable playing pitches but also because such games gave some diversionary therapy, even pleasure, to those of the military patients who were mobile. (I was destined to be one of them myself within a few months.) On the day of the match, several hundred patients voiced their Partisan enthusiasm or disgust from the touchlines. As a wing-half who took the throws-in, I made more contact than most with the spectators, especially the more agile of them who frequently recovered the out-of-play ball for me. These anonymous 'ballboys' earned a mere perfunctory "Thanks!" but on one occasion our eyes met in mutual recognition, if not in instant identification. For a seeming age I gazed into the gaunt, ageing face for some assistance, and had given up when he handed the ball to me and acknowledged my thanks with the single word, "Bitte!" A German! A sick prisoner of war? The POW of course! He was the one who had restrained me from entering the booby trapped house at Sarande! The word 'Sarande' was enough: he knew me then. He beamed. We shook hands and jabbered meaningless words to each other to the amusement of the other spectators, the bewilderment of the players and the piercing whistle-blowing of the impatient referee. It was a ludicrous, fleeting encounter which had a strangely satisfying finality about it. I did not see him again – team showers and immediate dependence on returning scheduled transport vehicles ruled out any hope of finding again a man who I knew I could not communicate with anyway – but I had made my gratitude known. And he knew I meant it.

Another Sort of Engagement

I must now halt the narrative of my further travels into an Italian winter and revert to an event I merely hinted at earlier, not only because its relevance had an important influence on all my future wartime thinking, but also because its place in time was so positively fixed. I wrote that 6 October, 1944 was significant. Although I didn't know it at the time, it was the day when I became engaged to marry Anne Hearfield.

Our sole physical contact, apart from the necessary closeness of dancing in the 1940s style, had been a frenetic, clumsy, and almost guilt ridden kiss outside Hull's Wenlock Barracks (no, not wedlock!) after a dance there two and a half years earlier. I know it will take some swallowing that such a brief encounter could have led to such a potentially binding attachment. War sets its own scenario, however, for fleeting, opportunistic romance by shortening the odds against one completing an anticipated average life span. In that respect, the Second World War was not a unique conflict. It was rich in impulsive, passionate romances, flourishing from chancier meetings than ours. They could generate as much ardour as normal peacetime courtships of much longer duration.

By mid-1944 correspondence between us had reached the state of mutual adoration as befits the relationship of long-separated lovers. And I do emphasise that I mean the old fashioned, sinless interpretation of the word. My diaries show that from mid-1943, except for very rare and understandable impediments, a daily letter was not exceptional... Neither maturity nor responsibility were very conspicuous in our written determination to marry immediately on my homecoming. We would worry about home and jobs on my later demobilisation. What naïvety!

Representations for the legal solemnisation of proxy marriages for those servicemen who were serving long, unbroken periods overseas were said to have been made to (and then by) the Forces' welfare associations, notably SSAFA (The Sailors', Soldiers' and Airmen's Families' Association). If they had been successful, I feel sure that the deed would have been done there and then. There must have been thousands of then enthusiastic couples who were ultimately grateful for heads ruling hearts on this revolutionary and controversial question. There were no mass, on-demand, Forces' proxy marriages: I do not know if there were any 'special cases' instances.

Whether or not we were still lost in that 1942 dream of Polka Dots and Moonbeams, the fact is that a single 'tiff' in writing – resulting from a silly, slip of the pen, badly-expressed sentence of mine – provoked the solitary brief interruption in an otherwise harmonious sequence of written, loving accord. The interruption lasted only for as long as it took to swap frantic letters of abject apology, and delayed only briefly our decision to become engaged. The formal recognition and announcement, it seemed, had to await the decorous – though never doubted – ritual etiquette of an exchange of letters between agreeably enthusiastic parents and the transfer home of some cash for an engagement ring and its carefully considered purchase ('Mum and Dad helped me choose it'). These formalities were not completed until 6 October, 1944. "The deed is done!" Anne wrote that day – words that I was not to read until the Army Post Office caught up with me towards the end of that month at the 22nd British General Hospital in Brindisi.

To anticipate your bewilderment at not finding 'Anne' appearing anywhere until May 1944, I need to explain that she was christened Mabel Anne, and that she had grown up answerable to the former name – her parents' first choice. Half a century ago, 'Mabel' was no more a fashionable name than it is now, even if one had then fallen into the foolish, contemporary trap of generalising in the denigration of all Land Army girls (one of which she then was) as being unfashionable 'swede bashers' (which she most certainly was not). So I complied with her wishes, which also met the accord of her friends, in agreeing that she would henceforth be 'Anne'. So the conspicuous 'Mabel' of two years' diary entries did not inexplicably drop out of my life in mid-1944, she had indeed become firmly established as the most important reason for it. Only the Mabel label had gone. What's in a name?

Fulfilment of the dream began to appear within the realms of possibility towards the end of 1944. The war in Europe was closing in on the German state itself; 'home' was not the remote speculation we had for years been afraid to think about. The Government had already published its White Paper on the plans for the post-war demobilisation of the Forces. Allied troops, having progressed across Northern France leaving only pockets of resistance at places like Calais to be cleared up later, were actually fighting on German soil. From the east the Russians had liberated most of Poland, accepted the surrender of Romania and Bulgaria and entered Yugoslavia to co-operate with Tito. The Allied air forces were dropping over a hundred thousand tons of bombs each month on German cities and installations. Only in Italy was progress against the enemy slow, mainly due to the diversion of Allied forces to take part in landings in the south of France in August and, of course, the atrocious weather and difficult terrain. The enemy were holding a line roughly across Italy north of Pisa and Florence. Nevertheless, we in Italy could see hopeful signs of an overland route home opening up soon, so that men with long, unbroken periods of service overseas to their credit were entitled to optimism for their prospects of home leave. There was always the constant niggling dread in our minds that, once Europe had been liberated, we would be sent to the Far East to fight against the Japanese. Any good news from that direction was valued by us much more than the poor devils engaged in that awful conflict would ever have imagined. The British 14th Army out there, labelled by themselves as 'The Forgotten Army' with some justification, had removed the Japanese from Indian soil and started the long trek back through Burma. The inexorable retaking of the Pacific Islands with exotic names by the Americans provided just as pleasing news items, until we later learned of the human cost involved in those fanatically opposed landings. Oh, yes! Things were going well.

"The 'Big Five' of us were at the head of the queue, and not even the freezing, whole-day journey in the back of a canopied truck across Italy, over winter-mantled mountains, diminished our vocal enthusiasm…"

Signals Over Salermo

In November 1944 an urgent call went out for volunteers for training as wireless operators, due either to an acceptance that communication had not been our strong suit in our few operations or to the agreeable, though farcical supply situation which saw us with more wireless sets than men to operate them. Such was the boredom and rancour prevailing at Rutigliano that six weeks at the Royal Artillery's Italian Training Depot, at a then-peaceful Salerno, held out pleasing prospects of a holiday by the sea. The necessary volunteers were very soon recruited. The 'Big Five' of us were at the head of the queue, and not even the freezing, whole-day journey in the back of a canopied truck across Italy, over winter-mantled mountains, diminished our vocal enthusiasm. But our first sight of the camp did! We hadn't reckoned on being in tents in a 'permanent' base camp in mid-winter. Nor had we realised what rigours an Italian winter had in store for us. And we were not by the sea – Salerno was ten or so miles away. The camp was at Eboli, sited inhospitably in the foothills of a mountain range, then almost perpetually obscured by torrential rain or enshrouding, chilling mists. Gypsies were said to live in profusion in nearby hillside caves. Whenever it was said, I felt sure it was in sympathy-invoking terms, but I soon began to envy the shelter enjoyed by the no-fool gypsies.

If Christ did stop at Eboli, I'll bet it was not for long – and it would have confirmed why I had immediately termed it a 'God forsaken hole'. Fortunately the course was absorbing, intensive, thoroughly well organised and rigidly disciplined. I don't think I was ever made to train harder during any other period of my army service. How else could anyone have taught me the basic rudiments of electricity? It is no fault of the RATD that such knowledge lasted only as long as the war. The instructors really were superb – not popular, mind you, but unswerving in imparting their very considerable knowledge. They were most dedicated in trying to ensure that we thoroughly understood the course, each stage of which was rigorously tested. Our impatient desire to get our hands on field telephones and wireless sets had to have been curbed until the theory and artillery communication procedures had been proved to be thumped home. This daily workload of instruction and testing made us almost fearful: the urgency conveyed such a sense of purpose that we each nursed a dread of failure and the stigma of being returned to our unit (RTU) which would be the consequence. That not one of us failed is testimony to the zeal of the instructors and the proven efficiency of the long established system of artillery communications in the British Army.

When the time came for field exercises involving the practical use of wireless sets, either humped on our backs or in the rear of 8cwt Morris Commercial trucks, the sense of achievement helped neutralise what would otherwise have been the demoralising effect of the steadily worsening winter weather. Memories of the cold and wet of Eboli will never leave me: they are reinforced by the absurdity of a 06:30 PT parade in shorts and vest. After an interminably long, farcical roll call from lists barely readable by a minute torch's glimmer and made farcical by bogus responses, the parade would set off into the blackness of night on a mile's stumbling run over hill and dale. If disappearance was simplicity itself, one had to weigh-up what advantage the alternative had to offer. Return to one's tent meant running the gauntlet of prowling NCOs, detailed specifically to nail any such malingerers for unwholesome fatigue duties. Running at least kept one's blood circulating.

After PT came the somewhat comparable abomination of ablutions. We stood on duckboards to use galvanised iron washing troughs which were, except for a corrugated iron roof, open to all the elements. Shaving at Eboli in the dark with ice cold water would always have been one of my more horrible reminiscences of the war, even if it had not produced the infuriating scenario for the loss of my captured watch. Stuffing the wretched thing in my trouser pocket to wash myself one miserable morning was the last time I had it in my possession. It was never seen again. It was some time later before I discovered that I hadn't got a pocket. Leaking acid, from a battery I had backpacked the previous day, had left a trail of destruction through my battle-dress to the less robust materials beneath. Pocket and patches of underclothes had disappeared; the battle-dress took a little longer to disintegrate. I suppose I shouldn't complain – the sacrifice of the fabrics was preferable to acid burns on my skin.

Happy diversions and pleasing relationships emerged from these times; it is never all doom and gloom. Jimmy, Topper, Archie, Steve and I found ourselves tented with two other characters whom I remember only as Bob and Jim. Our two new friends taught us the ropes at Eboli and immediately became an integral, affable and almost indispensable part of our group, although they were at Eboli for a different course of training than ours. A pair of natural comics, they were admirable foils for each other's wit, which readily blended with ours. They introduced us to a mysterious, Italian crewed train which stopped, I'm sure unofficially, at nearby sidings on a Saturday evening en route to Salerno. Scores of men from the camp scrambled across a Clapham Junction of lines to clamber aboard this 'considerate' train for their weekend binge, to be brought back equally mysteriously in due course. I didn't see anything of the city of Salerno, although we were regular passengers on the train.

Bob and Jim had established a friendship with an Italian family in a tenement suburb. That 'open' house, impossible of being found without their guidance, provided the venue for joyful musical booze ups which attracted a growing crowd of gregarious neighbours each successive Saturday. We produced the currency and cigarettes for the Vermouth and the grub; the music was provided gratuitously by the Italians (accordion and sometimes guitar); the singing was contributed by all non-stop! Neapolitan airs were happily juxtaposed with well lubricated renditions of alien songs such as 'You are my sunshine'. They were very happy evenings, bridging national barriers with an ease that politicians would probably find difficult to understand.

Needless to say, we were each fairly plastered by the critical time for our departure, but our hosts never once failed to make sure we got on the strangely unaccountable 'ghost' train, and none of them at any time ever took advantage of us (when robbing us or cheating us would have been child's play). They somehow arranged for the train to stop at Eboli's sidings, and they briefed one of the train crew to see that we all alighted there. It is no surprise that there is a dreamlike quality about those vermouth-misted memories of Saturday nights in Salerno. That bizarre puzzle about the request-stop train is the main stumbling block to belief that the episodes really did take place. One character who was very real at the RATD at Eboli in December 1944 was a young Lance-Bombardier called Harry Secombe, who had also arrived there late in November. Harry was just beginning to find his showbusiness feet, having done a few shows at places like Bari and Trani while still belonging to a combatant artillery unit, which had seen some fierce action in North Africa and Sicily. He'd had no easy passage. After his performance in the Christmas panto-type show at Eboli ('How Time Flies') he was recognised as having professional showbusiness potential and he spent almost all of his remaining Army service entertaining the troops in concert parties. I was not surprised.

He shone like a beacon among the others in the show, although their standards were certainly higher than we were used to seeing. He gave a talented comic performance as the Fairy Queen, as well as revealing a fine singing voice of such versatility as to provide passable impersonations of both Nelson Eddy and Jeanette MacDonald. It was at Eboli where, inspired no doubt by the freezing ablutions, he conceived and perfected his famous shaving sketch, which he himself admits launched him onto the West End stage after the war. After he had received his knighthood and was celebrating his 40 years as a performer, I sent my copy of the 'How Time Flies' programme to him, asking for his signature on it for old times' sake. Naturally, I accorded him all the formality of address due to his title: "Dear Sir Harry" etcetera. He sent it back, "To Wally, sincerely Harry Secombe – Lance Bombardier!!" The exclamation marks were his.

Christmas 1944 came in the middle of the course, and a few of the RSR contingent thought it worthwhile suggesting that the three day suspension of training might be more congenially spent with our unit back at Rutigliano. I didn't agree, I confess more from dread of the double truck journey over the mountains, but I was not very passionate about it, feeling that the regiment would surely refuse to supply the transport. I was outvoted on the first issue and wrong on the second, but I was horribly correct about the journey.

Despite wrapping up in every conceivable garment I could muster, I froze for most of the duration of those two journeys. Only the relative mildness of the east coast afforded any appreciable relief. It is difficult to find any justification for the trip, which amounted to little more than two awful days of travel and one so influenced by boozing that the venue for it could have been anywhere. Perhaps in my cynicism I have minimised my appreciation for the regiment's really serious attempts to provide us with a seasonal Christmas dinner, the enjoyment of a rather flippant domestic football match on the town's pitch, and the collection of a most welcome batch of mail which awaited me and had me guessing about when I would otherwise have received it. Quite a chore for a poste restante service, I thought.

New Year's Eve back at Eboli was much more memorable, although Jimmy always doubts if I could remember it. He contends that, if I could, I shouldn't. I had long intended that the stroke of midnight, marking not only the new 1945 but my own 25th birthday, would be the appropriate time for trying out my captured Browning pistol – its noise being expected to merge nicely in the decibels of revelry, thus causing no concern to anyone in authority. A few shots in the air would do the trick. The trouble was, apparently, that almost everyone doubted that I was sober enough to remember to fire in the air. Apparently, Topper suffered for years from recurring nightmares of my brandishing an untried weapon in a rather congested crowd of Hogmanay first-footers.

I do not expect anyone to believe that I was completely in control of my actions as I fired two innocuous rounds into the ebony black sky, removed the slim magazine and tucked away in my belt the cause of so much needless apprehension. The final two weeks of field training at the RATD were a positive delight. The acquired knowledge was put into practice with enjoyment stemming not only from the satisfaction one derives from attainments, but from some revelation of the astounding magic which 'wireless' had hitherto been to me.

Calling each other from distant vehicles was as exhilarating an experience as childhood memories of back yard communications along string attached to boot-blacking tin lids. If not quite so impressive in its proven results, even the fruits of mundane landline laying to Don five (DV) telephone handsets held its juvenile excitement for us. The pièce de résistance was undoubtedly the proving of the Appleton Layer. To gaze into the infinity of an azure sky, unblemished by the slightest wisp of a cloud, and expect to be convinced of the existence of an invisible, ionised layer up there (which was capable of bouncing radio signals like a squash ball does from a wall) taxed even the supreme belief we had in our admirable instructors. Only demonstration would convince.

Off we went in our truck, contacting base regularly and experiencing fading signals, until after about 30 miles the signal disappeared altogether. Then, as we travelled in the same direction, each further mile from base yielded progressively strengthening signals which, until at 60 miles away we could receive as well as at base. That proved the point about the Appleton Layer, yet never diminished the marvel of the mystery.

Hospital

When I became ill soon after my return to Rutigliano, it was initially no matter for concern. 'Gyppy-tummy' was hardly a rarity in the forces overseas, but I soon guessed that there was something different about this one. After the medicaments which the MO dealt me had produced no remedy, I was sent to the military hospital at Bari for some testing. A few days later a phone call from the hospital to the regiment had me rushed into a bed at the 98th British General Hospital at Bari. I was a diagnosed victim of amoebic dysentery. Dysentery was dysentery in my book, but apparently this was quite serious and a minimum stay of six weeks was assured.

My well scheduled programme required two weeks of complete inertia while receiving daily injections of the drug emetine, during which I could not leave my bed under any circumstances due to the drug's potency. Two weeks were spent just recovering by a very gradual return to physical activity, the limit of which was a walk to the toilet; then two weeks of daily enemas involving the retention for as long as possible the poured in, iodine-like antiseptic fluid called Yatrin, the ultimate ejection of which brought water to my eyes as the rasping fluid acted on the tender membranes surrounding the anus. It was like passing a bag of nails rather than a fluid.

The dedicated nurses – lovely Jewish girls from Palestine – and a couple of fellow sufferers told me that I would be tested again at the end of the six weeks and, if the germ were still present, the whole programme would start again. One poor devil was on his third six week schedule. I could sense that optimism was not very high and, as I had already become a shadow of my former self by the time I had been diagnosed and admitted, the prospect was quite grim. Yet all went well.

The discomforts were only brief interludes, the attentive nurses were positively charming and the food attractive and wholesome, while the luxury of a real bed was divine. Apart from the apprehension about the critical post-treatment test, I have no complaints about my stay in hospital when the alternative was Rutigliano. It was, however, a period touched by one very sad event and another which had equal shares of sadness and joy about it.

The 98th was a vast hospital, accommodating many more types of patient than the purely medical category that I was in. Many casualties of the fighting further north were being treated there, some unavailingly. Padres were busy people, administering last rites, writing consoling letters to relatives, and offering encouragement to patched up survivors. "Will Father 'X' please go to Ward 'Y' as soon as possible, please?" was the sort of announcement not infrequently interrupting the ward's programme of entertaining music pouring out from Radio Bari, innocently oblivious to the human tragedies. We all knew the grim significance of the announcement and, although it might bring some expression of sympathy from us for 'some poor sod', we were impersonally detached from his identity and he would soon be forgotten as just another anonymous 'casualty'.

That detachment ended one day, when a nurse came to me saying "That was one of your lads, who's just died." That he was a parachutist who had been making a descent from above the local airfield at Goiya was as much as she knew. I could not associate such an accident with any of the fully trained men of the Raiding Support Regiment, but I put in a request for the Roman Catholic padre (who had earlier been summoned over the radio) to come to see me. I learned from him the awful news that the victim had been the one-time member of my crew, Paddy Hayden. He had apparently answered a call for volunteers to make a demonstration jump for the benefit of trainees: the parachute failed to open. My mind instantly recalled Paddy's insistence that I should have details of his next of kin when we were on Vis. After allowing sufficient time for official notification, writing to his father was an uncomfortable experience. A both sad and happy experience came from one of the frequent visits I had from Jimmy, Topper and Archie, too. From the moment they entered the ward that day there was no mistaking that they bore good news.

"We're going home!" blurted Topper, whilst Archie unselfconsciously danced towards the bed with arms aloft like an 'Evening in Athens' performer. For an instant, I permitted myself the wild hope that 'we' might have included me – perhaps the regiment was being sent home –

but in my heart of hearts I knew I had guessed rightly that the lads had qualified by being in that select band of individuals who had not been home for more than five years. Rumours of implementing a scheme for the overland repatriation of such poor, deserving devils had been circulating for a month or so, but cynical disbelief about its realisation had been understandable.

It was not difficult to feel a part of their personal celebrations but my anxiety at what life at Rutigliano would be like without such loyal and companionable allies, together with their overt concern at leaving me in dock, tempered the proceedings. Their departure for home was so imminent that there was time for them to make only one further visit before they were on their way, Blighty-bound and pledging to visit both my family and my fiancée. All manner of emotions seized me as the lads paused at the ward entrance for a final wave, and I slumped beneath the sheets, feigning sleep but in truth trying to hide my grief from the others in the ward.

Topper, it seemed, had been similarly affected, a fact which did not come to light until some years later when a letter of his to my mother was discovered during the clearing up of my father's effects on his death. It was a letter of thanks following the dutiful visit which he, Jimmy and Archie had made to my folks as soon as possible during their first home leave for five years. Steve was going to be the only one left at the RSR with whom I had anything in common, and I was grateful to him not only for his visits to the hospital, but for organising a very special pleasant surprise for me. Surprise, it certainly was. Shock, perhaps, would be more appropriate. Just imagine my lying there, faithfully complying with the rules of calm inertia, which I was told must be applied when being treated with emetine, when my name sounded from an impersonal loudspeaker on that foreign wall. Our friend from Radio Bari had been nudged by Steve to broadcast a goodwill message and request. Knowing of my Benny Goodman interest he played 'Big John Special' for me – a wonderfully typical example of the Goodman band's arrangements for the late 30s, even if Goodman himself usually hides his personal light under a bushel in it. I think the shock to my nervous system must have registered a puzzling reading to the experts at Greenwich observatory and sent my own blood pressure graph-line off the paper. It was a kindly thought of Steve's.

At the conclusion of my finely scheduled six weeks of treatment, I endured a few more days of mental torture while awaiting the results of my final tests, which made the announcement of a clean bill of health all the more welcome when it came. Before departure, all patients for discharge had to appear before the hospital's senior medical officer, in my case a doctor with the rank of colonel. My genuinely expressed thanks for the staff's care and attention were met with a cautionary warning that they might prove to be premature. "They often have to come back with this complaint. Very difficult to get rid of, you know!" On that cheery note, I left. Happily, there never was a recurrence. The illness had taken its toll, however, leaving me almost two stones lighter and a frail shadow of my former self. Indeed, never at any subsequent point in my life did I return to my fully fit, pre-dysentery weight of 12 stone.

I walked out of the hospital on 26 March, 1944 with my discharge certificate recording 47 days of hospital treatment for 'Amoebiasis Dysenteric', on which the RSR's medical officer at RHQ promptly noted – after seeing my state of health – "I strongly recommend that this Corporal (sic) be given some leave at the earliest opportunity, 26.3.45". (My artillery, two stripe rank was Bombardier not Corporal). "Be sure you hand that in to your Battery Office," was his final exhortation. Well, I haven't done so, yet.

I still have that certificate which, from the moment I received it, I treasured as my document of entitlement to the anticipated delights of some leave in Rome. During my absences at Eboli and in hospital the Italian capital had, it seemed, become everybody's favourite place to spend their allocation of local leave. How they got there, incidentally, revealed a catalogue of initiative which, I suppose, typifies the devious sort of people the RSR was reputed to be. Road hitch-hiking and rail hoboing, with their various vicissitudes, yielded many a yarn, but for sheer enterprise one had to admire the first venture into air-hitching. The system was to hitch-hike 60 miles or so to Foggia, the very centre for most of the Allied Air Forces' activities in Italy; 'chat up' any obvious air crew personnel (British or American) one encountered in the Forces' canteens there; and flash one's parachute 'wings' to foster a kindred spirit. If your luck was in, you could scrounge a lift by air to Rome from crews on the supply run – an unofficial favour usually reserved for air force ground crew personnel. The liaison could usually organise the lift back.

Remarkably, although I am sure in breach of all manner of rules, the stunt was said to have been worked successfully many times through the personal contacts which materialised.

A contemporary story, the authenticity of which is unverified but worth relating, tells of one Rome-bound hopeful who could not believe his luck when he was offered, by an RAF crew, not a flight to Rome but a 'back tomorrow' trip to Blighty. Having been away from his wife for over three years, the potential pleasures of twelve clandestine hours with her far outweighed the physical and legal risks even if she might spend half of that time recovering from the shock of the unannounced appearance on her doorstep of the husband with a CMF (Central Mediterranean Forces) address. Timing, though fortuitous, had been perfect: he had arrived and departed during the hours of darkness, unobserved by even the nosiest neighbour. The fewer who knew of the highly irregular venture, the less risk there was of court martial for quite a number of those who had connived in it. The man's wife told nobody, not even her parents, and he was secrecy itself: only they and the plane's crew knew of the successfully engineered trip which had produced such unexpected happiness. How do I know about it? Well, nine months later he had to tell everybody: his wife produced a baby son! Our hero suffered no penalty. He had never been missed. It was the wife who had the explaining to do. The tail piece was that he still had time for five days in Rome too.

As fate would have it, I was not to see Rome until some forty-odd years later. Well, perhaps that is not strictly true. Within a few days of my leaving hospital I did see something of Rome's suburbs from a military railway train traversing the Eternal City's outskirts, en route to the north of Italy. But that wasn't quite fate's doing, nor did this remarkable change of events owe anything to sensible rationale or even 'the exigencies of the service'. It was the outcome of my impulsive resolve to abandon any intention of spending any more time than I could possibly help in purposeless inertia at Rutigliano, where I no longer had any friends. Only fate could have arranged that, on my way to the Battery Office with that coveted sickleave recommendation in my hand, I should be conversationally waylaid with the news that 'E' Battery, which had left five weeks earlier for an operation 'up north', were desperately looking for a relief wireless operator. I halted in my tracks, decided there and then to volunteer, was accepted, supplied with a No. 22 radio set manual, kitted out and given movement order to join 'E' Battery before I had time to realise that 1 April was but a day or two away.

There is no doubt that it was a foolish thing to have done. I was so ridiculously weak physically; the war appeared to be progressing rapidly to its inevitable conclusion in victory for the Allies; and to avoid anything likely to delay my homecoming in undamaged condition, I had sworn to volunteer for nothing more. Today, my motive would be expressed as a desire to 'grab a slice of the action' before the war finished – a last chance to be useful – to have played a part. Such madness was confirmed by everyone who knew me. But there I was, heading for action with the best and most successful battery in the RSR, in real artillery at last, manned with expert and experienced gunners and signallers, and equipped with perhaps the best communication gear which the Army had in all Italy. Exhilarating!

My memory of the journey is scant but vaguely reminiscent of my solo jaunts in the Middle East. I know I endured rolling stock which shunted and shuffled about as if to confirm the Royal Artillery's motto Ubique. We were coupled and uncoupled to and from variously trundling trains for several days of boredom, including that episode of being puzzlingly stuck outside Rome for hours of frustrating discomfort. Eventually, I found myself billeted in the very centre of a near-deserted Ravenna, in north-east Italy. In a school of course!

Lake Comacchio

The RSR's presence at Ravenna was demanded in its role as part of 2 Commando Brigade for a substantial special services raid in support of the British Eighth Army's final push against General Kesselring's stubborn resistance, then stolidly established (on the Allies' eastern sector) in the River Po Valley just north of where the River Reno flows into the Adriatic Sea. The whole area is a flat, featureless lowland landscape whose only natural barrier to military progress was water – the huge Lake Comacchio. The lake had been artificially enlarged by the Germans to flood a further area of lowland already a network of canals, lagoons and dykes. A narrow spit of land separates the lake from the Adriatic, and it was here that the enemy had reinforced strong defensive positions to prevent any right hook around the lake as a possible strategy for breaking the long standing stalemate further west.

Our Commando Brigade had been assembled to attack and eliminate these positions and to clear the important Spit for the onward progress of some of the Eighth Army's armour. The Brigade was known then as 2 Commando Brigade, not because it included 2 (Army) Commando but for the strangely euphemistic reason that as 2 Special Service Brigade, which it really was, its common abbreviation to '2 SS' had been thought too likely to invite odious comparisons with the loathsome German connotation of 'SS'. Only the British could conjure up such supposed sensitivity. One was tempted to ask, upset whom? The nasty Germans?

The Brigade was comprised mainly of four Commando units, namely 2 and 9 (Army) Commandos, and 40 and 43 Royal Marine Commandos. There were also splinter groups of the Brigade's supporting units at Comacchio, including our own 'E' Battery of the RSR, a troop of 'B' Battery's 4.2-inch mortars and sections of the SBS (Special Boat Squadron), then an integral branch of the SAS (Special Air Service). The area to the south-east of the lake but south of the River Reno, which was in Allied hands, was to be the start point for the assault on the spit at San Alberto.

The basic plan was something of a military paradox in that the Army Commando units would make the amphibious landings (from the lake, not from the sea) to coincide with the Royal Marine Commandos' – whose motto is Per Mare Per Terram – wholly land-based attack from the base of the spit, obviously only 'per terram' in this instance. My excitement, borne of the prospect of involvement in such an enterprise, was toned down slightly by my fear of not meeting the standards required through either my constitutional weakness (the journey had worryingly emphasised my fragility) or my lack of practical experience as a signaller. Napoleon was reported to have said, "The important secret of war is to make oneself master of communication." God, please help me!

Fortunately there was little time for speculation: being 'thrown in at the deep end' has a lot to be said for it. Yet, I must give credit to my new colleagues, who adopted me and nurtured my physical and technical rehabilitation with a deep understanding, far beyond the benefits which a relief operator, albeit a rookie, would bring to them. There seemed to be a splendid spirit of accord in the Battery, which I feel sure I correctly analysed as stemming mainly from a confidence in, and respect for, its officers, who had already proved their merit on several occasions. What a difference from 'C' Battery!

The Comacchio operation was obviously going to be the beginning of the last great battle for Italy. Its success would ease the Eighth Army's progress between Argenta and the lake through the so-called Argenta Gap. It was to produce two posthumous Victoria Crosses – a glorious chapter in Special Forces' history which might perhaps have convinced the many sceptics that such troops had justified their place in the overall plan of modern warfare. And yet, like most of our operations, its start was dogged by misfortune and immersed in confusion. From both of those categories, exclude the delivery of 1200 rounds of the wrong ammunition to our guns. That was simply foolish – but, then, it was 1 April.

I suffered no personal indignation at being allowed to adopt from the start of the operation the cutely proffered role of 'dogsbody'. Everyone could do with a little help, and I greatly needed not only experience but a little physical leeway – just a day or two in which to put some strength back into my pitiful frame. The initial role for our Battery's 75mm howitzers was to provide support at the base of the Spit for 40 and 43 Commandos' land-based attack northwards, and 2 and 9 Commandos' nocturnal landings from the lake onto the western shore of the Spit.

My signalling role was with 'G' Party (standing for 'Gun') distinctive from the 'O' Party (Observation Post or OP Party) whose importance in noting, assessing and conveying precise information and issuing fire orders to the guns was paramount, and demanded the experience of a competent wireless operating team. I knew that I would never be good enough for that, unless the war went on for a year or two more.

The Brigade had been in the line south of Comacchio for some five weeks and the men had absorbed some of the veterans of the hard slog of the Italian campaign, so vastly different from our usual brief, piston-like experiences of in-and-out special operations. This was not a Troop or Battery front, not even a Regimental or Divisional front, but one involving a whole Army – the illustrious Eighth Army. Famous regiments were in close proximity: the might of formidable armour was conspicuously within sight and sound.

Military Intelligence had pinpointed the enemy's defensive strong points on the spit, all seemingly fortified in anticipation of any Allied attack coming from the sea, not from the lake. For operational purposes each stronghold had been allocated a biblical name such as Matthew, Mark, Isaiah, Ezra et cetera. The lake was to be crossed by 2 and 9 Commando in small, outboard motor-powered storm boats and American Fantails – those tracked amphibious transportation vehicles which at first appearance resembled huge tanks, but whose hulls offered about as much armoured protection as would the skin of a rice pudding.

The movement of all these vessels overland in the last few days of March was a creditable exercise in logistics, which could hardly have escaped visual detection by Jerry then or whilst their use was being rehearsed. Comically optimistic attempts were made to mask the noise of such activity by superimposing the sound of real tanks aimlessly promenading for the sake of it and by blasting the music of Wagner over the Tannoy virtually non-stop. Personally, I have never been sure whether the latter ploy was meant to assail the enemy's ear drums or to attract – and thus divert – his interest. Why not Lili Marlene? Perhaps the Public

Relations profession had not been established then. We, for our part, had taken up position on 31 March and Jerry must have known something about that too, because some heavy calibre artillery shells fell among us and, indeed, several of them were so deftly deposited as to record direct hits on the 56th Division's artillery headquarters only 300 yards west of our position.

Next day, 1 April, was to see the start of the battle. Firing programmes were agreed at Brigade level and radio contact established with the called-up field guns of 142 Field Regiment (the Devon Yeomanry), to which it had been decided to attach us for artillery support purposes, and with 2 Commando Brigade HQ At 20:30 the men of 43 Commando began to move forward up the eastern side of the spit, on a tongue of land with the River Reno (which at this point took a northerly course to its outlet into the Adriatic) on their left and with the sea on their right. 40 RM Commando's attack up the 'inside' of the Spit (that is, on 43 RM Commando's left) was timed to go in as a feint to coincide with landings by 2 and 9 Commandos, on the Spit's west bank.

Unfortunately their plans went adrift, if you will excuse the following mixing of the metaphor. The shallow waters of the lake had been made even shallower by the Germans draining off some water to flood a wider area and, in an unseasonably dry spell, the loss had not been made good by rainfall. The high powered Fantails, which were to tow thirty-odd laden but unpowered assault boats across the lake, immediately became inextricably bogged down in the bankside mud and their use had to be abandoned. Subsequently, the launch of all the storm boats as towing vessels for the assault boats became something approaching a fiasco, too.

Both types of vessels looked admirably suited for the job as they floated with only a meagre, nine inch draught but, when loaded with their complement of men and equipment, they became stuck fast by the banks in a porridge of tacky mud. The canoe crews of the Combined Operations Pilotage Party (COPP), there primarily as route markers, hurriedly tested depths further from the banks and it was found that the boats would need to be floated out about a thousand yards into the lake before adequate clearance could be found.

So, for hours after the scheduled start time, human chain supply columns had to wade through the retentive squelch of the lake bed to carry equipment and outboard motors (which demanded even further draught) in a frantic exercise to load the storm boats with all the men and armaments, in time for their task. The slogging, swearing determination and endurance of every available man, each giving his all in this formidable, unforeseen task, still could not prevent 1 April becoming 2 April before the entire flotilla of seventy-odd boats were afloat. Even then the description 'flotilla', with its image of orderly marine assembly, was a misnomer. All semblance of organisation had disappeared in the dark, with craft drifting or being paddled about in glorious confusion, while the strictly emphasised instruction that all outboard motors must remain silent until the signal for their 'last minute' uniform switch-on. The scene was likened to the revellers' booze up at the conclusion of Henley Regatta, but one wag's comment was that it resembled the Serpentine on a Bank Holiday when a megaphone call from the shore bellowing something like, "Come in 24: your time's up!" would not have seemed out of place.

By 03:00 frantic signals were passed, suggesting that the officers afloat thought that the delayed start had self-aborted the landing operation, but the Brigade Commander would have none of that. The land based attacks were well under way; the artillery programme, long started and progressing, could not be wasted; and, furthermore the Brigade Commander must have asked himself whether the water levels would be any higher tomorrow or in the foreseeable future.

By the primitive expedient of bawling from boat to boat, the vessels' passengers learned with understandable dismay of the confirmed decision that the raid was still 'on'. With much further shouting, the boats were collected and lashed together. Then they were towed by the storm boats until the outboard motors could be started in unison. Finally, with the engines making a resounding din, they were navigated (thanks to the efforts of the COPP canoeists) to their planned landing point on the spit. Incredibly, hardly any hostile reception awaited them, apart from deadly mines. Perhaps Jerry had concluded that the ostentatious racket could only be a 'feint' for the more substantial sea landing he persisted to expect.

It was here at about 04:30, while the Comacchio regatta took place, that we played our little part in adding our four guns to the artillery barrage of more than a hundred which kept German heads down and created its own noise and smoke screen. 250 rounds per gun was no small contribution from us. I busied myself in every way possible, yet missed no opportunity of breathing down the neck of my wireless operator mentor to familiarise myself with the practical application of Eboli's already manifestly excellent training. I fetched and carried, made tea and prepared compo meals for the 'workers', deftly avoiding (or did it avoid me?) one of three enemy shells which fell perilously close to us at 05:45, narrowly missing our makeshift cookhouse but destroying some signalling stores.

From midnight the news had been good, except for the cavortings on the lake. 43 RM Commando were initially 'going well': by 06:00, they had captured strong points 'Amos' and 'Ruth'. Despite a delayed landing, 2 Commando had taken the bridge at the point known as 'Peter' on the Canal Bellochio after wading and slithering through appalling conditions at their landing points from boats manhandled as far inshore as the mud banks would permit. They too were soon making agreeable reports of success. The attack of 40 RM Commando had started just before 05:00 and the reports from here were also guardedly 'favourable'. Meanwhile, 9 Commando's landings, having been augmented by their rounding up of some of 2 Commando's 'missing' boats which had been swanning around like so much flotsam, had similarly overcome the atrocious beaching conditions and were reporting success and, in particular, the capture of many prisoners.

By the end of the day 2 April, almost half of the spit had been taken up to the point where it was divided by the Bellocchio Canal, which presented the next and more formidable barrier behind which the enemy's resistance could be greatly stiffened. News of the British successes diverted us from our natural wish to sleep, but in our relatively passive role we were able to snatch catnaps from time to time. I took the opportunity to gain more experience on the radio sets by doing relief stints for dozing comrades, but mostly it involved no more than being on 'listening watch'.

During the day 43 RM Commando had successfully crossed the Reno. Attempts to ferry our guns across had been abandoned, not only because of the inadequacy of available rafts – a problem which it was considered might ultimately be overcome – but mainly from the discouraging recommendations made to our officer (who had crossed for reconnaissance purposes) by 43 RM Commando's Adjutant about the conditions to be faced on the opposite bank. It seems that swamp conditions to the west denied vehicular progress to all but the amphibious Weasels, whilst mines barred progress in most other directions.

A party of men from an anti-tank unit attempted to clear the mines, but had found too many to make their task a practically rewarding one in the limited time available. We were glad – amateurs at that game are to be discouraged. At about 21:00 a well meaning guide directed us further up the tongue to a beach on the Adriatic shore, where we were confronted by an impassable, three mile stretch of soft sand, separating us from a raft which would have suited our purpose! So it was not until 03:00 on 3 April that we had the guns across the Reno, the enterprising Royal Engineers having then miraculously slung a pontoon bridge across it in the middle of the sector. Our mobility then seemed assured, particularly as six extra Jeeps and trailers had been allocated to us prior to the crossing. This remarkable surfeit of transport increased my opportunity to make myself useful, but the satisfaction which this produced was short lived. We had not progressed very far before the omnipresence of such a variety of enemy mines stifled our zest: this indirect sort of weaponry was causing more casualties than the direct enemy fire – and the mines certainly more fears. The ever-present possibility of detonating one was terrifying.

Fortunately, an officer in charge of one of 43 Commando's supply column had reached similar conclusions and, in turning back, had persuaded our officers to do likewise. An emergency conference of officers then decided that our way northwards should be up the left side of the spit in close support of 2 Commando. At first light, whilst we were brewing up, about a dozen Germans casually walked onto the site, frightening the life out of me until it was obvious they were unarmed, docile and wished to surrender. As they were mainly officers and senior NCOs it was a rather encouraging incident, once the shock had subsided.

For most of the morning, we were poised to implement the fire plan based upon new targets beyond minor canal crossings which had been made at 'Amos' and 'Peter'. The guns opened up at 12:30 but this was hastily stopped as a reported false start. All hell was let loose by our gunners and mortar men at 14:00, after which 2 Commando and 43

RM Commando achieved all their objectives and advanced further up the spit towards the Valetta Canal (Canale Valetta), meeting stiffer opposition at every yard. They finally stabilised their line for the night by digging in about 2000 yards short of the canal which then separated them from their prime objectives on the northern banks: Porto Garibaldi and the road which linked it with the Germans' other stronghold, the small town of Comacchio.

It was during that day's vicious battles, where the enemy's defences had to be tested, that 43 RM Commando's posthumous Victoria Cross was won by Corporal Thomas P. Hunter. The official citation describing this man's astonishing bravery and firm resolve conveys some notion of the military situation and topographical features – or more correctly its lack of features. Our guns had played no part in the evening battle, embarrassingly because communication had broken down with the Observation Post – reconnection not being effected until after dark. Not my fault, I hasten to add.

By first light on 4 April, our OP had established himself somewhat precariously in the upstairs of an already partially demolished house, which by its conspicuousness in so barren a landscape must have been well ranged and targeted by every enemy gun for miles around. Only close proximity with these daring observers brought appreciative awareness of their cool courage. The OP officer soon registered three specific targets in the area of Comacchio and Porto Garibaldi, and it was heartening to be bashing away at them at various intervals throughout the day. In fact, until 02:00 the next morning (5 April) when the compelling need for sleep overcame even the excitement of action. That day, however, Eighth Army command had recognised that basic human need by replacing the two Commando units in the line with 24th Guards Brigade.

On the morning of 5th April, all British troops were surprised to be ordered to withdraw temporarily from their forward locations by 09:30, because of a planned bombing attack by the RAF on Porto Garibaldi. This was one occasion when withdrawal did not adversely affect morale. Right on time, the Boston bombers plastered the tiny port, inflicting damage described as 'heavy'. So flat was the countryside that we could see only rising smoke and dust: typically, our OP wanted to inspect for himself, for within half an hour he was signalling again from the dubious haven of his half house, re-registering the targets for that night. He must have thought that continuing the withdrawal was a waste of time, or he had supreme confidence in the accuracy of our air crews, for when a further planned attack by dive bombing and machine gunning Spitfires and Thunderbolts went in at 17:00, he refused to leave his crows' nest so that he would be able to pin point for future 'stonking' the locations of the German 88mm anti-aircraft guns from their muzzle flashes. His skill, high sense of duty and opportunism assumed even greater value after dark.

When the Guards were ordered to cross the canal in assault boats at 21:00, in order to test Porto Garibaldi's defences following the air raids, we really began to justify our existence. Initial support fire of 120 rounds per gun on one target area was followed at 23:00 by more specific calls for shelling areas which had been giving serious trouble to the Guards. This included counter artillery battery work, and neutralisation mortar and Spandau machine gun emplacements. Such was the strength of the opposition met by the Guards – which at least proved that Porto Garibaldi was still substantially defended – that the assault was called off in order to minimise casualties. The remainder of the night was quiet; the German's seemingly wished to conserve their artillery ammunition for a purely defensive role.

Morning brought news that we of 12 Troop were immediately to be withdrawn to Ravenna for a rest. I welcomed this more for the prospect of sleep than for any feelings of safety felt at being a mere twenty or so miles south of the hostile battle line. I drove a Jeep and trailer in that convoy for the short journey south to Ravenna, and remember it well for the titanic struggle to sustain my wakefulness for the whole of that drive. Before food, drink or even the normally exciting prospect of reading a waiting stack of accumulated mail from home, I flopped on my blankets without undressing and disappeared from the world for three parts of a day, not insignificantly tranquilised by the satisfaction which one derives from the feeling of having been useful.

Refreshed and relieved, I assiduously devoured my assortment of mail, which by Army Post Office standards was commendably recent in view of the successive redirections made necessary by my rapid transfers, firstly from hospital back to 'C' Battery at Rutigliano and then to 'E' Battery, located some 400 miles to the north and in a battle zone. Oh!

and how different was the mood at home then. At last people were beginning to permit themselves the luxury of optimism. 'Blackouts' had ended; 'bus service timetables were having a look of normality about them; and Services' demobilisation projections, at that time appearing in the newspapers, were being studied avidly. The end of the war in Europe was so imminent that 'take care' sentiments expressed in the letters we received were much more meaningful. "Don't you dare volunteer for the Far East!" became more a threat than a mere exhortation from Anne.

Aware that the respite from battle would be minimal, I set about responding, uneasily restrained more than ever before by the confounded shackles of censorship. There was so much that I wanted to reveal, let alone answer, but I knew I could barely hint at what I was doing. It was all the more annoying because I knew that all my correspondents thought me to be cosily skiving 400 miles to the south. My chagrin was further compounded by the fears which had suddenly clouded my enthusiasm. I think it was the menace of the mines which accounted for changing my erstwhile fatalism or faith – I knew not which – to sheer terror and self-condemnation for having needlessly placed myself in such a situation. It had always been relatively simple to ascribe the prospects of a direct hit from a shell or a bomb to fate: there's a lot of space out there! But treading on a mine was a self motivated action, no matter how well the menace had been concealed. There was only oneself to blame – one's own stupid fault – and I had promised to do nothing stupid. I did not suffer alone. Each of us was affected by what I can only describe as this last lap, irony syndrome. Only the gloomiest of pessimists could envisage the war in Europe lasting much more than a month. Weren't the Russians almost at Berlin's gates and the other Allies well across the Rhine, racing eastwards to meet them?

Yet the will to finish off our theatre's contribution to the overall plan was tinged with a caution verging on dread that we would 'cop one on the last noggins'. There was no sign of a German surrender in Italy. The formidable arch-defender of the Italian peninsula, General Kesselring, had been transferred to Germany for treatment for accident injuries and retained on the Western Front for a more urgent and critical exploitation of his undoubted skills. Hitler's 'stand firm' instructions were then being obeyed by a similarly experienced exponent of stubborn resistance, General Von Vietingholff-Scheel, the obstinate defender of Cassino, where many Allied graves left testimony to the General's reputation.

The German defences, then spread across northern Italy at its widest, had been effectively dug in since December on a shrewdly chosen line for a stand, where the Appenine mountain range in the west and Adriatic-bound, south-west to south-east flowing rivers such as the Senio, Santerno, Sillaro (before they joined the Reno) and the River Po's own multiplicity of tributaries presented their own natural obstacles as far north as Venice. The good sense which pervaded 'E' Battery from top to bottom, and which made me so pleased to be a part of it, showed itself in officialdom's wise recognition that catching up on lost sleep at Ravenna carried a higher military priority value than the formality of parades or drills.

'Recovery' was the only order of the day – at least for a couple of days. Then, the shape of things to come was revealed by our hurried familiarisation with the Fantail tracked amphibious vehicles. Two days later the Troop was split into two Sections, as Section Three and Section Four. Section Three immediately (10 April) returned to the line on the spit to find a complete stalemate at the Canale Valetta with our old friends of 43 RM Commando, having taken over again from the Guards on the south bank. The relief in the dark must have been carried out efficiently, for the enemy paid no attention to the exercise – "a quiet night" is recorded. Captain Gervers – our OP – was back in his half demolished house again.

The splitting of the Troop provided me with the very opportunity for which I had volunteered. Placed in charge of the 'G' party signals of Four Section, I had two splendidly trained signaller gunners to help me, Bob Myers and Les Lounds. To be truthful, I helped them but since I had the stripes the glory was mine, as was the Type 22 radio set. Whatever 'Operation Cinderella' was, or was expected to have been, I never did learn, but the Fantail acclimatisation training for which it was intended was not wasted when that operation was peremptorily cancelled. Poor Cinders! Two days later 'Operation Impact Royal' took its place. That sounded much more impressive in prospect than either a fairy tale or a pantomime. Perhaps it was thought that we might quit at midnight with one foot bare.

"What rich and easy pickings would our slow, cumbersome and poorly manoeuvrable craft be for the Germans' deadly 88mm guns when we moved in to land."

Operation Impact Royal

On 11 April, we had no sooner rejoined Section Three and watched them blasting enemy positions across the canal than we were directed back to Ravenna at 16:00 for 'Impact Royal', leaving Section Three in support of the new holders of the south bank positions. That was the first operational contact with organised Italian resistance units, then bolstered with Allied armaments. They were in the line as temporary relief for a desperately tiring and depleted 43 RM Commando. Military fingers were said to be crossed in the hope that the Germans on the north bank still believed that they were confronted by British forces of some repute, such as Commandos or Guards. To supplement this bluff, Section Three stonked away as ordered at the German forward defensive locations from 21:00 to 23:00, which obviously had the desired effect on an otherwise quiet night. To be fair to the Italian 28th Garibaldi Brigade, their tenacity, courage and menacing zest for the opportunity of settling long-simmering scores with their erstwhile Allies and occupiers deserved to be applauded, not disparaged.

I was not to know very much of the happenings on the spit, however, for the next eight days: 'Impact Royal' had all my attention – and apprehension. By 9 April, 1945, 2 Commando Brigade's activities on the spit had created the intended diversion within the grand plan for a massive Allied breakout from the front, which had been fairly static since December 1944. The great Allied offence, from the Tyrrhenian coast to the Adriatic, would involve the US Fifth Army and a truly cosmopolitan Eighth Army made up of troops from Britain, Canada, New Zealand, Poland, India, South Africa and Brazil, plus the Gurkhas, a Jewish Brigade and units from the reformed Italian Army.

On that day, the first major objective of the Eighth Army had been achieved – the crossing of the River Senio. By the 13 April, the day when we embarked upon 'Operation Impact Royal', the Santerno and Sillaro

Rivers had similarly been crossed. Not for much longer would we be the most northerly Allied troops in Italy, for 5 Corps 56th Division were over the Reno behind us and heading for the Argenta Gap, towards the revised western banks of Lake Comacchio.

To counter this Allied territorial gain, the Germans had further flooded the countryside south of the famous highway, Route 16, so that there remained only a theoretical two mile land gap between the city of Argenta and the lake. This became renowned as the Argenta Gap, but in terms of military usefulness the gap was much narrower, due to quagmire conditions of huge areas of land which were only partially covered by the flood water. The gap amounted to little more than the elevated Ravenna/Argenta road (Route 16). The rest was not, perhaps, a lake, but it was certainly a massive bog. Prominently raised, and thus conspicuous, roads criss crossed the area like Dutch dykes, rendering them vulnerable to enemy artillery. The further north we could force enemy guns, the more useful the roads became to our armour. Hastening and harassing the Germans' retreat was the object of 'Impact Royal'.

At 16:00, on 12 April, we received formal briefing for our part in the raid in which we – together with a Battalion of that famous infantry regiment, the Buffs (The Royal East Kent's) – were placed under the operational command of 9 Commando. The preparation of our stores and ammunition began immediately, and by 22:00 the Section – guns and OP – had arrived ten miles away at the rendezvous of Porto Corsini. We had taken a number of diversions to confuse the curious and to minimise congestion by ensuring that troops did not all arrive at the embarkation area at the same time. Embarkation took place sufficiently far from San Alberto's quagmire to make sure that the unjustly maligned Fantails could be tried, tested and afloat beforehand. For the task in hand they were irreplaceable: weighty artillery pieces, Jeeps and trailers, enough 75mm ammunition and the necessary complement of personnel had, by midnight, been enthusiastically and efficiently distributed among the craft by the American officer in charge of the Fantail Squadron.

Allocated to the RSR were five Fantails: numbers 1 and 2 each carried a 75mm gun and 100 rounds of ammunition; numbers 3 and 4 each had a Jeep, trailer and 50 rounds aboard. The fifth had been designated a 'follow up' vessel, scheduled to arrive six hours later unaccompanied, bearing reserves of ammunition and stores, and with only two men aboard.

The rest of the personnel for the operation and their small-arms – eleven men as crews for the two guns, and four men and an Officer (Lt. MacFadyen) representing the gun party of command signals and support – were evenly distributed among the other Fantails. Any spare space which did not jeopardise the safe carrying capacity of the vessels was filled in with ammunition. The whole of our OP party was conveyed in the same Fantail as 9 Commando's HQ personnel. By 04:00 we were waterborne, following marker craft which also placed floating smoke generators at frequent intervals.

I cannot recall what timetable information had been given to us, but I have a strong recollection of my anxiety at the arrival of dawn with no landing beaches in sight and, worse still, the emergence of full daylight with the conspicuous convoy inexorably chugging its ponderous way to nowhere. What a target! Where was the Luftwaffe? For a tense couple of hours, though, our operation seemed a very reckless exercise to me. We did not know it then, but virtually all its aircraft had been transferred to defend the Fatherland. What rich and easy pickings would our slow, cumbersome and poorly manoeuvrable craft be for the Germans' deadly 88mm guns when we moved in to land.

It would be generous to attribute our relatively unmolested landing to the excellent information gleaned by our intelligence experts; it would probably be true too, in this instance, but it was always fashionable to deem as eccentric (at best) the assessments coming from an organisation which boasted of wisdom in its very title. 'Information' would have been more appropriate, whilst attracting less hostility from the cynics. Be that as it may, when we approached fairly firm landing 'beaches', after five hours of being waterborne (if not always moving), a couple of German 88mm guns opened up on us. They were obviously intent on picking off one Fantail after another, but their early success at spectacularly knocking out one on our extreme left was not repeated.

It transpired, to our intense relief, that the main thrust of the 56th Division's attack from the south-west of the lake had been more successful than we could possibly have imagined in the time available. The Division's artillery was already in range of the enemy defences we faced on landing. Their stonking, and the prompt arrival of RAF fighter bombers, must have made Jerry aware that the more immediate menace came from land and air, not from water. Whether his guns had been spiked by the 56th Division's artillery or by the RAF, I know not. It was likely that any German guns which had escaped the onslaught were withdrawn to more suitable positions to stem the progress of Allied tanks and infantry rapidly advancing up the newly mapped west bank of the lake.

Whatever the reasons, our charmed arrival was not a subject for speculation as at 11:30 the Fantails, except for the sad, smoking and exploding specimen on our left, disgorged their vital cargoes of guns, Jeeps, trailers, ammunition, wireless sets, rations and assorted impedimenta of war onto a soggy, dubiously traversable 'beach'.

Within an hour we had good reason to be grateful for any potential obstacles to progress onto dry – or certainly, drier – land. At 12:15 the enemy decided he would again turn his attention to us, and his closeness was a great surprise. Mortar shells started plonking among us, mercifully sinking into deep mud before exploding, thus minimising the distribution of their shrapnel. Two enemy tanks, obviously summoned up to deal with the fragile Fantails, immediately introduced us to their deadly 88mm guns, whilst distant field guns started to bracket on such exposed and congested targets.

Fear is an excellent spur. The speed at which that vulnerable 'beach' was cleared of the contents of four Fantails and personnel, as well as the 'six hour follow up' load from the fifth, was nothing short of incredible. With no serious casualties, orderly dispersal ashore had been achieved with some measure of concealment among farm buildings and trees. More Fantails had been hit after unloading but, mercifully, most were chugging their way out of range on their return voyage whence they came, their crews' ears burning with our praise for their stoic acceptance of the dangerous work they did. Gun party and OP party found themselves jumbled in close proximity in a cluster of farm buildings and, long before I could set up communications with anyone, the brilliantly experienced stalwarts of the OP boys had established wireless contact with 9 Commando HQ.

The guns were soon moved 200 yards away, dug in and camouflaged: the OP needed the height of the buildings, and scattered dispersal was vital in the interest of safety. Information received from 9 Commando told of mixed fortunes. 56th Division had certainly progressed overland, with a Battalion of the Queen's Infantry Regiment, supported by two tanks, already astride the road between the lake and the small town of Menate, itself the last village of any note before Argenta. On the other hand, the Buffs had stumbled on too far after their earlier landing and found themselves surrounded by rather fortuitously redeployed enemy units.

Our instructions were to hold fire, to conceal our firepower and positions until selected priority targets became available. At least it gave us time for communication between guns and OP to be established. By 15:00, when enemy shelling and mortaring intensified, our ordered inertia became frustrating, yet neither our OP nor the Division's experts could locate the source of the firing and there was little anyone could do to rescue the Buffs. Spitfires made a general machine gun strafe on enemy positions at 17:30 in an attempt to winkle them out, but defiant German shelling at dusk (as if to display the seeming ineffectiveness of the air strike) also made plainly visible where those weapons were – a point not lost on our ever alert OP.

After dark, the Queen's made considerable progress towards the beleaguered Buffs. Several enemy strong points were taken, until heavy Spandau fire from one emplacement caused many casualties and a halt had to be called for. Divisional HQ then decided that it was more a job for tanks on the morrow at first light. It had been a momentous 24 hours, and in safe retrospect I still marvel at how little sleep one could exist on.

14 April was hardly less significant. By 09:00 Allied tanks, aircraft and artillery, including our own 75mms, had driven the Germans back – that is, those who did manage to retreat. Fifty prisoners had been taken by the Queen's in their successful relief of the Buffs. Successful it surely was, but the cemeteries at Ravenna and Argenta yield tragic evidence of the human cost in young lives suffered by both regiments on 13 and 14 April 1945.

Canals were again the defensive barriers behind which the enemy retreated and reformed, Canale Campazzo and Canale Marchetto being the next obstacles. The next objective for 9 Commando was the liquidation of an enemy bridgehead astride the Canale Marchetto, with fire programmes hastily arranged for our guns and those of the prominently involved 65th Field Regiment of the Royal Artillery to support an attack scheduled for that night.

While 9 Commando were forming up for the attack at 23:00, the preliminary bombardment was started, but hurried signals that our shots were falling short so infuriated our OP that he commanded an instant, five minute ceasefire. He was almost laughing into the microphone to report then that the short firing continued during our respite, enabling him to report smugly that the Divisional gunners had the adjusting to do. Just after midnight (14/15 April), however, all firing was abruptly stopped when it was reported that 9 Commando were ready and anxious to attack the bridge well before the arranged fire plan was due to be lifted. They found the bridge intact, and had succeeded in crossing with about half a dozen men when the bridge was blown up with delayed action fuses.

All hell was let loose by the guns of an enemy tank, attacking the Commandos who were poised to follow their comrades across the bridge. With casualties mounting from heavy firing on both sides, the attempt to form a bridge head was abandoned at 04:45. The two OP's – ours and the 65th Field Regiment's - got together before first light to try to spot opportunity targets for that day's shoot, but heavy morning mist ruled out such action until 10:00, when the enemy, moving about in the open, was intermittently engaged without much effect. Indeed, heavy German gun fire was put down among us for most of the day – a day in which it had been resolved that another attempt to cross the canal would be made that night at two other points, where it might be shallow enough to wade or cross in small boats. The crossings would be attempted by the Scots Guards on the left and by 9 Commando near a small transformer station to the right of the previous night's objective. As if to show his resolve to defend the crossings at whatever cost, the enemy succeeded in bringing up a patrol at dusk to make a further demolition at the main bridge, resulting in its complete destruction.

Such action seemed to do nothing to diminish the enemy's feverish resistance to that night's attempt by the Guards and 9 Commando on the alternative targets. From 23:00 to 03:00 the battle raged. Again, the attack had to be called off: all our boats and rafts had been sunk by mortar and machine gun fire, whilst wading had proved impossible in effective numbers due to the adhesive quality of the deep muddy bottom of the canal.

I have never been able to discover how this localised episode of war was resolved. 9 Commando and my own unit were withdrawn from the area on the evening of 16 April to return to Ravenna. The Queen's Regiment relieved the Commandos. Tired almost to stupefaction, we were glad to be out of it. Reaching Ravenna at 02:00, this time wholly by road, only sleep mattered. For us, 'Impact Royal' was over. Could it be the end of the Second World War for us, too? Morning would be soon enough to know: for what was left of the night, we slept.

"My first emotion was far from the modicum of rejoicing which Churchill suggested we were entitled to permit ourselves – it was one of holy terror."

Operation Roast

Meanwhile, as they say back on the spit... Section Three had had their share of action within the narrow confines of the area bounded on the west by the lake, on the east by the sea and, it seemed interminably, to the north by the still unassailable Canale Valetta. The targets for their guns had been plentiful, if mainly opportunistic rather than tactical. Targets varied from enemy working parties and conspicuously active gun crews and OPs, to a 'house in Comacchio where the Germans go for meals'. One source of constant nuisance was a mortar-harbouring cemetery. The identification of targets showed the unceasing and superb vigilance of Captain Gervers, their OP. I think the Germans must have agreed with such compliments, taking formidable measures from the north bank in an attempt to rid themselves of this persistent irritant by supplementing their normal daily onslaught of artillery and mortars on the night of 18/19 April with what amounted to our first experience of rocket fire. Their explosions left huge but shallow craters and sprayed the area with lethal fragments. They posed the question, where were their firing sites?

When we of Section Four took over from our Section Three colleagues on the spit at 15:00 on 19 April (after 60 hours 'rest' at Ravenna), that question became Lieutenant Newton's problem. His on-site conference with Captain Gervers, though certain to have originated some valid theories, happily proved needless as we were not subject to further rocket fire. The German artillery was not taking a holiday, however, and for most of that evening we were subject to heavy shelling from one or perhaps two heavy calibre guns and two 75mms, as well as mortar fire from the cemetery. As I write this, it occurs to me that I cannot recall casualties. There were victims among Section Three during their three weeks up the Spit, but I can only conclude that my unfamiliarity with the names of my new colleagues which filtered to me encouraged an easy 'but for the grace of God' detachment from the reality of such tragedies. The RSR's war diaries, too, are scant and inconsistent in the recording of casualties.

Nevertheless, escape in our immediate vicinity during those artillery duels was nothing short of remarkable. The dreaded possibility of a direct hit, which would surely have demolished us all, was treated as a fatally rare phenomenon, more akin to a strike of lightning – an absurd analogy among artillery men who understood the deftness with which a modern gunner could bracket his fire, with the combined aid of his precise instruments and shrewd observation.

At 09:50 on 20 April the first hint of an enemy withdrawal from the north bank of the Canale Valletta came in a signal from Tactical Headquarters, which suggested that the previous night's heavy shelling and mortaring was most likely a cover for a general withdrawal from positions on the opposite bank. Infiltrating Italian Partisan patrols sent out to investigate had reported however, that Porto Garibaldi was still very much in the hands of a considerable number of Germans and, indeed, the Partisans were soon signalling for help for about twenty or so of their colleagues, trapped by hostile machine gun fire in a confined area near the town's church.

We plonked over a number of smoke shells, under cover of which, and thanks to their own local knowledge, an effective escape was made with only one or two casualties. The remainder of the evening and night was uncannily quiet and, when morning came and our shelling of a pillbox and a house the previous day had brought no response, hopes rose that an enemy evacuation of the north bank had been effected.

This time our hopes were realised. At 10:30 Tactical Headquarters signalled a halt to firing whilst civilians bearing white flags approaching from Comacchio town were investigated. Their report that the town was clear of Germans prompted small boat crossings of the canal west of Porto Garibaldi by unopposed Partisan patrols. An hour later, the Italians were joyfully milling around on the canal's south bank opposite Porto Garibaldi without attracting enemy fire. We knew then that the three week long stalemate was over. Means of crossing the canal were exploited and ferrying vessels commandeered in competitive zeal before the renowned bridge building techniques of the Royal Engineers could swing into familiar action.

By afternoon Lieutenant Newton had been across and back again, bemoaning the fact that no means could be found to ferry over his Jeep to enable him to probe northwards to establish his next Observation Post. His frustration was compounded by news from Tactical Headquarters that no sightings of enemy south of Pomposa (about seven miles away to the north) had been reported, while he was firmly grounded on the south bank for the night. The fury of the man! For most of us, however, merely standing on the raised south bank represented achievement.

That afternoon we buried the bodies of two British soldiers. One we recorded as Private Crouch of the Special Boating Squadron (SBS). From reading books 40 years later, I am convinced that he must have been the Corporal Crouch (of the SBS) reported killed in the raid mounted by the SBS on the dykes leading to the town of Comacchio on 9 April, in which its flamboyant leader, Major Anders Lassen, was killed in winning Comacchio's second posthumously awarded Victoria Cross. Major Anders Lassen was a Dane, then only 24, who had already earned himself the Military Cross and two Bars.

April 22 dawned to reveal the miraculous appearance of a miscellaneous collection of dozens of craft, ranging from the sideless platform ferries (so useful to people like us with artillery pieces and Jeeps to get across) to hastily home-made floats (some of which didn't). But even such mishaps provoked taunting, humorous jibes, which recently had been in short supply. Comical, park-lake cavorting scenes were present again, but this time in an atmosphere of bustling exhilaration and 'let's get at them' enthusiasm. Our tiredness was temporarily forgotten amidst purposeful, teamwork activities, the complete opposite of the forgivable lethargy which stalemate induces. We did not need to have it explained to us that this was the bell for the last round of the fight.

Starting at 09:00, all of Four Section's guns were across within an hour: eight Jeeps sent to us from 2 Special Service Brigade HQ followed immediately. Soon after midday most of the Battery were two miles north of Porto Garibaldi at San Guiseppe, where a halt was called pending further news of the extent of the German withdrawal. At 16:00 the Battery Commander, Major Ross, arrived with the remainder of the Battery, further bolstering our collective morale. It was decided that the guns would park up in the village for the night, while reconnaissance was made in several directions. To my delight I was allocated (with a backpack radio set) to Lt. MacFadyen to explore the next village, Vaccalino. It was a trek into evening which I shall never be able to erase from my memory. It was, incidentally, the closest I came to any officer in the unit and his friendliness was a refreshing experience. I was consulted as an equal on what 'we' should do, although his intuitive grasp of the situation and apparent indifference to imminent danger exposed the vast differences in our battle experience and attitudes. By the time our expedition into the unknown had been completed, my admiration for the man bordered on hero worship.

About a mile along the wholly exposed and mainly undeviating road, a cluster of three or four houses on each side of the road raised the first question: "Well, what do we do? Risk brazening it out with a frontal approach in the middle of the road, or skirt and try to arrive among them unseen?" Lt. MacFadyen asked. I could not imagine that we could come upon the houses from any angle without being observed by anyone on vigilant lookout within. He shared this opinion. "OK. March on?" he ventured, with the suggestion of a smile and no semblance of a command. "March on," I confirmed. The smile became more than a suggestion: it was a seal of approval. The manifold display of improvised white 'flags', one dangling from almost every roadside window of each dwelling, ought to have eased my tension as we neared the houses, but it did not. Thoroughly exposed, I mused about how I could contract the whites of my eyes.

Marching on in complete silence, we had passed the first house which stood singly on the left side of the road and were proceeding between the first two houses opposite when something of a verbal commotion erupted from the house on the left. "Inglesi! Inglesi!" It was a female voice and belonged to an excited elderly lady who emerged, soon to be followed by her equally agitated, and apparently even more elderly, male partner. Their alarm was more obvious, in the flow of jabbering Italian which poured from each of them, than the joy of liberation which might have been more to be expected. A proliferation of, "Attenzione! Attenzione!" stopped us in our tracks. Although our normal vision could have been called into question if we had not observed the crudely laid mines across the road a few yards further ahead, our hearts went out to the old couple who, it transpired, had been looking out for the liberators since the departing Germans had hurriedly sown their final, lethal crop twenty four hours earlier. The leading vehicle of a night convoy might easily have fallen victim to the odious menace: a vehicular hold up would have resulted even if the mines had been spotted in time. Even more useful information was forthcoming from the endearing old couple. Behind the houses, the rocket firing site was revealed which had been abandoned only 24 hours earlier. One problem solved!

With our best 'Grazies', we thanked the two Italians. We stopped only for as long as it took to signal news of our discoveries back to San Guiseppi and, gingerly skirting the mines, we moved on towards our intended destination – as we were anxious to get on before darkness fell. The identical dilemma confronted us at the approach to Vaccalino, but 'March on!' was barely a subject for discussion. I signalled that we were going in. The village houses lined both sides of the road in the haphazard dispersal typical of a Saxmundham or a Deddington, as I remembered them in 1941. Not a living soul could be seen or heard as we entered this eerie avenue of slightly fluttering, white flags of peaceful submission. If there had been room for humour in my mind I would have thought, 'like Aberdeen on a flag-day'. Had the village merely been evacuated in anticipation of an Allied preliminary bombing or shelling to precede the imminent entry of our infantry and armour? Instinct told us not.

There was no escaping the uncanny feeling of scores of eyes anxiously scrutinising us. Ridiculously, we discussed this impression in corner-of-the-mouth whispers, which contrasted with the clattering of our army boots as we strode side by side, down the middle of the road, deep into the village. The murmurings of human voices began rather like the first sound of a high, distant aircraft approaching from the rear. We turned to look behind us and were not surprised to see heads popping out from windows and doorways like quizzical rabbits emerging from burrows.

Then, gradually, the people made their tentative appearance. Cumulative questioning and answering whispers were the start of the ascending babble; opinions were being voiced; decisions were being made. And then – yes! We were the liberators – perhaps not the mass of victorious marching columns and trundling trucks they had dreamt of for months as the termination of occupation, but they decided that we were unmistakeably the British. Here at last! Only two of them, but they'll do! In seconds, we were engulfed in chattering, cheering, hugging, kissing and weeping confusion, as the population emerged from its brick and mortar observation posts, from which our progress along the road had been observed for probably as much as the last half mile of our walk. German stragglers had infrequently passed through the village during the previous 24 hours, hence the anxious, concealed spotters who wanted to be sure. Then, amazingly, came the most incongruous sound of all: "Where've yow bin?" assailed us in the broadest of Birmingham accents from an almost reprimanding, middle aged lady.

A smothering kiss from her delayed my answer, however, before she answered herself by explaining that we had been eagerly expected a day earlier. I thought that her astonishing presence there made my obvious question more deserving of answer than her rhetorical one. She just had time to start explaining that she had married an Italian just before the war. Then representatives of officialdom pushed their way through the crowds and were marshalling us to the village bar, not primarily for drinks – although they duly materialised – but to show-off their cowering prisoners.

'Officialdom', in truth, had probably enjoyed not much longer tenure of the village than we had. They represented Partisans infiltrated from due north who had asserted instant control over the hapless, leaderless villagers, newly freed from the yoke of German occupation. For all that, they were just as much a part of the celebration and moving emotions of gladness and relief which followed. Perhaps it would be an exaggeration to say that the prisoners were glad to see us, but there was no mistaking the momentary expression of relief which our British uniforms evoked, more particularly from the four alleged Italian Fascists among them. The reasons for their relief were soon to be comprehended. The remaining six wore German uniforms, but were mainly pathetic specimens of the Turkoman unit which had provided so much of the opposition on the spit. One of the Germans was a Russo-German interpreter, who was anxious to integrate himself by passing on as much information as possible regarding troop dispositions, weaponry and minefields. Almost in unison, they had risen to their feet in a gesture of appeal to us to take them away from their fearsome custodians, whose appearance did not belie them.

The captors were not deficient in guile either, being aware that the captives in German uniform had to be seen to be benefiting from Geneva Convention protective treatment, but knowing, too, that we were powerless to restrain them in their treatment of their own nationals. With totally gratuitous brutality, the Fascists were bludgeoned to the ground – blatant cruelty which disturbs me to think of even today. Only the absence of knowledge, then and now, of how justified the tit was for the tat, eases my conscience at doing nothing to stop this overt display of barbarism against these defenceless wretches, presumably carried out to impress us. Accidentally or anonymously spilt blood is ugly enough; the violence of this occasion, and the seeming pleasure with which the scene was enacted, was sickening, just sickening. You will have gathered, I was a pathetic warrior. Drinks helped! And there were plenty of drinks, which swelled our tin God image as much as our bladders. Gratefully, we were spared the decision making.

As darkness fell we were signalled back to San Guiseppi, with instructions not to lumber ourselves with prisoners, who would be collected on the morrow when the troops in strength would take over the village. Conversation was minimal as we marched briskly back, relaxed and without the tentativeness which had attended the outward venture. The darkness, to which our eyes soon became accustomed, obscured any possible intrusions into our personal reflections during a varied and illuminating couple of hours. One of the things we had learnt from the prisoners was that Pomposa was virtually clear of Germans, which encouraged the impatient Partisans of the Garibaldi Brigade in San Guiseppi to push on northwards that night.

Major Ross decided that we would spend the night in San Guiseppi, and withdraw the next morning south to Ravenna to utilise the better network of newly accessible roads west of the lake, in order to join the then accelerating pursuit of the northward retreating Germans. The chase was on! It was a chase not merely to complete the annihilation of German might in Italy – the only logical purpose of which we were aware at the time – but also for an important political reason of which we were blissfully ignorant for a long time to come. The goal was to reach Trieste before the rapidly advancing Partisan forces of Marshall Tito, who were driving westwards through north-western Yugoslavia – virtually unopposed. South Slav designs on annexing this area of Italy, as one of the prizes of victory, had apparently been common knowledge among the Allied leaders. Presumably, on the proverbial principle that possession is nine tenths of the law, whichever power first occupied the area stood the better prospect of retaining it.

By noon the next day (23 April) we were back at Ravenna, delayed ironically by temporary difficulties in recrossing the Valetta canal, this time from north to south, on one of the improvised 'ferries'. Two hours later the whole Troop was belting unexpectedly north on a relatively unimpeded Route 16 heading for Codigoro, a small town no further north than Pomposa, but considered easier to reach via Alphonsine, Argenta, Porto Maggiore (where we had a brew up break), San Vito and Migliarino. Codigoro would provide a better platform for further advance. Due to the post-war growth of the region as an area of seaside holiday resorts, a modern main road due northwards from Ravenna to Venice now takes the coastal route through Pomposa, not via Codigoro, and actually includes an impressive fly over across the vital Canale Valetta at Porto Garibaldi. How times change!

We had travelled about 60 miles that day in 1945 to end up only about ten miles from the San Guiseppi we had left 24 hours earlier. Our three ton supply vehicles could not be ferried across the Po River tributary at Massa Fiscaglia, a mile or two short of Codigoro, where the drivers cursed in totally unreasonable impatience for the morrow. Then, the splendidly efficient Royal Engineers would sling a Bailey bridge across what to them was a mere temporary, if challenging, obstacle. Interestingly, our role in this area was in support of the Cremona Group, a unit made up of regular Italian Army soldiers. It had been assembled to operate under Allied military command as a disciplined uniformed military unit (distinct from Partisan guerrillas, who had their own useful role to play).

By 07:00 the next morning (24 April) our OP had found targets for us to blast in support of the Cremona Italians, who had left Codigoro at first light to attack a village to the west of the town, and Ariano, about six miles to the north, where the Germans were making their next stand. It did not last long. The three ton lorries reached us by 09:00 with ammunition, water etcetera, and our guns were in position and firing on machine gun positions in Ariano until noon, when the town was entered by infantry. It was taken with its main road bridge intact, but not before our very own OP team had had their share of street fighting, using their Bren gun like hardened infantrymen.

In spite of the volatility of the situation, signals were passing with immaculate efficiency and I was beginning to revel in my unaccustomed usefulness which, although far from matching the confident slickness of my admirably expert colleagues, considerably reduced the feeling of being more burdensome than valuable which had typified my early days with the Battery. Such was my growing familiarity with procedures and with my improved dexterity as a radio operator, that I joined with the rest of the gun party's clamour for another gun with which to join in the fight. A Troop's manageable establishment of weaponry stood for nought in the disarray of the enemy's retreat and our harassing pursuit. Surely, in the battlefield turmoil, an abandoned enemy artillery piece could be salvaged and added to our fire power? The bureaucrats at desks in Woolwich Arsenal or Whitehall need never know. Sure enough, the OP Jeep duly trundled onto the gun site towing a 75mm anti-tank gun together with a small supply of ammunition. I cannot recall whether the gun came without sights, or whether the sights it came with were deemed inoperable due to our ignorance of how to use them, but I loved the touch of whimsy when, after the formal fire instructions for the battery guns came over the air from the OP, they were followed by such unconventional (and sometimes, frenetic) signals as, "Cook's Gun" – as our weapon was aptly designated. "Cock the bloody thing up a bit!" Too often, it seemed, our merely directionally 'pointed' shots came too close to the OP for comfort.

Any notion that the enemy was finished is discounted by the records which show that the guns of 12 Troop fired 700 rounds on the day of Ariano's taking. The targets were stubborn pockets of resistance, including Spandau nests, infantry FDLs and anti-tank guns which had already claimed two of the Cremona Group's Bren carriers at San Basilo after the crossing of the bridge – but progress was inexorable. Our gun positions were changing almost hourly. The Italians took fifty prisoners that day and captured much weaponry, including two of the offending anti-tank guns.

One evening, during this skirmish and chase period, we were able to relax over our freshly brewed tea and even find enjoyment in the undisturbed consumption of our by then monotonous compo rations. We sat on the incongruously still intact, beautiful, mosaic patio floor of what remained of an elegant North Italian villa. The obstinate German troops had evacuated it only a few hours earlier. With the rumbling of new artillery battles then reassuringly distant, only the delightful, soothing sound of the territorially impartial birds' songs intruded the local silence. As if by mutual agreement, conversation seemed superfluous; each of us, in his own way, reflected again on survival through another day towards victory and peace. It was all so tranquil. At least it was until the man I shall call Phillips appeared on the scene. Phillips was the single, battle shy irritant in 'E' Battery, and I had been warned about his capacity to skive off when things became dangerous. With patently exaggerated casualness, he had dropped his question carefully – too carefully, for our liking.

"Why aren't we burying that dead Jerry outside?"

"Where?" we chorused in complete, spontaneous unison – a predictably concerted reaction of surprise after we had spent a few hours rounding up the miserable, acquiescent prisoners and locating their dead for them to bury. It annoyed us enough to think we could have missed one of them, but the thought that 'Windy' Phillips had detected such a lapse made our disbelief more a matter of wishful thinking. He must be mistaken.

"He's in the slit trench in the front garden," the posturing Phillips answered with irritating nonchalance. "Come on, I'll show you," he added.

Exhausted as we were, the five of us were soon on our feet, our curiosity prompting us to follow the by then positively strutting Phillips into the garden. He was right! The German was in a half upright position in the trench with his head slumped onto his chest, wholly out of sight to anyone not actually at the trench side. I felt sure I had looked there and mentally chastised myself for this embarrassing aberration. But before we had time to communicate our incredulity or indulge in any self recrimination, Phillips had gone – gone like a madman, disappearing on the double into the villa at the speed of a frightened gazelle. Again, there was no time to register our surprise, beyond our glances of bewilderment and questioning, shoulder shrugging gestures, before he emerged with undiminished pace but this time brandishing a Sten gun, which he was fumbling to cock as he raced towards us.

Surely to God, he wasn't going to riddle the already lifeless body? (It occurred to me that a dead German would be the only one he would tackle.) There has to be some dignity in death, even with one's enemies. He must be stopped! He was still incoherently jabbering with excitement as we brought him down, disarmed him and demanded an explanation for such extraordinary behaviour. After all, he was unlikely to be suffering from what might otherwise appear to be the symptoms of battle fatigue.

He struggled to speak, the words coming only with the difficulty of one in a state of fear. "The last time..." he gulped, "...the last time I saw him," he pointed to the German, "he... he... he didn't have a helmet on." It didn't take long to discover that our 'dead' German was, in truth, a sleeping one. Obviously, he had crawled into the trench for safety from some undetected, but less secure refuge after our search, but before Phillips emerged from his personal funk hole and spotted him during his cosy stroll around the then cleared garden. No doubt Phillip's movements had briefly awakened the German enough to cause him to replace his helmet subconsciously. Then, dimly aware that he seemed to be in a blissfully peaceful sanctuary, he had lapsed into a deep sleep of exhaustion, from which we had great difficulty in rousing him. Phillips never lived it down.

25 April was notable for a couple of unconnected reasons. It was the day when the south bank of the River Po itself was reached by the Cremona infantry, and by our own indefatigable OP. Having spotted entrenched Germans only 300 yards from the north bank, he ordered our guns within range at a place called Letombe and by noon we were engaging this target and others, including a factory area from which firing had earlier been observed. Somewhat dangerously, he directed our fire to some south bank targets still harbouring Germans. He must have had supreme confidence in our ability not to wander in our aim. Naturally, the erratic 'Cook's Gun' was excluded from the fire plan. Considerable small arms fire heard on the right was soon explained as the work of the Partisans. The 28th Garibaldi Brigade obviously wanted a share of the Cremona Group's glory.

The day's second incident of note was the remarkable appearance on the scene of the RSR's Commanding Officer, Lieutenant-Colonel Meynell. Although he had been in command of the Regiment since November, when he had taken over from Lieutenant-Colonel Devitt, it was the first time I had seen him – and, as it happened, the last. Without the slightest knowledge of his previous record or proven prowess, it would be wholly wrong of me to express an opinion about him in either of these aspects. Perhaps I had been in the wrong places when he had put himself about.

There is, however, one act of his for which I shall never forgive him. It was he who had immediately decided that our beige coloured berets were not distinctive enough, although they had aptly and correctly associated us with our similarly 'lidded' airborne sister units of the Special Air Service, Special Boat Squadron and (the reformed) Long Range Desert Group, all of Middle East origins. He had all our berets dyed brown. From that date onwards, the Raiding Support Regiment had no readily discernable affinity with any other unit: one had to be near enough to read the regimental title flashes on our shoulders to guess even our nationality, let alone our Special Service role. Even at close proximity, identification was not always correctly made. Unaccountably, we were henceforth regularly confused with Polish troops. I remember on my first home leave after the war's end, stepping off a Glasgow tram car and hearing the conductress being contemptuously assailed by her off duty companion with, "There ye are! I telt ye it could no' be the Rangers' Supporters Regiment."

26 and 27 April were exciting for those involved, yet frustrating in their relative military fruitlessness at a time when we almost demanded swift achievement of ourselves. The rivers continued to be the obstacles to any rapid pursuit of a gradually disintegrating enemy resistance. Queues at the Po and later the Adige would have been barriers enough, with limited ferrying capacity available, but an untimely order from Brigade Headquarters, recalling our very generous allocation of Jeeps, meant that we would only move forward one section at a time. That meant doubling back and rejoining queues which showed a typically British preference for first come, first served, before considering any question of military priority. Perhaps it had merit in diplomatically avoiding arguments about priority. There was a gloriously fluid confusion about those two days: I have chosen the words carefully. Fluid it surely was, but for once it was a confusion marked less by fear or inefficiency than by sheer ebullience. The glory came from the realisation that we were, at long, long last, without the slightest doubt, winning.

Once the Allies had crossed the Po, the enemy's subsequent rear guard actions were deemed less significant in delaying our advance than were the physical bulwarks of the rivers themselves. We became conscious of being part of a much wider scenario: overhead, our unopposed bombers and fighters were devastatingly active; around us, Eighth Army Divisional signs, so reassuringly familiar from Middle East days, confirmed our more comprehensive involvement. Stunned and exhausted prisoners were beginning to wander through our lines in such profusion that no one seemed to have time to round them up. It must have been reminiscent of the scenes just prior to the Dunkirk evacuation, but with the roles reversed. As soon as we crossed a river or canal we were in action. Our OPs were finding targets galore. Ammunition supply difficulties aggravated our impatience at any minimising of our effectiveness, yet several hundreds of rounds were being fired each day.

All the bridges across the Po had been blown, yet within eight hours of the first Allied infantry crossing in assault boats (at 05:30 on 26 April) we had our guns across and, by 17:00, had one gun in action north of the evacuated town of Adria. By the 28 the south bank of the Adige had been reached at San Pietro, with the enemy already completely out of range. An early crossing with the guns then proved to be impossible, and by 20:30 all intention to do so was abandoned until strengthened ferry vessels could be found. We had reached the end of our northwards progress – we had, indeed, virtually reached the end of our war, although we were not aware of it then.

The following day, whilst the guns were directed to move south to Il Bosco and apparent inactivity, the OP party had the envied satisfaction of being asked to join the 56th Division's right flank probing column (comprising four tanks, several tracked Bren carriers and a Company of the Queen's Regiment) in a drive towards Venice. They actually reached Mestre, before a defiant last stand by the enemy blocked any further advance – at least until those reliable stalwarts of the Italian campaign, the New Zealand 2nd Division's street-fighting veterans arrived on the scene to deliver the coup-de-grâce.

The RSR's contribution in Italy ended near Mira, fittingly in a skirmish involving those other notorious cavaliers of Special Forces, Popski's Private Army, whose two casualties that day were probably the unit's last in the Second World War. When the OP party, cheated of their sight of Venice, was ordered back via Padua to join us at Il Bosco, 'E' Battery became wholly re-integrated and ready to start its ordered return to Ravenna.

Starting at 09:00 the next morning, the tedious recrossing of the Po seemed to take an age in the tricky, vehicle by vehicle stowing on the ferrying rafts. Our testy impatience owed more to postponing the prospect of sleep in a bed, than to the absence of the stimulus which had attended the outward, though even more improvised, crossing. By nightfall my war had ended in dreary anti climax with our arrival at the billets in Ravenna. In desperate search of sleep, I resolved that I would attend to the world 'tomorrow' – 1 May 1945.

Two days later the German forces in Italy formally surrendered, following 24 hours of near farcical discussion about who was competent among them to tender formal surrender. It was really academic, because by then most of their senior officers, including General von Arnim, had already given themselves up to the Italian Partisans in the region of Padua. Their forces in Yugoslavia held out for only a few more days – a very significant few days of political tension involving the critical issue of the occupancy of Trieste: another story! On 8 May – thenceforth known as VE Day (Victory in Europe) – the whole German nation capitulated. Hitler had killed himself in his Berlin bunker. Mussolini's lifeless body was hanging upside down, alongside that of his mistress, Clara Petacci, in the Piazzale Loreto at Milan, their bodies still being grossly violated. Italian Communists had executed them as they had vainly tried to flee to asylum across the Swiss border. It really was all over, at last!

The broadcasting of Churchill's historic announcement of the end of hostilities in Europe has since been repeated so many times that I honestly cannot remember if it was the original transmission I heard, though it is extremely unlikely that it was. However, the finality of its message was too well disseminated, too effectively documented and too epoch-making in its implications to remove any lingering suspicion that it might be yet another rumour, although disbelief was understandable. I recall being alone and sitting on the edge of my self-made bed in the school at Ravenna. My first emotion was far from the modicum of rejoicing which Churchill suggested we were entitled to permit ourselves – it was one of holy terror. If there are any acceptable justifications for self-centredness, comprehensive involvement in a battle must surely be one of them. Any relief I felt at survival was suddenly neutralised by the realisation that, although I had luckily escaped Scot free, nobody at home knew of it. I had forgotten about everyone else. Had I even told them that I had left hospital? (Old letters reveal that I had).

In a way, I had also forgotten about myself, at least to the extent of ignoring what five weeks in action had done to my already weakened constitution. I was sick from delayed action fear, too. 47 years later, in April 1992, I attended a commemorative reunion in the Comacchio area as a guest of veterans of the Italian Army's Cremona Group – an invitation they had made to 43 RM Commando which was extended to me. The almost mandatory visit on these occasions to the war cemeteries, this time to those at Argenta and Ravenna, made me recall – and repeat – the shudder of relief which vibrated through my frame that day in May 1945 when the foolhardiness of my volunteering to be there, and exposing myself to such avoidable risks, had finally penetrated my understanding. The dates on those gravestones brought all this back to me. I hadn't realised how many men had died in that last week of April 1945. Their families would have been celebrating the end of hostilities before the War Office could possibly have had time to confirm and communicate the news of those tragic deaths. I know that the life of a fatal war casualty is just as effectively extinguished whether he was killed on the first or last day of a war, but oh, the poignancy of a last lap demise!

The days which immediately followed the end of hostilities in Europe were days of forgivable anticlimax. We weren't recently experienced in a peaceful existence. Only the fearsome prospect of then having to concentrate all of our resources on the complete defeat of Japan in the Far East niggled against the almost alarming possibility of going home. I dreaded the former and had my moments of anxiety about the latter, dearly as I craved to see home again after three years of wondering if I ever would.

Blighty signalled the imminent need for the sort of decisions which I knew I was pathetically ill-equipped to make, and which left me in limp indecision. "We'll just have to wait and see." Why worry about matrimonial possibilities before ensuring that the faces still fitted? Why concern myself about post-war jobs when my only work experience – and that well forgotten in six years – was in a commercial avenue which showed all the signs of being a cul-de-sac? Prophetic reasoning! The Liverpool Cotton Exchange was one of the first avowed casualties of the Socialist era which resulted from the 1945 General Election, when I had contributed my proxy vote to put Labour in power.

Where would I live if the outcome of either of those posers meant that I could not live in the family home in Fleetwood! Then my thoughts strayed to the millions of Joe James', Malcolm Simpsons and Paddy Haydens who would not be around to worry about such trivia – and I had a little cry. Well, more than a little really; it just flowed. It was as though I needed to shed tears – a sort of duty to pay tribute to them, although spontaneous and uncontrollable.

I honestly cannot remember any kind of Victory celebration. Much less significant happenings in the past would have proved the excuse for a booze up. Perhaps all the 'knees up' sessions were in areas where fighting had ceased much earlier, or at home where the finality of it all was concentrated on the day of the actual announcement. Our recent involvement in the fighting must have had a sobering effect, for when we learned that we were to return to the Bari area almost immediately we could not get away from Ravenna quickly enough.

I think that it must have been my physical condition which prompted to someone that I should be on the advance party. The strange thing is that I was the advance party, and although I can clearly remember driving well that solo, 400 mile journey in a Jeep on 12 May, I cannot recall what my terms of reference were, nor could I imagine what use I could have been without some substantial authority. Perhaps 'E' Battery merely wanted to rid themselves of me in my physical condition as a potential casualty, but I was back with them again within a few days, presumably in possession of some valuable information to the convoy for its journey south. The trip was unnecessarily extended to take a couple of extra, deviously routed days, mainly to reconnoitre as many NAAFI establishments as could be found on the way. Here the yarns were spun, shamelessly exaggerating our sustained period in military action which had denied us access to any NAAFI rations of beer and cigarettes for weeks on end. Sometimes it worked – true as it nearly was – but for some inexplicable reason every NAAFI in Italy seemed to have no other beer than Guinness that week. (Only officers and senior NCOs could draw spirits.) Guinness was not to everyone's taste, but nobody refused a NAAFI ration and I found myself buying options which left me with three cases of the stuff by the end of the journey.

This coincided nicely with my rejoining 'C' Battery, then installed right alongside the Adriatic in the dilapidated former monastery of San Vito, just a couple of miles south of Mola-de-Bari. There I was given the extraordinarily explicit, yet most unmilitary instructions, to 'relax'. With cases of Guinness beneath my bunk bed, the seemingly ever present, glorious sunshine of Southern Italy in May and superb swimming facilities in a clear Adriatic at hand, without having to leave the camp, the life of Old Riley was at last mine, whilst I obeyed to the letter the command to unwind.

From the date of my appointment to the near sinecure of the job as NCO in charge of food rations, my health improved and rapidly began to restore me to normal weight and vigour. I had learnt a few tricks at transit camps about inflating the numbers of the camp's personnel for rationing purposes. Each day, I appeared with my truck at the Royal Army Service Corp's food rations' supply depot, housed under the arches of Bari's magnificent sports stadium, where my guilt must have shown but my figures of personnel were never challenged. Perhaps the normally stringent service Corps clerks had seen and been sympathetically affected by some of the Order of the Day accolades which were soon being put out by High Command in recognition of our services. It will surprise nobody to learn that those most unmilitary of regimental instructions – to simply 'relax' – were carried out with a thoroughness and enthusiasm rarely encountered in the Army.

Sun, sand, sea (and additionally, for me, stout) by day; Bari, beanos and booze (mainly Vermouth) by night. Only guard duties on the monastery and the tasks necessary for feeding a regiment had to be performed; the other batteries had drawn the short straws that would see them on irksome prisoner of war camp guard duties. After about a month or so of this real hedonism, the short 'honeymoon' was abruptly ended. Not knowing quite what to do with us, the War Office eventually – and probably, sensibly – decided that the Raiding Support Regiment had completed the job for which it had been formed in Palestine two years earlier. Instructions were issued for the Regiment to be disbanded forthwith. Field Marshal Alexander, in a communication dated 26 June, said that he "was indeed sorry" and he added: "The famous fighting reputation you have made for yourselves in this theatre is an enviable one and I shall always be proud that you served under my command." This rather flattering compliment was conveyed to us by the Regiment's Commanding Officer (by written notice, of course) when informing us of the War Office's decision and the practicalities of its implementation. The most important 'practicality' from the men's point of view was home leave.

We were to be sent off in groups at weekly intervals for a month's leave in Blighty. Two months later there would be, so to speak, no 'green bottles on the wall', (not even my Guinness empties). After our leave came to an end we would have to return to Italy. We were dismayed by that decision, and some reacted with belligerence and anger, but when we had calmed down we could understand the reason for it. The work of armies of occupation was just beginning. The maintenance of internal law and order, the controlled distribution of essential supplies such as food, the restoration of the public utilities such as power, light, water, and telephones, and the supervision and redirection of prisoners of war and displaced persons, were all matters which would require vast 'armies' to organise and control. That work would go on until a constitutional civil government could take over from our alien, military administration.

Most of us were well aware of all that. Nevertheless, we felt that it ought to be somebody else's job. "We've done our whack!" was another variant of the 'why me?' syndrome – a common affliction in the Services. Perhaps it was the remarkable concession which had been attached to the order that averted the riot. The promise was that we would be treated as the very special troops we had been, and be offered choice in the jobs we were to perform for the remainder of our service! With 'old soldier' scepticism, we could not believe that we would be anything other than anonymous numbers, rather than persons, when dumped in Royal Artillery, Infantry, Royal Engineer base camps or transit camps, once we were back in Italy unitless. Ah! but wait, there was yet another sinister proviso. Excluded from all these arrangements were to be "…those of you who might be required for service in the Far East."

It had never been too distant in our minds that Japan was showing no signs of capitulation, though by then she was taking a severe mauling from the Americans in the Pacific. We knew nothing then of atomic bombs. Furthermore, the likely qualifications (or disqualifications) for service in the Far East were unknown to us. I endured the period of waiting to find out, with a dread akin to taking a stroll through a minefield. Happily, my fears proved to be unfounded: I did not go to the Far East, nor can I recall any of the RSR being sent there.

So it was that on 27 July 1945 I found myself on a crowded, northbound, military train that would take me to a huge barracks complex in Milan's suburbs, for assembly with thousands of other servicemen. There we waited for the train to take us home for the month's leave we had been promised. Emotion and excitement must have been the dominant sensations because I cannot recall my travel companions, nor can I even remember what must have been touching partings from men who had been my friends for a year and a half, and whom I would probably never see again.

Even with the authorising travel and destination documents in my pocket, and with all the signs of imminent fulfilment – notably the special leave complex itself – there was still an air of doubt pervading the very atmosphere. I can remember spending a leisurely day strolling around the city of Milan, wholly enthralled at the magnificence of Il Duomo (the cathedral) and that most imposing of railway stations. I also recall strolling through the nearby arcade of shops, marvelling at the fanciful display of luxury goods whilst pondering upon the source of their supply in a war ravaged Italy. The crowded, special troop train on which I left Milan for Switzerland seemed like a magic carpet to paradise, in spite of a slightly niggling apprehension which competed with the more obvious mantle of relief and happy expectancy which clothed us all.

We had all been taken away and compelled to spend several years of our young adulthood far from family, friends and home. It must be difficult for anyone who has not had that experience to understand how anxiety could in any way intrude on the overwhelming sense of relief, which truly attended the realisation that we were going home at last. But it did – and some prophetic justification, as it happened. However, my mind was soon diverted from such intangible worries by the dramatic impact of the grandeur of the Italian Alpine scenery, which seemed to be on show for my especial appreciation during a couple of hours at the beautifully located mountain town of Domodossola, where we were allowed off the train expressly to receive and enjoy a remarkably well organised and amply satisfying meal. Domodossola seemed to have been unblemished by the war – an admirable choice for a journey break. Then Switzerland!

Cleanliness, orderliness, efficiency, no shortages and, above all, astounding natural beauty were the immediate, inescapable signs of a European world I had never known. I think I could be forgiven for thinking that here, in the very heart of a devastated Europe, had been planted a haven of peace and plenty to display what living could be like if nations would cease the nonsense of self destruction. The Swiss hydroelectric-powered train of impeccable cleanliness and bewildering modernity sped on its barely vibrating way across that magnificent panorama of mountains and lakes. I feel sure that it stopped at more town stations than were necessary for our journey, merely to expose us to maximum mass feting by the local people. Ours was certainly not the inaugural 'special' leave train, yet the platforms were massed with elegantly groomed – and above all, generous Swiss, who bestowed on us gifts of food, confectionery, cigarettes and drinks, as if we were the first great saviours of mankind.

Strangely, this bounteous display of capitalist affluence failed to incite in me any feelings of envy or covetousness, even though I had just used my first voting rights (by Forces proxy) to help elect a Socialist government. The Swiss experience was simply one of sheer wonderment, perhaps only comparable with my similar acceptance of such unattainable delights from the Hollywood dream factories of the 1930s.

Only in one respect was the Hollywood analogy fortunately faulty: the glamorous, female, fashion plate allure we encountered on the platforms might have been fleeting, but for that moment it was real, not a mere celluloid image of such charm. The Swiss girls hailed us (invariably in faultless English) and to prove their reality, they responded, not merely soliloquised; they smiled at us in a universal language of joy. This glimpse of paradise ended abruptly at the Swiss border. It was a treasured experience whose uniqueness, in deprived lives such as ours, made it too remote to either 'spoil' us or fire us with ambition or covetousness. It was simply another unreal world that one could never imagine ever seeing again.

Predictably, war had left depressing scars of devastation on the places through which we had passed on our journey across France. It had also affected the demeanour of its people. Come the evening of that eventful day, the train having been shunted into a secluded siding, I slept my first night in France (after an excellent meal) on the floor of a village schoolroom, sharing the experience with hundreds of other dumbstruck troops. Once again, the halt had been arranged and administered with commendable efficiency, which cushioned the few rather ungracious comparisons of this remote, austere and rather sad, suffering village with the splendour of Domodossola. It had filled its function well – and after all, who cared? Blighty tomorrow

Return Home

Halfway across the Channel, I flung overboard my .38 Browning pistol with a sadness which might have deserved to have been associated with the loss of an old friend. Unaccountable sentiment for loot! There had been just one too many dire warnings on the ship's Tannoy system, about the horrors awaiting anyone caught smuggling unauthorised fire arms into the country. I had ignored the final amnesty concession notice at Boulogne, where I had been quite prepared to risk it. Cowardice caught up with me at sea. Well, it was a sort of compromise cowardice. My smooth, palm-fitting .22 Beretta pistol, seemed to be worth the risk; the crude, conspicuous Browning, was not. The Beretta would not be easy to spot even in a search; the huge, ugly Browning would be difficult to miss.

Nevertheless, it was a tormenting decision which resulted in the .38 glugging to the bottom of the Channel, probably to join a few others, instead of gracing the mantelpiece as a trophy of war. As might be expected, there was the mental shin kicking when there was not the slightest suggestion of a searching at Folkstone. Commendably, all the efforts of organisation had been put into rapidly boarding us into the waiting trains seemingly poised to get us home as quickly as possible. Without any delay our train was speeding through the Kent countryside, heading for London's Victoria Station. Houses en route still displayed 'Welcome Home' posters and flew Union Jacks, which oddly reminded me, with no little emotion, of the send off of the Scottish dockers as the 'Awatea' slipped down the Clyde, to who knew where or what, three years earlier, when indisputably we were losing the war.

I was to return to Italy at the end of my leave and would have another seven months to serve on the Continent before I was demobilised, but I consider that my story really ought to end in 1945, with my arrival home on leave in one piece. However, if you have read this far, I flatter myself that you would not need to be an avid reader of Mills & Boon novels to be interested in the romantic consequences of my homecoming. I could hardly leave you in suspense on that score.

You will recall that Anne and I became engaged to be married on 6 October 1944, while I was serving in Albania. I had last seen her in May 1942. As soon as I reached my new family home in Fleetwood, I dashed off a letter to announce my arrival. Like most homes at that time, we did not enjoy the luxury of a private telephone: romance had to rely on the postal service. A hasty and excitable exchange of letters soon fixed the arrangements for me to spend some of my leave at her home in what the wartime censor would have called 'an East Coast Port'.

My fiancée and I duly met at the main railway station in her home city. After being apart for so long, we both wondered whether we would we be able to recognize each other? Would surprised travellers be treated to the hackneyed Hollywood romantic version of the returning serviceman's homecoming? We all know the sort of thing: the worried peering into the milling throng, the tentative sighting, the momentary uncertainty, the headlong rush towards each other – checked just in time to avoid a damaging collision – and all culminating in a long, emotional embrace. Instead, we recognised one another without difficulty. After all, there could not have been many soldiers in that city wearing the distinctive brown beret of the Raiding Support Regiment. We 'pecked' clumsily, grasped trembling hands, and conversed nervously about such banalities as the quality of my train journey, the vagaries of the weather and the regularity of the buses needed to take us to her home.

I experienced all the sensations of pent up ardour, but it just did not seem to be the time or the place to demonstrate it. My fiancée must have thought that way, too. Neither of us was a demonstrative person but, whatever our individual motives might have been for controlling our emotions – even if only that good old English reserve – control them we did.

Before I had been sent abroad, I had not had a chance to meet any of my sweetheart's family, so introductions had to be made when we reached her home. I recall with crystal clarity the warm welcome I received from her mother, a charming, lovely woman who still looked surprisingly young. There must have been several other members of the large family present, but I am ashamed to say that I cannot honestly remember any of them now. The man I already thought of as my future father-in-law was still serving at sea in the Navy. I always regret not having met him. His reputation and his letters to me marked him as a responsible and rightly proud family man, possessed of a wry sense of humour and a shrewd worldliness. I like to think that we would have been close friends.

I may have been rather anxious, hesitant and preoccupied, but I could not fail to notice that my future wife's radiant beauty had been enhanced by a self assured maturity which, happily, did not completely mask the many reminders of the demure charm, and wide eyed, impressionable and innocent youthfulness which had attracted me three-and-a-half years earlier. We dined, and passed away the evening in small talk and exchanging comfortable platitudes. Nevertheless, that first evening was bound to involve a certain amount of nervous tension, and I was relieved when it was time to retire to bed. I guessed that she was also glad to get the first evening of our reunion safely out of the way. Any lingering doubts I might have had about our engagement had been completely dispelled: indeed, I could hardly believe my own good fortune. How long would it take to finish the war against Japan? What kind of job would I be able to get in 'Civvy Street' after demobilisation? How would my future employment affect my long nurtured ambition for our early marriage? These were the kind of questions which disturbed my mind and made it difficult to get to sleep that night.

At breakfast it was obvious that my girl had been crying, and her mother's pleasing calm had given way to deep concern. A family crisis? Bad news about one of them? It had been decided that my fiancée and I would take an early morning walk, obviously to give her an opportunity to give me a private explanation of whatever was troubling them. Between the front door and the garden gate, I became very worried to see her obvious anguish as she again became engulfed in tears. Through the tears she unburdened herself of the heartbreaking news she had to impart. It was obviously a painful task for her. She did it in few words, but with implacable resolve. She told me that I was not at all what she had been expecting. As soon as we met, she had known instantly that the reality did not match the dream. After talking it over with her mother, she had decided that I must be informed of her disillusionment at once. To record merely that this news left me stunned is probably a classic understatement. It also provides a clue to the reasons for my rejection. I was in a situation that I could neither fathom nor effectively deal with. I was simply demolished. It never occurred to me to say, "Well, go on then, tell me what the Hell's wrong with me," in the hope that I might miraculously have been able to put things right. I could only say, "All right, if that's how things are, when do you want me to go – now, tomorrow or when?", or something like that. The totally defeatist 'hero'! "You can't go today! Please, not today!", she implored. "We must have at least the day and the evening together to talk about this." And that is what we did, but we never managed to 'talk about this'.

She would not or, as she subsequently insisted, could not offer any explanation beyond the generalisation that I was quite 'different' from the image of me she had conjured up from my letters, spread over three long years. I have never been quite sure whether she succeeded in her noble efforts to spare my feelings. I sometimes think I would have preferred to have heard the worst, though I'd heard quite enough.

We spent the evening in a cinema in the city. There my tentative caresses and pent up longing were soon replaced by self-restraint as I realised, that her unresponsive acquiescence arose only from pity. That night I suffered from an embarrassing and inexplicable nosebleed, which left blood all over my pillow. It was almost unstoppable, and I disturbed the whole household with my efforts to staunch the flow and mop up afterwards. I suspect that the whole scene might have suggested – if only briefly – that I had cut my throat! I departed for Fleetwood the next morning – to the terrible distress of her mother, incidentally.

I left the scene of that awful 48 hours, initially feeling more damaged than deprived. Then I experienced a reaction as false as that which sometimes follows an unsuccessful interview for a job, when a damaged ego seeks to ease the pain in the lie, "I didn't want that wretched job, anyway" ...when all along you wanted it desperately. In all truthfulness, when the stunning effect of my rejection had worn off, it did not prove too difficult for me to understand the cause and to measure the effect, given that I have always been absolutely sure that there was not 'another man' waiting in the wings. My sweetheart's terrible distress at the time, and later events also, proved that. I had stumbled naïvely into the minefield of reintegration into civilian society – a traumatic experience for many returning servicemen who for years had known no other social life than that appropriate to tent, billet or barracks. Those of us who had been overseas for several years must have presented an even more frightening prospect. No matter how loving the former relationship might have been, not every wife or girlfriend had the moral fibre, let alone the tact and talent, to take on the task of our rehabilitation into civilian life. Those who did tackle the job were to earn my heartfelt admiration: those who could not even face trying had my complete understanding and sympathy. Even tackling the job and initially succeeding could have its future pitfalls, where the teacher turned preacher and damaged the ex-serviceman's pride by not knowing when to stop.

Instead of the authoritative, 'man of the world' whose image I must innocently have projected through my letters, my girl had found herself confronted by a self-conscious, tongue tied 'alien'. Ignorant of most of the social graces, unaware of my own shortcomings, I had suddenly found myself plunged into a bewildering vacuum where I had to start thinking for myself. For example, I had to learn how to initiate and maintain polite and rational conversation with virtual strangers, when for the first six years of adulthood my behaviour had been regulated by military discipline, and social communication had been restricted to exclusively male, banal banter.

There is little doubt in my own mind that my fiancée had innocently exaggerated my qualities in proudly describing me to her friends. She had been shocked to find that I was not going to be able to live up to my advertised reputation – at least not on my first meeting with them. Ought we to have detected some kind of early warning in the very restrained way in which we had first greeted one another at the railway station? I was a social yokel. I would have been an embarrassment to her. Yet, even as I left for home feeling emotionally bruised, I had already begun to experience a strange, almost uplifting, sense of freedom from the anxiety of having to make a decision about marriage and all that would entail. Perhaps that was evidence of my callowness, which must have been so readily discerned by my sweetheart herself. Hurt as I was, there was plenty of room in my heart for admiration at the courage she had shown, when merely 21 years old, in acting so maturely, just as there was sympathy for her dreadful disappointment and for her unenviable predicament in having to explain matters to her relations and friends. It was the last I ever saw of her.

The immediate damage to my self-esteem was considerable, yet in comfortable retrospect I have been able to reflect with only minimal regret on a love affair so barren that I calculate that, in the whole three and a half years of our association, we had been in each other's company for not more than a grand total of 48 hours. In the long term, the manner of our break-up probably did me more good than harm. In saying that, I know it begs the question whether I could have been really in love with the girl at all.

The ending of the affair clearly indicated to me that my woefully unprepossessing presence must have given her an unpleasant jolt. I was forced into an urgent and radical self-examination. I had to do something about myself quickly. I needed to supplement my elementary school education, to become more articulate and to obtain qualifications for earning a living (which I eventually achieved in accountancy). I realised that I needed to become more observant to pick up patterns of social behaviour that were worthy of imitation. Ignorance may be bliss, but becoming aware about what one is ignorant of is absolute hell. That awareness was the spur!

My romance had one other compensation. It had kept me writing much more than I would normally have done. If it had not been for the millions of words which flowed from my wartime pens, writing would probably have become just an irksome chore instead of the pleasure-giving exercise it has been for me ever since. My darling seemed to have a compulsion to write almost every day. That played an important part in giving me the incentive to write in reply. I do not regret that all that writing turned out to be fruitless. I do regret, however, that the increasing intensity of our correspondence ultimately led to the exclusion of all others. I am ashamed to say that I lost contact with most of my friends – and even some relatives – during that final year of the war. I had never thought consciously about the style of what I wrote, nor worried myself about the deficiencies in my knowledge of the rules of grammar. It may be a proverbial exaggeration that practice guarantees perfection, but it is surely axiomatic that abstention creates nothing at all. I simply wrote.

My sudden and unexpected return to Fleetwood, and the depressing announcement of my rejection, came as something of a bombshell to my almost disbelieving family. That week's momentous news of atomic bombs being dropped on Hiroshima and Nagasaki may have been of greater significance historically, but to the Fleetwood Joneses those events paled into insignificance compared with my own disaster.

On 15 August 1945, I was spending a few days with Eddie Keeley and his sympathetic family in Leeds when news came that Japan had surrendered unconditionally. World War Two was finally over. I need hardly say that I was not the only person considerably the worse for alcohol at Eddie's massive local pub, situated at the end of Osmondthorpe Lane. It was my first real experience of victory celebrations. The Keeleys were there in their scores, and for once I was made to feel a hero – at least until oblivion took over.

Another part of my leave was spent in Glasgow with Jimmy Irvine, and I was once again able to enjoy the company of Topper and Archie. The news of my broken romance came as a genuine shock to Jimmy. His first reaction was one of sincere sympathy, but he soon reverted to his normal, puckish character by decreeing, with a certain amount of relish, that as the rebuff had taken place while we were still at war with Japan, and as it was the second time during the great conflict that I had been 'given my cards', I could actually qualify for double membership of his cynical, flourishing, yet mythical 'Brush-off Club', to which he admitted those of his friends who had become romantic casualties of the war. I suppose he could have called it the 'Never Mind Club' or the 'Other Fish in the Sea Club', but the very suggestion of its existence usually had the effect of taking some of the sting out of such disappointments. He maintained that I had presented him with a difficult precedent. Did I qualify for a DBO (Double Brush-off) or a BO (Brush-off) and Bar? Either way, it was agreed that it was a rather rare distinction which we celebrated, in due course, at a convivial investiture in Glasgow. With us on that occasion was Topper, who had been dealt a similar fate on his return home. That it could happen to Topper, whose many qualities I so much admired, made my own brush-off seem much more tolerable. We were in good company. Archie had been rejected on his return, too! I hope that does not read like some kind of stiff upper lip pose, or an attempt to trivialise what was an unhappy event by any standard. Our demoralising experience was shared by lots of other returning servicemen.

I am convinced that my mother never really got over her

disappointment at the news of my failed romance. When my leave finally came to an end, and I had to say goodbye, it was to be the last I would ever see of her. Already worryingly ill when I left, she was to die the following 3 February while I was still abroad. Due to the ineptitude or indifference of the Army Post Office, I knew nothing of her final illness until several weeks after she had died and been buried. By that time I could not argue for compassionate leave with the 'powers that be'. With my final release from the Army only weeks away, it would all have been rather pointless. It is not too extravagant to suggest that war had claimed another victim. I do not blame anything or anybody else.

As I travelled overland back to Italy in early September 1945 I was still reflecting on, and trying to come to terms with, the events of that momentous month's leave. When I reached a remote Royal Artillery Base Camp near Benevento, I was amazed to find that the clerks had actually heard that men of the Raiding Support Regiment were to be given special treatment. Winter had arrived early in the south of Italy. The Nissen huts were unheated; it seemed as if I was always wet, and I was perpetually cold – suffering, in fact, from probably the worst cold I have ever had.

"I'm told that I must ask you what you would like to do for the rest of your service," the clerk informed me, without managing to conceal his distaste for such restrictions on his otherwise autocratic power in determining the fate of others.

I could not think of anything more imaginative to say than, "I want a nice indoor job for the winter."

From such inauspicious interviews are destinies determined. Early in November, I was sent to Vienna for clerical duties with the Allied Commission for Austria, firstly at the historic Schönbrunn Palace, then in the imposing House of Industry. The premises in Schwartzenberg Platz had been requisitioned by the four Allied powers (Britain, USA, France and the Soviet Union) to house the inter-allied secretariat of the Commission. Mixing with such notables as the American General Mark Clark, the Russian Marshal Koniev and the British General McCreery, I had found my indoor job for the winter of 1945-1946.

My former sweetheart had maintained contact by writing to me occasionally during the remainder of my leave in the United Kingdom, and she continued to do so during the autumn after I had returned to Italy. At first she wrote in sympathetic and apologetic terms, obviously trying to soften the blow for me. Then, during the winter when I had been moved to Austria, her letters became more frequent and more affectionate, suggesting – and latterly even pleading – that we should 'try again' on my demobilisation. Replying to those letters became progressively more difficult. Continuing to act the role of a mere pen pal became impossible. My love for her, which had been a very painful emotion for me, was beginning to revive, given a resuscitating kiss of life by her letters, but I knew that, if I were to meet with a second rejection, the effect on me would be far more dangerous than the first.

It was only after I realised that my standing in her eyes was again increasing, ominously in direct ratio to the length of time we had been apart, that the warning signs were heeded. The correspondence had to be brought to an end, once and for all. In the end I must have flattered myself that I had accidentally acquired the knack of which Shakespeare wrote:

> "For these fellows of infinite tongue, that can rhyme themselves into ladies' favours, they do always reason themselves out again." [Henry V, Act V, Scene ii]

I have always hoped that my sweetheart eventually married the man she wanted and deserved. I have no cause to be vindictive, yet I know that it must read like the churlishness of the spurned for me to say now, after being rejected, that I am glad that I was not the one. I know that my damaged dignity would have added to the disharmony when the inevitable marital conflicts arose. I would then have recalled, with flushing embarrassment, the slight to my pride of that initial dismissal, no matter how justified it may have been. I have never been in agreement with the 'I'll make you love me!' school of rejected suitors. It is not a recipe for married bliss to have persuaded someone against their own instinctive inclinations. I still like to think of love as a spontaneous phenomenon, not as a subject for persuasive debate. I know, too, that I belong to the faint hearted brigade: chasing has never been part of my repertoire. But I confess that I shall always be curious to know what kind of man eventually measured up to her expectations – and how I would have compared.

Along with other servicemen in Release Group No. 27, I was

eventually demobilised in March 1946. I then had to begin the difficult readjustment to being a civilian once more. While serving in Vienna I had met one of the British secretaries, a member of the Auxiliary Territorial Service. She has been my wife for the past 45 years, mother of my three daughters and grandmother of my nine grandchildren. But that, as they say, is another story.

Reference

1. Jones memoirs, book 1, unpublished MS, p.11, 34-35, 98 and 155

2. Jones memoirs, book 1, unpublished MS, p.34-35

3. Jones memoirs, book 1, unpublished MS, p.98

4. Jones memoirs, book 1, unpublished MS, p.155

5. The five Batteries, which comprised the Raiding Support Regiment, gave it a range of capabilities. 'A' Battery was armed with 12 Vickers medium machine guns, 'B' Battery with 18 three-inch mortars, 'C' Battery with 18 0.5 inch Browning heavy machine guns, 'D' Battery with 4 Italian 47mm anti-tank guns and 'E' Battery with 8 American 75mm mountain pack howitzers. Even the heaviest weapons of the Regiment were portable, with the howitzers of 'E' battery being able to be disassembled and transported by aircraft or packhorse into mountain regions. The Italian 47mm anti-tank guns were renowned for their ruggedness and ability to be transported across difficult terrain.

6. The Browning .50 is an air-cooled, belt-fed, heavy machine gun. Its heavy weight places limits on its potential use. These usually involve fixed mountings on vehicles, aircraft and on tripod mounts in defensive positions. Firing large projectiles at high velocity, with a high rate of fire, the .50 is a formidable weapon in defence and, despite the weight problem, in attack. It is still in widespread use today.

7. Increasingly drawn into the Nazi orbit in the late 1930s, Yugoslavia was attacked by Axis forces on 6 April 1941. The country was divided into zones controlled by the Germans, Italians, Bulgarians and Hungarians and a Croat puppet regime. The latter's reign of murder against Serbs, Jews and others rapidly provoked the emergence of Partisan resistance. The British initially backed the Serbian Chetnik resistance that owed its allegiance to the Royal Government in exile in Britain. By the end of 1943, amidst growing concerns about the inactivity of the Chetniks, and questions about their loyalty, the British Government transferred its support to the more broadly based Communist-led Partisan movement.

8. Under King Tomislav in 925 AD, Vis was incorporated into Croatia. In the Middle

Ages, control of the island was contested by a number of rulers before falling under the control of Venice. Under Venetian control the island was known as Lissa. On 13 March 1811 a Franco-Venetian fleet was defeated off Lissa by a force of Royal Navy vessels. The Second Battle of Lissa took place in on 20 July 1866 between the Austrian and Italian fleets. After World War II the island became one of the principal naval bases of the Yugoslav fleet. After the break up of Jugoslvia in the 1990s the island became part of Croatia. Wine production, fishing and agriculture remain the bedrock of the local economy.

9. Josip Broz Tito (1892-1980) was born in Croatia. In October 1940, after spending a considerable period in Moscow, he became political secretary of the Yugoslav Communist Party. It was not until after the German invasion of Russia in June 1941 that the party began to engage in military resistance against Axis forces in Yugoslavia.

10. In late 1943, with Allied forces firmly established in Italy, German forces along the Eastern shores of the Adriatic began to prepare for an Allied invasion of the Dalmatian coast of Yugoslavia. With a strong guerrilla movement to support a landing, an invasion of Yugoslavia offered the allies the chance for a rapid advance into the Balkans. German policy concentrated on attempting to destroy the guerrilla movement and denying the Allies potential landing sites. To this end the Germans began to occupy the islands along the Dalmatian cost. Korcula was seized on 23 December 1943 and Hvar the following day as its Partisan defenders withdrew. By February 1944 only the western most island of Vis remained unoccupied, its ports crammed with schooners which the Partisans had used to withdraw from other islands. Vis held a military, political and symbolic value that both sides recognised. Walter Jones did not realise the significance of his destination in February 1944, nor was he aware that in Berlin a date between 20 February and 1 March had been fixed for the invasion of Vis and the elimination of the mixed British and Partisan garrison.

11. British torpedo and gunboats based at Vis caused the Germans considerable trouble. They disrupted German traffic in the Aegean and along the coast of Dalmatia. This led Admiral Doenitz to press for the capture of Vis. On the night of 11 October 1944, four Vis-based MTB/MGBs scored fought one of the most successful small boat actions of the war when they destroyed 11 enemy vessels including one 'S' boat. A further three 'S' boats were also damaged in the attack. Cooper, B., The Battle of the Torpedo Boats, Pan, London, 1970. Pp.241-248

12. Tito arrived in Bari, Italy, during the night of 3-4 June accompanied by his dog, his staff, a Russian mission and a British military representative. During the night of 8-9 August 1944 he crossed to Vis on the British destroyer HMS *Blackmore*. He 'escaped' from the British controlled airfield on Vis in a Russian aircraft to General Korneev's Red

Army headquarters in Romania on 18-19 September. See Phyllis Auty, Tito: A Biography, Longman, London, 1970. p. 237. and p. 242

13. By June 1944 up to three squadrons of Spitfires could use the island's runway at any one time, although they were not usually stationed there overnight. Vis report for 13 June 1944, TNA:PRO Defence p.2/700

14. A seaborne invasion of the Island of Vis was considered the most likely form of German assault. To counter the threat, the approaches to Vis harbour were fortified along with the island of Ravnik. Three Bofors guns were sited on the coast of Vis opposite Ravnik to further disrupt any attempt at a landing. The garrison at Ravnik, which was armed with 0.5 Brownings and six pounder anti-tank guns, was instructed to hold to the last. See Churchill, T., Commando Crusade, William Kimber, London, 1987. p. 176

15. Walter Jones was not the only appreciative onlooker to the birth of this unusual naval craft. A Royal Naval Officer on board Motor Gunboat 658 later commented: "LCI 254 had a magnificent canvas funnel at a rakish angle, and two large canvas gun turrets", Reynolds, L.C., Gunboat 658, William Kimber, London, 1955. p.170

16. Anne was planning her second holiday at Walter Jones' parents.

17. The AB 64 is a soldier's combined identity record and pay-book. Jones must have lost his.

18. Diary Entry for Monday 21 August 1944.

19. Invaded by Italy on 7 April 1939, it was not until 1942 that a large scale guerrilla movement began to emerge under the encouragement of Tito and the British Special Operations Executive. With the removal of Mussolini from office in July 1943, some elements of the Italian Army followed the orders by Marshal Badoglio, the new Italian Prime Minister, to join the Partisan movement. The Germans rapidly flew in forces to reconstitute a line of defence in Albania. By early 1944 they were firmly back in control of the coast and major cities with the guerrillas contesting control of the interior. In September 1944 the overall strategic position compelled the start of a withdrawal of German forces from Albania.

20. In his memoirs Churchill states that he "was surprised to receive a peremptory order to report… [to Brigadier General Davy's] headquarters at Bari", after advising the Director of Military Operations at General Headquarters Middle East that he would face considerable difficulties in taking his Brigade across to Yugoslavia to attack retreating German forces. His distaste for Davy was evident in his relation of the story of how Davy had been on the destroyer HMS *Eclipse* which had been sunk on 24 October 1943. Churchill commented waspishly, "Unfortunately someone saw fit to fish

him out." See Churchill, T., Commando Crusade, William Kimber, London, 1987, p.259

21. As the Raiding Support Regiment's Report for the Sarande Operation, 22 September to 17 October 1944, noted: "Initially the operation was designed to last for 50 hours and consequently kit and personal equipment was taken to last that period. Considerable discomfort was afforded the Tps. taking part when the operation became of greater duration." TNA:PRO WO170/1364

22. The after action report by 2nd Special Services Brigade on operations in the Sarande area went to considerable lengths to describe and blame the terrain for the difficulties faced by British troops. "To understand all of what followed in Albania, it is necessary to get some clear picture of the terrain. Maps and air photographs had already revealed the high mountains rising steeply from the shore to over 2000 feet, intersected with sharply defined valleys filled with thick woods and tangled bushes. But neither the maps nor the photographs had shown the difficulties of moving about in this country. Not only were the woods extremely thick, but there were very few paths through them, and no reasonably easy means of keeping direction. The mountains were not only high and rocky, but their surface was so uneven that anybody walking there was in constant danger of breaking an ankle. In parts, the surface consisted of innumerable pointed rock projections about nine inches high and six inches apart, so that one either had to walk from rock point to rock point… or else step between the rock points… In either case, walking was painful and dangerous, but yet men had to carry equipment, food and ammunition over these rocky surfaces, for no mule could traverse such ground." Report by 2nd Special Services Brigade, 22 September to 30 October 1944, TNA:PRO Defence 2/700.

G.H. Bennett

G.H. Bennett, is Associate Professor at Plymouth University where he has taught history, including that of the Second World War since 1992. Author of more than 20 volumes on Military, Diplomatic and Political history he has appeared in documentaries on the Second World War as well as historical series such as *Who Do You Think You Are* and *Combat Ships*. He is also a regular contributor to BBC National, Local Radio and to Gem Collector TV.

BIBLIOGRAPHY

Index

A

Afrika Korps 16

Albania 14, 158–159, 161–162, 183–184, 194, 196, 259

Argenta 245

Artillery Regiment, 111th Field 165, 179

B

Bari 48, 153, 200, 209, 214

Beirut 19

Beretta pistol, .22 258

Bisevo 78, 126

Bol 99, 112–113

Borsh 159, 162, 166–168, 171

Brac 54, 92, 94–97, 105, 112, 120, 128, 181

Brown, William Laird 45, 58

Broz, Josef 128

Butcher, Fred 65

C

Caserta 146

Chetniks 55

Churchill, Brigadier Tom 77, 158, 162, 194

Churchill, Colonel Jack 64

Codigoro 245

Commando 82–83, 90, 94, 96, 171, 173, 181, 184, 195

Commando, 40 Royal Marine 162, 172, 174, 182

Commando, 43 Royal Marine 63–64, 66, 68, 120, 230

Commando, No. 2 54, 64, 91, 113, 158–159, 172, 174–175, 179, 181, 194, 230

Commando, No. 9 231

Commando, No. 10 63

Corfu 158–160, 182, 188, 196

Coyle, Lieutenant 180

Crete 54

D

Davy, Brigadier 130, 162, 194

Delvine 159–160, 165–169, 172, 182, 196

Dilwara MV 44, 49

Drvar 92

E

E-boat, German 73

Eboli 208–209, 215

Elliott, Colonel 137

Everton FC 9

F

Fishwick, Ray 67–68, 77, 80, 132

Flight Sgt. Kent 22–23, 25–28, 32

Flying Fortress bombers 76

Foggia 157

G

GHQ Middle East 37

Giles, Commander Morgan 137

Goiya 213

Grant, Charlie 150, 188

Green, George 70

H

Haden, Paddy 65, 93, 106–107, 111, 252

Hayden, Paddy 213

Highland Light Infantry 97, 120

Hospital, 98th British General 201, 212

Houndforce 194, 162, 196

Hvar 54

I

Irvine, Jimmy 65, 85, 147, 150, 153, 174, 179, 188, 200, 208, 210, 213–214, 264

Italian 28th Garibaldi Brigade 230

Italy 49

J

Jones, Albert 8

K

Keeley, Eddie 147, 264

Kelly, Corporal 'Spike' 41–43, 101–104, 106–107, 109–111, 114, 117–118

Kirkwood, Willie 45

Kirkwood, Willie (Kirky) 59, 71, 93

Komiza 56–58, 66–67, 73, 81–83, 93, 123–124, 127, 133–134, 147–149, 151

Korcula 54, 136–141, 144, 147

Kos 54

L

Lagosta 138–139

Lake Comacchio 231

Landing Craft Infantry 52

Landing Craft, Assault 93

Landing Craft, Tank 93

Leros 54

Lockheed Hudson 23

Lockheed Lightning 80–81

Long Range Desert Group 13, 19, 147

Lord Haw Haw 19

Loundon, Captain Bob 90

Lundy, Archie 45, 65, 70, 93, 98, 101–102, 108–109, 132, 146, 148, 153, 174, 188, 194, 196, 200, 208, 213, 264

M

Macchis 84

Machine Gun, .50 inch Browning 59, 66, 83, 92, 95, 98, 100, 105–106, 112, 122, 134–135, 138–139, 141, 158, 166–167, 169–174, 180–181, 183, 195, 210, 268, 270

Maclean, Brigadier Fitzroy 128

Marco 126, 132, 135, 150–151

Migliarino 245

Mihajlovic, Draze 55

Milka 72–73, 117

Minkley, Bud 77

Mljet 54, 88–89, 91–93

Mola 152, 156, 194

Monopoli 49–50, 52, 158

Motor Torpedo Boats 73

N

Nahariya 19, 25, 34, 40

Nahariya' 22

Naharyia 21

Nidova Gora 97

O

Orebic 136, 141

P

Parker, Charlie 86, 89

Parsons, Captain 180

Partisan 56–58, 61–63, 65, 68, 72, 77–78, 87, 90, 92, 96, 113, 137, 148, 183

Peljesac 136

Ploesti, Romanian oil installations 76

Podselje 59–61, 63–66, 71, 86, 92, 122–123, 125, 132, 134, 149

Pomposa 244

Prosiec 135

R

Ramat David 21–23, 25, 68

Rangers, American 134

Ravenna 250–251

Ravnik 122–125, 127–128, 130, 132–135, 140, 146, 148–149, 151, 164

Rice, Douglas 86, 89

Robinson, Wally 70

Roger, Bert 45, 65, 88, 90, 93, 101, 103–104, 107–110, 148, 188

Roko 71–72, 149

Roman Candle 24, 28

Royal Artillery Light Anti-Aircraft Battery 63

Rukavac 92–94, 122–127, 130, 132, 135, 148, 150–151

Rutigliano 152, 196, 198–200, 212–214

S

Salerno 199

San Guiseppi 244

Sarande 159–160, 162, 165–168, 171–173, 179, 181–182, 184–185, 194–196, 201

Shen Vassil 165, 179

Sirjon 60–61, 66, 71

Skates, Spike 85

Sofia, rail installations 76

Solta 54, 64, 65

Special Air Service 13

Special Boat Service 13, 19

Spumanti 52, 157, 200

SS Brigade, No.2 162

Stephenson, Bernard 157, 200, 208, 214

Subasic, Dr. Ivan 129

T

The Royal East Kent (Buffs) 231

Tito 54–56, 58, 61, 113, 128, 130, 146, 244

U

Usherwood, Lieutenant Commander 165

Ustasi 56

V

Vis 54, 56, 59, 61–62, 64–66, 69, 71–73, 77–78, 81, 83–84, 86, 89, 92–93, 97, 100, 111, 113, 116–117, 120, 122–124, 126–129, 132–134, 137–139, 146–149, 165, 198–199, 213

W

Wellington bomber 24

William Laird Brown (Topper) 52, 58, 65, 82, 84–85, 133–134, 147, 153, 188, 200, 208, 210, 213–214, 264

Winch, Charlie 45, 59, 65, 87, 93, 150–151

Women's Auxiliary Air Force 23

Y

Yugoslavia 14, 55–56, 64, 72, 77, 92, 122, 128–129, 136, 145, 148, 151, 177, 194, 204, 244, 251

25-pounders 93, 97, 100, 102, 105, 109, 112, 120, 135, 137, 141, 172, 177, 179–180, 183

PB ISBN 978-1-7394402-0-6
HB ISBN 978-1-7394402-1-3
Ebook ISBN 978-1-7394402-2-0
Publication date July 2023

A Most Irregular War
SOE Burma, Major Trofimov's Diary 1944–45

Richard Duckett
Richard is a graduate of the Universities of Essex (BA, 2000) and Reading (MA, 2001), and was awarded a PhD in 2015 by the Open University. He has published two books on the Special Operations Executive in Burma, and continues to lecture widely on the subject.

GH Bennett
Harry is Associate Professor at Plymouth University where he has taught history, including that of the Second World War since 1992. Author of more than 20 volumes on Military, Diplomatic and Political history he has appeared in TV documentaries on the Second World War.

In early 1945 small teams of Allied special forces soldiers were parachuted into the Burmese jungle far behind enemy lines. Their task was to work with local tribespeople who had suffered at the hands of the Japanese occupiers and the majority Burman population to raise irregular forces for guerilla warfare. Their goal was to assist advancing Allied forces by disrupting the rear area of the Japanese Army as it tried to hold the Allied advance. Recruiting, training, supplying and fighting with indigenous peoples Allied special forces created powerful local forces that learnt all the skills of demolition, ambush and infantry attack. As the war in Burma turned into a rout for Japanese forces in 1945 those forces, instead of trying to disrupt the rear areas of the enemy, found themselves squarely in the way of the retreating Japanese Army trying to get out of Burma. The fight would turn desperate as Allied special forces and tribespeople stood against a Japanese Army in headlong flight. This is the story, through the unvarnished diary and photographs, of one of those Allied special forces soldiers.